ASP.NET MVC 4 Mobile App Development

Create next-generation applications for smart phones, tablets, and mobile devices using the ASP.NET MVC development framework

Andy Meadows

[PACKT] **enterprise**
PUBLISHING   professional expertise distilled

BIRMINGHAM - MUMBAI

ASP.NET MVC 4 Mobile App Development

First published: July 2013

Production Reference: 1160713

Published by Packt Publishing Ltd.
Livery Place
35 Livery Street
Birmingham B3 2PB, UK.

ISBN 978-1-84968-736-2

www.packtpub.com

Cover Image by Abhishek Pandey (abhishek.pandey1210@gmail.com)

Credits

Author
Andy Meadows

Reviewers
Shailendra Chauhan
Shiju Varghese

Acquisition Editor
Mary Jasmine Nadar

Commissioning Editor
Llewellyn F. Rozario

Lead Technical Editor
Neeshma Ramakrishnan

Technical Editors
Mausam Kothari
Rikita Poojari
Amit Ramadas

Project Coordinator
Arshad Sopariwala

Proofreader
Christopher Smith

Indexer
Hemangini Bari

Graphics
Abhinash Sahu

Production Coordinators
Manu Joseph
Nitesh Thakur

Cover Work
Nitesh Thakur

About the Author

Andy Meadows has been in a love affair with technology since his third-grade teacher introduced him to her TRS-80 Model III in 1981. After several months of typing "Go North" on the keyboard, he began his foray into BASIC programming. The TRS-80 Model III begat a Commodore 64 and an introduction to Pascal. By 1988, he was spending his summers earning money by writing software in C for local small businesses.

While attending college at the University of Georgia, Andy developed his passion for web development and, of course, beer. His first web application was a series of CGI scripts that output content for NCSA Mosaic and by 1994, he was designing web interfaces for global information systems.

After college, Andy wandered listlessly through the IT world spending time in several verticals using several different languages, but he always returned home to web development. In 2002, he began his foray into mobile development beginning with native Java development, and quickly moving into the mobile web space where he began marrying his two passions: mobile web development and .NET.

Since then, Andy has worked on several projects involving mobile development, web development, or both. He is extremely excited about the future of the mobile web made possible by the newest generation of mobile devices. He is currently working at a startup in Atlanta, where he lives with his wife and two children.

Acknowledgment

Writing this book was one of the biggest challenges I have ever undertaken. When originally approached with the idea for this book, I was hesitant. I'd heard horror stories about the sheer level of effort and commitment it takes to complete this task, but after consulting with the family I decided to try. Let me tell you, those stories are wrong. It was much, much more difficult than I had heard, but more fulfilling than I could have imagined.

The biggest commitment I had to make when writing this book was time. Lots and lots of time. Fortunately, I was blessed with a wonderful supporting cast.

I would first like to thank the people at Packt Publishing for their gentle encouragement and guidance through this process. They were truly a pleasure to work with, and their level of commitment to their authors and a quality product is evident in every action they take.

To my reviewers, thanks for the candid feedback—both critical and complimentary. This book is better because of you.

To my wife, Amy, and my two children, Noah and Nate, who permitted me to undertake this venture, thank you for your patience and support. And thanks for letting me take over practically every room in the house at one point in time as I attempted to find my muse. I sure must have done something right at one point to deserve the unconditional love you have shown through the long days at work, followed by the long nights in front of the computer. I love you all.

About the Reviewers

Shailendra Chauhan is an N-Tier Application Developer & .NET Consultant in Noida, Delhi, Gurgaon NCR region, India. He has 4.5 years of experience in building web applications using Microsoft Technologies including ASP.NET, MVC, C#, jQuery, SQL Server, WCF, Web API, Entity Framework, and many more web things. He loves to work with Internet applications using Microsoft technology and other related technologies.

He likes to share his experience and knowledge through his blogs www.dotnet-tricks.com and www.windowsappstutorial.com, which he started in Jan 2012. He strives to be the best he can be. He always tries to gain more knowledge and skills in Microsoft Technologies. He always keeps up with new technologies and learning new skills that allow him to provide better solutions to problems.

Shiju Varghese is a Microsoft MVP and a Technical Architect, specializing in Cloud, Mobility, and Web technologies. His current technology focus is on Windows Azure, ASP.NET MVC, Node.js, HTML 5, and CQRS. Shiju is passionate about building Cloud apps on the Windows Azure Platform. His areas of interest include Cloud Computing, Enterprise Mobility, Agile software development, Domain-Driven Design (DDD), Test-Driven Development (TDD), and Web application scalability. Shiju has been working with .NET technologies since its inception.

Shiju works as a Technical Architect in Marlabs Inc where he is focusing on Cloud apps with Windows Azure.

Thanks to my lovely wife, Rosmi, for her support and motivation. I would also like to thank my daughter, Irene Rose.

www.PacktPub.com

Support files, eBooks, discount offers and more

You might want to visit www.PacktPub.com for support files and downloads related to your book.

Did you know that Packt offers eBook versions of every book published, with PDF and ePub files available? You can upgrade to the eBook version at www.PacktPub.com and as a print book customer, you are entitled to a discount on the eBook copy. Get in touch with us at service@packtpub.com for more details.

At www.PacktPub.com, you can also read a collection of free technical articles, sign up for a range of free newsletters and receive exclusive discounts and offers on Packt books and eBooks.

http://PacktLib.PacktPub.com

Do you need instant solutions to your IT questions? PacktLib is Packt's online digital book library. Here, you can access, read and search across Packt's entire library of books.

Why Subscribe?

- Fully searchable across every book published by Packt
- Copy and paste, print and bookmark content
- On demand and accessible via web browser

Free Access for Packt account holders

If you have an account with Packt at www.PacktPub.com, you can use this to access PacktLib today and view nine entirely free books. Simply use your login credentials for immediate access.

Instant Updates on New Packt Books

Get notified! Find out when new books are published by following @PacktEnterprise on Twitter, or the *Packt Enterprise* Facebook page.

Table of Contents

Preface

Today's web developers are faced with a multitude of challenges in delivering their product to market. Once upon a time, applications only needed to look and function properly within Internet Explorer. Today's applications must not only function within multiple browsers, but on multiple operating systems running on multiple devices.

ASP.NET MVC 4 Mobile App Development is meant to serve as a guide to successfully building web applications that target current desktop browsers and browsers meant to consume the mobile web.

ASP.NET MVC 4 Mobile App Development walks you through the process of creating a web application from concept to delivery.

What this book covers

In the first section of this book, we build a fully functional sample application to manage and share recipes for homebrewed beers. *Chapter 1, Developing for the Mobile Web*, begins with a discussion on the importance of understanding how to develop for the mobile web. You are then given a brief history of how we arrived to at the mobile web of today. The chapter ends by discussing all of the constraints we, as developers, must acknowledge if we are to successfully develop applications for the mobile web.

Chapter 2, Homebrew and You, introduces you to the domain of homebrewing and BrewHow — our homebrew recipe sharing application. From our understanding of this domain we build the requirements for our application and then examine how ASP.NET MVC 4 and its new features will help us develop it. We conclude the chapter by setting up our environment to launch our mobile emulator to design and test our application.

Chapter 3, Introducing ASP.NET MVC 4, introduces the MVC pattern. We then discuss how it is implemented within ASP.NET MVC 4 as we begin to build our application. By the end of this chapter the initial shell of our application will be complete and running inside our desktop and mobile browsers.

Chapter 4, Modeling BrewHow in EF5, walks us through creating a data model for BrewHow. We begin by discussing the new features and improvements of Entity framework and create a data model and database for our domain using the code-first model in EF. The model and database are continually refined through the use of migrations until the needs of our application are met and our application is consuming data from LocalDB.

Chapter 5, The BrewHow Domain and Domain-driven Design, introduces us to the tenets of DDD. We apply these tenets to BrewHow by creating repositories, view models, and domain entities to enforce the boundaries between persistence, logic, and display.

Chapter 6, Writing Maintainable Code, begins with a discussion on the SOLID principles of object-oriented design; principles that serve to facilitate the writing of maintainable code. We then review the topics of Dependency Injection and Inversion of Control as tools to help us SOLIDify the BrewHow codebase. This chapter ends by applying these principles and tools to the codebase leveraging the extension points provided to us by ASP.NET MVC 4.

Chapter 7, Separating Functionality Using Routes and Areas, provides a detailed discussion on this key piece of technology in ASP.NET MVC 4. We examine how, by leveraging routing and areas, we can create meaningful SEO-friendly URLs and separate the functionality of BrewHow into discrete units of work for the content contained within BrewHow. We then exercise our knowledge by adding support for user reviews.

Chapter 8, Validating User Input, looks at the server-side support for data validation contained within the .NET Framework's `System.ComponentModel.DataAnnotations` namespace. The data model and view models are modified to support the use of these attributes so we can validate input on the client side and again once the data has made it to the server. We also explore how these technologies help protect BrewHow from common web attacks such as CSRF and XSS.

Chapter 9, Identifying and Authorizing Users, introduces the new membership functionality available in ASP.NET MVC 4. BrewHow is modified to support user authentication using the new membership functionality and we then modify the application to allow authentication using a Google login. We end the chapter by tying together the BrewHow data model with the membership data model so we can associate recipes and reviews with the users that created them.

Our application is now functionally complete and has met all of the requirements set forth in *Chapter 2, Homebrew and You*. In the second section of the book we take a look at a few advanced features provided by ASP.NET MVC 4. *Chapter 10, Asynchronous Programming and Bundles,* explores how we can design the server-side portion of our application to get information to our users more efficiently and with less wait time—something critical for mobile applications. To accomplish this, we begin by examining and then implementing support for asynchronous actions. We then examine the support of minification provided to us in the form of bundles.

Chapter 11, Coding for the Real-Time Web, investigates how we can use always-on connectivity to provide the illusion of a desktop application within BrewHow. We then leverage SignalR to simulate push notifications from the server to BrewHow.

With our application fully optimized to deliver content to mobile devices, we can now begin the third part of the book. *Chapter 12, Designing Your App for Mobile Devices,* discusses how we can use the next-generation of web standards, HTML5 and CSS3, to create responsive markup to present our content to users in a manner best fitting the device on which they are viewing it.

Chapter 13, Extending Support for the Mobile Web, extends the concept of mobile design to our servers as we explore the mobile view support built into ASP.NET MVC 4. We then extend this concept to target specific mobile devices using the new support for display modes.

Chapter 14, Improving the User Experience with jQuery Mobile, shows how BrewHow can be converted to a mobile web application that looks and feels as if it were native to the device. We look at some of the controls provided by jQuery Mobile and apply them within the context of everything we have learned to build a fully polished and functional mobile application.

Chapter 15, Reader Challenges, presents how BrewHow could be extended to be an even richer experience for the user. We discuss how full-text search technology could be integrated into BrewHow, how we might provide support for social networking, and how we might even extend BrewHow into a truly native mobile application. The readers are then encouraged to undertake these tasks themselves.

What you need for this book

To build the sample application within this book you will need a copy of Microsoft Visual Studio Express for Web 2012. To view the sample application you will need a web browser capable of supporting HTML5 and CSS3. The sample application in this book was tested using the current version of Google Chrome and Opera Mobile Emulator running on Windows 8.

Who this book is for

This book is for any individual wishing to learn ASP.NET MVC 4 and its role in developing applications that target the mobile web. The material in this book assumes the reader has familiarity with the .NET framework and exposure to C#. If you are new to ASP.NET MVC and want a good solid introduction, if you want to learn what's new in ASP.NET MVC 4, or if you want to learn how you can modify your web applications to support multiple devices this book is for you.

Conventions

In this book, you will find a number of styles of text that distinguish between different kinds of information. Here are some examples of these styles, and an explanation of their meaning.

Code words in text, database table names, folder names, filenames, file extensions, pathnames, dummy URLs, user input, and Twitter handles are shown as follows: " In prior versions of MVC, all of the application bootstrap code was located in the Global.asax code-behind".

A block of code is set as follows:

```
.white-go
{
    width:31px;
    background:url('img-sprite.png') 0 0;
}

.orange-go
{
    width: 31px;
    background:url('img-sprite.png') -32px 0;
}
```

When we wish to draw your attention to a particular part of a code block, the relevant lines or items are set in bold:

```
public interface IBrewHowContext
{
  IDbSet<Models.Recipe> Recipes { get; set; }
  IDbSet<Models.Review> Reviews { get; set; }
  IDbSet<Models.Style> Styles { get; set; }
```

```
IDbSet<Models.UserProfile> UserProfiles { get; set; }

    int SaveChanges();
}

public class BrewHowContext : DbContext, IBrewHowContext
{
    public IDbSet<Models.Recipe> Recipes { get; set; }
    public IDbSet<Models.Review> Reviews { get; set; }
    public IDbSet<Models.Style> Styles { get; set; }
```

public IDbSet<Models.UserProfile> UserProfiles { get; set; }

```
    public BrewHowContext()
        : base("DefaultConnection")
    {
    }
    /* ... */
}
```

New terms and **important words** are shown in bold. Words that you see on the screen, in menus or dialog boxes for example, appear in the text like this: "Select the **ASP.NET MVC 4 Web Application** icon and provide a name and location for the new project in the **Name** and **Location** text boxes respectively".

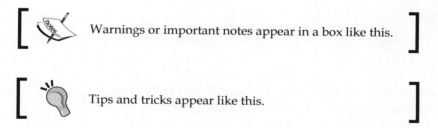

Warnings or important notes appear in a box like this.

Tips and tricks appear like this.

Reader feedback

Feedback from our readers is always welcome. Let us know what you think about this book—what you liked or may have disliked. Reader feedback is important for us to develop titles that you really get the most out of.

To send us general feedback, simply send an e-mail to feedback@packtpub.com, and mention the book title via the subject of your message.

If there is a topic that you have expertise in and you are interested in either writing or contributing to a book, see our author guide on www.packtpub.com/authors.

Customer support

Now that you are the proud owner of a Packt book, we have a number of things to help you to get the most from your purchase.

Downloading the example code

You can download the example code files for all Packt books you have purchased from your account at http://www.packtpub.com. If you purchased this book elsewhere, you can visit http://www.packtpub.com/support and register to have the files e-mailed directly to you.

Errata

Although we have taken every care to ensure the accuracy of our content, mistakes do happen. If you find a mistake in one of our books—maybe a mistake in the text or the code—we would be grateful if you would report this to us. By doing so, you can save other readers from frustration and help us improve subsequent versions of this book. If you find any errata, please report them by visiting http://www.packtpub.com/submit-errata, selecting your book, clicking on the **errata submission form** link, and entering the details of your errata. Once your errata are verified, your submission will be accepted and the errata will be uploaded on our website, or added to any list of existing errata, under the Errata section of that title. Any existing errata can be viewed by selecting your title from http://www.packtpub.com/support.

Piracy

Piracy of copyright material on the Internet is an ongoing problem across all media. At Packt, we take the protection of our copyright and licenses very seriously. If you come across any illegal copies of our works, in any form, on the Internet, please provide us with the location address or website name immediately so that we can pursue a remedy.

Please contact us at copyright@packtpub.com with a link to the suspected pirated material.

We appreciate your help in protecting our authors, and our ability to bring you valuable content.

Questions

You can contact us at questions@packtpub.com if you are having a problem with any aspect of the book, and we will do our best to address it.

1
Developing for the Mobile Web

If you are at all interested in developing web apps in the future, it is important you understand the increasing role played by mobile devices, and how to develop apps fitting their capabilities. I'm saying this not to scare you into buying my book (though I hope that you are currently reading your purchased copy), but to underscore the fact that mobile computing will play an increased role in the lives of every connected person.

To appreciate the growth in mobile usage, one should consider the iPhone. The iPhone, typically heralded as the smartphone that began the current mobile computing revolution, wasn't introduced until 2007. At the end of 2008, more than a year after its release, mobile traffic accounted for less than 1 percent of the global Internet traffic, which was not much of a revolution.

However, by the end of 2010, mobile traffic accounted for nearly 5 percent of all the Internet traffic, and at the end of 2012 it was nearly 13 percent. Halfway through 2013, mobile traffic has passed 15 percent of all the Internet traffic. This trend is roughly a multiplier of 1.5, year-over-year, and is likely to accelerate.

In the 4th quarter of 2012, iPad sales reached approximately 140,000,000 total units shipped, approximately 3 times the total number of iPhones shipped. The iPad was introduced 3 years after the iPhone, and just 3 years after the tablet revolution was launched by the iPad, total tablet shipments in the 4th quarter of 2012 surpassed both desktop and notebook shipments.

As developers, it is important we understand and embrace this mobile revolution or else we will be run over by it.

Throughout this book, we will be building a fully functional web app using ASP. NET MVC 4, HTML5, and CSS3 to support both desktop and mobile computing platforms. We will begin with building the desktop version of the web app but will be keeping mobile considerations in mind.

Once our desktop app is complete, we will modify it to support the mobile web using concepts such as responsive design and media queries. During this modification, we will examine the new features of ASP.NET MVC 4 we can use to better target mobile web devices.

In the last chapters of this book, we will modify the app to support a truly mobile experience using jQuery Mobile. It is my goal that, by the end of the last chapter in this book, you will have a complete understanding of what it takes to develop for the mobile web, and the tools to take your mobile web apps to the next level.

In this chapter, we will begin by examining a history of the mobile web. This understanding is essential in appreciating the unprecedented growth in the past few years. This chapter will also highlight some of the constraints that existed, and still exist, when trying to target the mobile devices of yesterday, today, and tomorrow. We will end with a preview of the new platform support in Microsoft ASP.NET MVC 4.

Our journey into the mobile web begins now.

History of the mobile web

Without knowing how the mobile web started, it's impossible to appreciate the ease with which we can develop for mobile devices. If the mobile web works at all, it is a feat in itself, and it took the convergence of several technologies to make it all possible.

The Nokia 9000

The Nokia 9000 is, arguably, the first mobile web device. Developed by Nokia in 1996, this phone weighed in at a whopping 14 ounces (397 g), and was powered by an Intel i386. It was equipped with a 640 x 200 pixel gray-scale LCD. This phone allowed owners to send faxes, send and receive email, and surf the web. It also came equipped with terminal and Telnet applications for accessing mainframe systems.

Market fragmentation

During this time, Nokia was in competition with Ericsson and others for control of the mobile data space. The Nokia 9000 was designed to use Narrow Band Sockets, a communication protocol developed and championed by Nokia. Information that was to be displayed on the Nokia 9000 was returned to the phone using **Tagged Text Markup Language (TTML)**, a markup language that content providers could use to optimize web pages for mobile devices by removing extraneous information from the display and transmission.

At about the same time, Ericsson had developed **Intelligent Terminal Transfer Protocol (ITTP)**. ITTP was Ericsson's proprietary markup for the mobile web.

It became evident to the major phone manufacturers that market fragmentation was going to be inevitable unless they could develop a common standard to enable the mobile web on their devices.

WAP 1.0 and WML

On June 26, 1997, Nokia, Ericsson, Motorola, and Unwired Planet publicly announced that they would be cooperating on a **Wireless Application Protocol (WAP)**. WAP 1.0 was to be an open protocol that any vendor could implement, and this new protocol would enable mobile device manufacturers to connect to the IP-based world of the Internet from mobile devices that had an inherently high rate of data loss during communication.

Wireless Markup Language (WML) became the standard for designing applications that ran on WAP 1.0, and was a second-generation derivative of HTML and XML.

However, WAP and WML had some shortcomings. The protocol and companion markup languages were designed for very slow data networks and very limited display capabilities. If your device had limited data input capabilities and a low-resolution display, then WML served you well, but with the advent of smart phones and mobile web browsers, derivatives of their desktop counterparts, WAP 1.0 and WML became less relevant.

WAP 2.0 and XHTML MP

As the convergence of mobile phones and PDAs gained momentum, new standards were needed to support the growing use of web-enabled mobile devices. To support the new browsers that began to ship with mobile devices, a new markup language was required.

In 2001, **eXtensible HyperText Markup Language Mobile Profile** (**XHTML MP**) was adapted from XHTML Basic by the WAP Forum (now part of the Open Mobile Alliance) to replace WML as the default protocol for WAP.

 While WAP became the standard in the United States, United Kingdom, and Europe, the standard in Japan, i-mode, was developed by NTT DoCoMo.

The new standards were short-lived. Today, most mobile devices ship with browsers supporting the latest HTML standards including HTML5 and CSS3, but it is still a good practice to deliver content to target the broadest market possible.

Continued development constraints

Having modern browsers on our phones, tablets, and other mobile devices doesn't mean we should make no accommodation for users of the mobile web. There are still many real-time constraints placed upon mobile devices which we, as developers, should take into consideration when writing mobile web apps. We can't simply shrink down the desktop version of our web app and provide a satisfying experience to the user. One must keep in mind when developing mobile apps that the mobile devices on which our app is being executed have different processing, network, and presentation constraints than their desktop counterparts.

Processing constraints

Today's mobile devices have several times the processing power of the Apollo Guidance Computer that put humans on the moon. They do not, however, have infinite processing power and have much less processing power than the common PC has at its disposal.

To accommodate the lack of processing power, mobile web apps should refrain from running highly intensive JavaScript functions, image manipulation, or any other processor-intensive operations in your app unless it is absolutely necessary to the functionality of the app.

One way to reduce the load on the client is to make certain determinations on the server before returning content back to the mobile device. This practice, referred to as server-side browser sniffing, allows the application to return web pages and content targeted for a specific device, and limits the need to do browser capability checks on the client. It is during this time that you can also preprocess data that would be returned to the client for processing otherwise. This is a shift from current web development trends where data is typically submitted to the client for processing.

By reducing the amount of content that is returned to the client by the server, you also mitigate some of the network constraints inherent to mobile devices.

Network constraints

While today's mobile networks rival, and in some cases surpass, speeds available to home-based broadband networks, your users may be constrained by data limits, speed governance, corporate policy, or some other constraint on the limit or speed at which they can retrieve data on their mobile device.

Mobile networks also inherently lose more network data in transmission than land-based communication. This data loss has two effects on the application and the user experience. Firstly, packet loss requires the TCP/IP stack implementation to request resends for lost packets and increases the amount of data that must be sent across the network. Secondly, your app needs to be written such that it can survive failed requests because it's guaranteed to happen.

How do we, as developers, ensure that our mobile web apps provide a great user experience on such a network?

Content compression

We can start reducing the amount of data representing content we're sending to the client by compressing it on the server side.

Server to client compression

Content compression can occur as part of the communication between client apps and web servers that support it. Content compression works by serving static, and occasionally dynamic content, and compressing it using **gzip** or **deflate** before returning it to the requesting app.

For a client to indicate that it can accept and process content, it must send an `Accept-Encoding` HTTP header with the request with the types of encoding it will accept.

```
Accept-Encoding: gzip, deflate
```

Enabling compression on the server is vendor and version-specific. It should be noted that while enabling compression on the server for communication does reduce the amount of data the server must send, it increases server processor utilization.

In addition to compression, we can also reduce the amount of data that needs to be sent to the client through a process called **minification**.

Minification

Minification is the act of removing extraneous white space from our HTML, CSS, and JavaScript files. Minification is not compression in the typical sense. The benefit of minification is that while you have reduced the amount of data you are sending to the client, it is immediately usable because nothing functional from that data has been removed.

Some minification techniques can also serve as a way to obfuscate JavaScript making it harder for people with ill intent to decipher what your code is doing. This is accomplished by parsing the content that is being minified and renaming long variables to between 1 and 3 characters.

Think Security

Never perform any action on the client that requires you to expose keys, usernames, passwords, or other sensitive information. Transmitting this information to the client is inviting mischief.

Image optimizations

Images make up a large percentage of the content your app will be serving to the client. Outside of minification, image optimizations may be one of the fastest ways to reduce the size of your app.

Lower color depth

Perhaps the easiest way to optimize images on your site is to reduce their color depth. Most images on the web are icons that can easily be represented with images of 8-bit or 16-bit color depth. With that said, it is an art more than a science. As today's mobile device displays increase their pixel depth, images of poor quality can detract from the functionality of your site and may discourage some users from using it.

CSS image sprites

An image sprite is a single image (that contains multiple images) that might be used on a site. The image sprite is then referenced by the stylesheet with different image offsets to only show a portion of that image. The following image from the Packt Publishing website (www.packtpub.com) is an example of an image sprite:

This image is actually a single image that contains two images for the site to use. Both images are 31 x 31 pixels. From this image we can create the following two styles:

```
.white-go
{
    width:31px;
    background:url('img-sprite.png') 0 0;
}

.orange-go
{
    width: 31px;
    background:url('img-sprite.png') -32px 0;
}
```

Firstly, note that the styles both have a width that is limited to the width of the actual image we want to display, that is, 31 pixels.

The white-go class sets the background image of the element which is applied to the sprite and sets the offset of the image to be the top-left corner, that is, 0,0. Since the image is restricted to 31 pixels wide, the viewer of the image will only be presented with the portion of the image containing the white go button.

The orange-go class has a negative offset to the image display telling the browser to show 31 pixels of the image starting at pixel 32. This displays only the orange image.

Both images may be reused by the app by applying the defined styles to the elements within the HTML markup, but the true benefit is that the app only made one request to the server to retrieve both images.

Data URIs

Data URIs (**Universal Resource Identifiers**) allow you to put content data directly into a URI link. The URI is formatted using the `data:[<mediatype>][;base64],<data>` format. From RFC 2397, the data URI scheme is defined as follows:

> *The <mediatype> is an Internet media type specification (with optional parameters). The appearance of ";base64" means that the data is encoded as base64. Without ";base64", the data (as a sequence of octets) is represented using ASCII encoding for octets inside the range of safe URL characters and using the standard %xx hex encoding of URLs for octets outside that range. If <mediatype> is omitted, it defaults to text/plain;charset=US-ASCII.*

Assume we want to embed the following simple image in a page using a data URI:

Hello,
Data URI!

If you were to embed the image above as a base-64 encoded PNG data URI into a page on your site, you would construct a data URI in your HTML source.

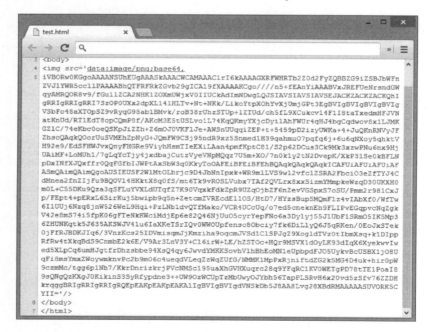

This provides the browser the benefit of not having to make a separate request to retrieve the image. With some clever JavaScript and CSS you could reuse the content of the URI without submitting another request to retrieve the image or embedding the image twice into the page.

As part of the page content, there is a second added benefit: the image data is compressed when sent from the server to the client as part of the web server's gzip compression.

 Data URIs are not supported in all browsers. If you elect to use data URIs in your site, make sure that your target market's primary browser supports them.

Content Delivery Networks

A **Content Delivery Network (CDN)** is a distributed network of servers that exist solely for returning static content. CDNs can reduce network load by hosting static content that is commonly cached and reducing the amount of data an application sends and receives for any given request.

Cached data

If you are using common third-party libraries such as jQuery, the mobile device executing your app may have already loaded that library from a third-party CDN. If the device has already retrieved the data you want to load, there is no need for the client to retrieve it again from the server. It can simply load it from the cache. There are several free CDN networks available for common content. As of this writing, Microsoft hosts a large amount of common third-party content on its CDN, of which a listing may be found at http://www.asp.net/ajaxlibrary/cdn.ashx.

As a routine point of maintenance, you will want to make sure the CDN you are using for shared content continues to provide the content. If they remove the content, your app will eventually degrade or fail.

Less traffic

A CDN is also useful for your proprietary static content. If you are using cookies within your site, every HTTP request to the domain specified in the cookie will retransmit the cookie data. Static content has no need for this data and it is consuming bandwidth that could be used elsewhere. If you move the static content of your site onto a different domain than the domain(s) on which your cookies reside, you reduce the amount of data sent to and from your app.

Don't make them wait

While it is critical to limit the amount of time any user has to wait to load your app's content, this is especially true of mobile web apps.

Presentation constraints

Processing constraints and network constraints help define how you implement your background services, but it is what the user sees that typically defines their experience. When presenting the content of your app to the user you need to keep in mind there are very real constraints placed on how information is presented to the user.

Single window

For starters, you only have a single window in which you can work. This means you should not be creating content that requires pop-up windows. Pop-up windows will open up in new tabs on most mobile browsers and those browsers may have limits as to the number of tabs open at any given time.

It is far better to stick with a simple navigation paradigm, and reduce the amount of data you present to the user at any given time. The user may have a few more screen touches to navigate through your application, but if you make the behavior consistent then it is unlikely your users will notice.

Lower resolution

With the exception of the newest mobile devices on the market, most devices do not have the resolution of their desktop counterparts.

Comparing standard phone form factors, the iPhone 5 has a screen resolution of 1136 x 640 pixels and the Samsung Galaxy S3 has a resolution of 1280 x 720. Of the popular 7-inch tablets, both the Kindle Fire HD and Google Nexus 7 have a screen resolution of 1280 x 800. Only the largest tablets such as the 10-inch third generation iPad (2048 x 1536) and the 8.9-inch Kindle Fire HD (1920 x 1200) come close to matching a desktop's display capability.

By way of comparison, the iPhone 4 and iPhone 4S have a resolution of 960 x 640.

While these resolutions seem respectable for mobile devices you must keep in mind that these resolutions are presented on screens that are substantially smaller than a desktop monitor, meaning not only is the number of available pixels for your app reduced on these smaller displays, but your app needs to present content, text, and buttons larger than it would to a desktop browser. This is partly because of the increased pixel density of the mobile devices, and partly because the input mechanism to these devices is your user's finger.

Content spacing

Designing a system to support touch instead of traditional input methods of mouse and keyboard mean that your buttons need to be larger, and a larger area of padding must surround any area of the screen that is designed for interaction with the user. This means your user interface and user experience must account for a large percentage of spacing.

Viewing the mobile web

While most of us own one, two, or perhaps three or more mobile devices with which we can browse the web, we need to develop our mobile web applications to support the broadest number of devices possible.

Market percentage

It is important for us to look at what technology is being used to browse the mobile web, so that we can target our mobile app appropriately. Currently, Android and iOS dominate the mobile OS market, but the newest version of Windows Mobile is gaining market share. Supporting the common browsers on these operating systems should be sufficient for most application needs.

Browser variants and compatibility

How does one target these specific browsers? All of these systems allow third-party browsers to be installed on them, so we cannot look at OS percentages as the sole determining factor when looking at compatibility.

Fortunately, while there are multiple browsers available for these platforms, there are only a handful of layout engines with which we must concern ourselves.

WebKit

WebKit is the layout engine for the majority of the web. Safari, Chrome, the Android Web Browser, Dolphin HD (a popular third-party Android web browser), Blackberry Browser 6.0+, and even a version of the PS3 software all use WebKit. If you target WebKit without any vendor-specific extensions, you will be supporting a huge segment of the web.

Trident

Internet Explorer uses the Trident engine to lay out HTML content. If you have done any Windows desktop development you might know this engine by the name MSHTML.

Trident has received a new version with every release of Internet Explorer since Internet Explorer 7. Both Windows and Windows Mobile share the same version of the engine. Internet Explorer 10 and Internet Explorer Mobile 10 use Version 6.0 of the Trident engine.

Gecko

Gecko has been around since Netscape 6, and is the current layout engine in Firefox, and several other Mozilla Foundation projects.

Presto

The Opera browser and the Nintendo DS/DSi use the Presto engine. This engine is only available as part of Opera but cannot be overlooked. Opera was the dominant browser on the mobile web and, depending on whose statistics you believe, continues to be the number two or number three used mobile browser today with over 20 percent of the market (no single browser currently eclipses 25 percent).

Emulating the mobile web

Since we will be implementing our mobile app on a desktop or laptop, we will want to emulate the mobile devices we are targeting. We can do this by installing emulators for each platform on our development machine, or by faking the mobile browser experience within our computer's browser.

Mobile device and browser emulators

Mobile device simulators provide us the best means of testing the functionality of our app within a mobile browser without having access to a physical mobile device.

Opera

The Opera Mobile Emulator has the smallest footprint of any emulator available. This is in large part due to the fact that there is no emulation of a mobile operating system. The installation comes with support for various device and browser version variants allowing you to test your app's look and feel on any device on which Opera Mobile is offered. There is also an optional install for Opera Dragonfly. Dragonfly allows you to debug your CSS and JavaScript as well as tune the performance of your app inside the emulator.

The Opera Mobile Emulator may be downloaded at `http://www.opera.com/developer/tools/mobile/`.

Android

The Android SDK, available at `http://developer.android.com/sdk`, comes with a mobile device emulator you can use to test your applications on the Android platform. The SDK requires you to install several third-party tools, JDK 6 most notably, to be fully functional.

iOS

If you do not have access to a machine running OS X, you cannot emulate the iOS environment with the official Apple SDK tools. Third-party emulators do exist, and you can find them by consulting your local search engine. Mac users may download the iOS emulator as part of Xcode (Apple's IDE) at `https://developer.apple.com/xcode/index.php`.

Windows Mobile

Microsoft provides a rather comprehensive set of tools with its Windows Mobile SDK. You can download and install the Windows Mobile SDK at `http://dev.windowsphone.com/`.

The user agent

Outside of an emulator, the easiest way for us to view the mobile web for multiple browser and device variants is by manipulating our desktop browser's user agent. The user agent is contained in an HTTP header the browser sends with any standard request for content to identify itself to the web server. The following line is a representation of the User-Agent HTTP header that Internet Explorer 10 submits to a web server with each request:

```
User-Agent: Mozilla/5.0 (compatible; MSIE 10.0; Windows NT 6.2;
Trident/6.0)
```

It cannot be stressed enough that altering the user agent is only marginally beneficial for testing the application. Even though mobile browsers are often built on top of the layout engines of their desktop brethren, you cannot assume that these engines will behave the same. The mobile engines are often ports of the desktop engines, and may have been altered or tweaked due to mobile device constraints. They may even not be written in the same language. Due to these issues, it must not be assumed that WebKit == WebKit. It does not. Because of this you will want to test your application using actual mobile devices, and all browser variants for which your mobile web app is targeted before pushing a product out to a production system.

With that said, let's examine how to set the User-Agent string of Internet Explorer, Safari, and Chrome so that they identify themselves to a web server as their mobile version.

Emulating Internet Explorer Mobile

To emulate Internet Explorer Mobile from the desktop, you will need to access the developer tools. To do this, you can either press *F12* in Internet Explorer or click on the settings wheel in the top-left corner of the window, and select **F12 developer tools** from the menu options.

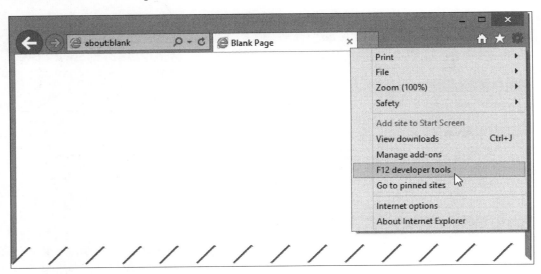

Internet Explorer will then present a dockable window containing the Internet Explorer developer tools. In the tools window, click on **Tools** from the menu, and then select the **Change user agent string** menu option. You will be presented with a list of preconfigured User-Agent strings within Internet Explorer. You may also enter a custom User-Agent string by selecting the **Custom...** menu option.

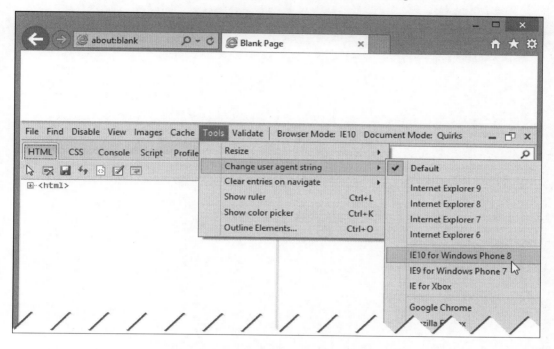

Internet Explorer will revert to the default User-Agent string after you close all browser windows and exit the process. This is important to remember when you are debugging your mobile app using Internet Explorer.

Emulating Mobile Safari

To set the User-Agent string in Mobile Safari we first have to enable the mobile tools. To do this, open the preferences pane for Safari by pressing *Ctrl +* , or by clicking on the settings icon in the top-left corner of the window, and then clicking **Preferences...**.

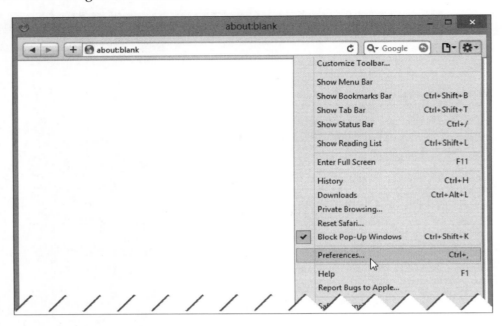

On the Preferences window, click on the icon labeled **Advanced** to display the Advanced Preferences pane, and ensure that the checkbox captioned **Show Desktop menu in menu bar** is checked.

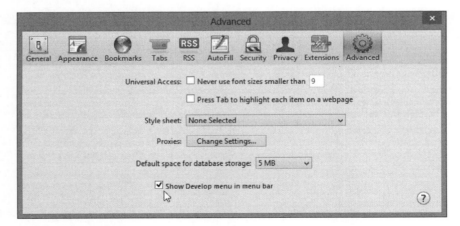

After you close the window, you will have a new **Develop** menu available. Clicking on the menu and hovering over **User Agent** will open up the known User-Agent strings for which Safari has built-in support. If you do not see the User-Agent string you wish to target, you may provide a custom User-Agent string by clicking on the menu item labeled **Other...**.

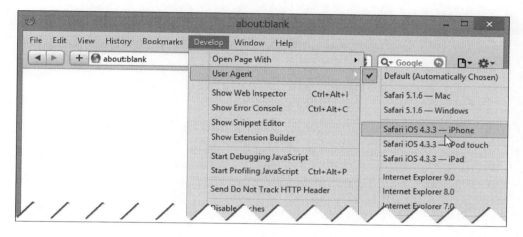

It is important to note that Safari, like Internet Explorer, will restore the value of the User-Agent string to the default value after you close the browser window.

Emulating Chrome for Mobile

Like Safari, Chrome has built-in developer tools that are immediately accessible by pressing *Ctrl + Shift + I* or by clicking the customize icon in the top-right, selecting **Tools** and then clicking on the **Developer tools** menu item.

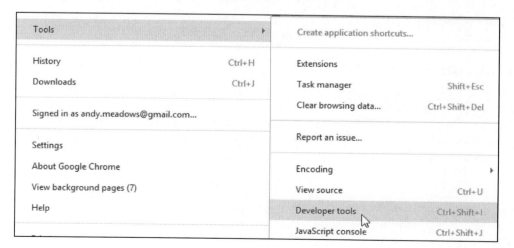

Clicking on the **Developer tools** menu item will display a docked window at the bottom of the browser. In the bottom-left corner of this window is a small gear icon. Clicking on the icon will display the settings for the developer tools in an overlaid window. The window has three tabs: **General**, **Overrides**, and **Shortcuts**. Click on the **Overrides** tab, check the checkbox labeled **User Agent**, and then select the User-Agent string you wish to use from the drop-down menu.

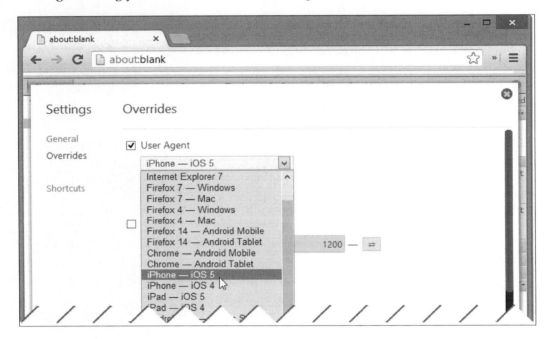

Like Safari and Internet Explorer, you can create custom User-Agent strings to be used by the browser. Unlike those browsers, Google Chrome will remember the User-Agent string to be used if you close all the windows.

Emulation in this book

When using user agent emulation, all samples in this book will emulate the mobile Safari browser used by iOS from within Chrome. This is in small part due to Chrome using the same layout engine as Safari, but is primarily due to the developer tools that are built into the browser itself and the fact that it is more widely installed on computers running Windows than is Safari.

When using a mobile emulator, we will use Opera Mobile emulating a Samsung Galaxy S II—a device that has a screen resolution of 480 x 800, and has 216 pixels per inch.

We will also show screens from a few physical devices such as iPhone 4, iPhone 5, and the Asus Nexus 7 Android tablet.

You should feel free to run the samples in the book against any browser or emulator mentioned above.

Support for the mobile web in ASP.NET MVC 4

Microsoft has unprecedented development support for the mobile web with Visual Studio 2012 and ASP.NET MVC 4.0. Out-of-the-box, the latest environment supports:

- HTML5 and CSS3 (standards crucial to developing responsive mobile web apps)
- The ability to merge, compress, and transform JavaScript and CSS files to minimize browser requests and bandwidth requirements
- New convention support to target specific mobile platforms
- As part of the new mobile application project template, jQuery Mobile integration into your mobile app projects

All of these improvements to Microsoft's development environment directly address the constraints with which we, as developers, engineers, architects, and content designers, must concern ourselves. If you couple these improvements with the improvements in .NET 4.5, .NET users such as us can now target the mobile web better than ever before.

Summary

In this chapter, we learned why it is important as developers to embrace the mobile web and ensure that our apps support it. We began with a brief history of the mobile web and the constraints still placed upon developers like us to ensure an optimal user experience when viewing our sites through a mobile browser. We also learned how to emulate the common mobile browsers from our desktop and received a glimpse of what Microsoft has provided in support of the mobile web with the new ASP.NET MVC 4 tooling, Visual Studio 2012, and .NET 4.5.

In the next chapter, we will create the shell for our app—a homebrew recipe sharing app called BrewHow—and configure our environment to run the app within an emulator.

2
Homebrew and You

In this chapter, we will discuss everything you need to know to build our sample app, a recipe-sharing site for homebrewers. We will begin with a discussion on homebrewing in order to understand the domain of our sample app. From our understanding of the domain, we will determine requirements. We will then create the solution for our app using one of the new MVC 4 (Model-View-Controller) project templates and examine the output of the template to discuss the notable changes between MVC 3 and MVC 4. Finally, we will configure Visual Studio to launch an emulator and a desktop browser simultaneously when starting our app.

Understanding the homebrew domain

The brewing and fermentation of malt that creates the delicious beverage commonly referred to as beer has been around since ancient Egypt. Beer is comprised of four ingredients: water, malt, hops, and yeast. This simple combination of four ingredients can produce a wide variety of beverages and it is this quest for variety that has sparked the homebrew and craft brew movement so active today.

Knowing your ingredients

Any good recipe starts with a list of ingredients. A beer recipe will start with the list of grains to be used, any adjuncts (special ingredients such as coffee, chocolate, fruit, or spices that will give the beer a new flavor or enhance an existing characteristic of the brew), the strain of yeast to be used, and hops used for bittering and aroma.

Malt

Malt is any grain that has been allowed to begin the germination process. It is the germination of the grain that allows the grain to produce enzymes that can convert starches contained in the grain to sugar and break down protein to feed the yeast. It is the converted sugar of the malt that gives beer its sweetness and it is the same sugar that is converted to alcohol during the fermentation process.

Yeast

Yeast handles the conversion of sugars into alcohol. When brewing beer one must always consider that the yeast is alive. Proper handling of yeast, in addition to the sanitization of brewing equipment, is essential to brewing a successful batch of ale or lager.

Ale versus lager

Beer is either classified as ale or lager. The classification is based upon the type of yeast used to ferment the beer. Lager yeast ferments beer from the bottom of the chamber and is active at cooler temperatures than yeast used to create ales. Ale yeast ferments from the top and is most active at around 70 degrees Fahrenheit. The warmer fermentation temperatures of ale yeast require less special equipment than lagering yeast and, as such, most homebrew recipes are designed to create ales.

Hops

Hops are a type of flower used in recipes and lend to the distinct aroma and bitterness that most people associate with beer. As with grains and yeast, hops come in several varieties and each variety is measured by the aroma and bitterness that their inclusion in the recipe brings to the beer.

Hops also aid in the prevention of spoilage of beer as they create an environment within the brew that is favorable to the yeast used to ferment beer.

Brewing

The brewing process takes our raw ingredients and transforms them into unfermented beer. There are three steps in the brewing process, namely, mashing, sparging, and the boil.

Mashing

Mashing is the process of soaking cracked malt in water in a temperature-controlled environment. Temperature control is important as different proteins, enzymes, and by-products are produced and released from the malt depending on the temperature at which the malt is maintained. These by-products of the malting process affect the body, head retention, clarity, and alcohol content of the beer being produced.

The mashing process may be a single infusion or step infusion. Single infusion mashing holds the ingredients at a single temperature throughout the process. Step infusion, however, requires the brewer to alter the temperature of the ingredients throughout the mashing process to better control the release of proteins, enzymes, and by-products released from the malt.

Sparging

Sparging is the process of separating the spent grains, termed grist, from the mash and is essentially straining the mash into another container. Additional water is poured over the grist to free up any remaining starches, proteins, or sugars. The resulting liquid is called wort.

The boil

Once you've obtained your wort, the wort must be boiled. The boil typically lasts 60 minutes and is meant to sanitize the liquid to create an optimal environment for the yeast. It is during the boil that hops are added to the beer.

Early addition of hops to the boil increases the bitterness of the beer. Later additions contribute to the aroma of the beer.

Fermentation

After the boil, the wort must be cooled quickly, typically to 70 degrees Farenheit, before we can add the yeast. After cooling, the wort is moved into a fermenter and yeast is added. The wort is then kept in a quite corner at a temperature beneficial for the strain of yeast used to ferment, typically for two weeks.

Bottling and kegging

We now have beer; it's flat beer, but beer nonetheless. To liven the beer up, we need to feed the yeast before we put the beer into bottles or kegs. To do this, we put a little priming sugar into the beer or into the bottles or kegs. Feeding the yeast with sugar will allow for the production of CO_2 and its production will carbonate our beer.

That's all there is to making beer. After two weeks, in the bottle or keg, the beer should be sufficiently carbonated to open up and share with your friends.

Now that we have a deeper understanding, appreciation, and love for beer, let's go build an app to allow us to share recipes to the world's mobile devices.

About our mobile app

We just arrived at the homebrew supply store and, low and behold, we left our recipe at home. That's the last time this is going to happen. We're going to build an app that allows us to retrieve recipes on our phone.

The recipes created and stored in our app will also provide a means for us to teach others about the brewing process and what makes good beer. To that end, we will name this app BrewHow.

App requirements

For us to be successful in our mission to create a great beer recipe site for the mobile web, we need to know the requirements that, when met, will determine success.

Adding, editing, and deleting recipes

How good is a recipe-sharing app without the ability to add and edit recipes? Our site will allow us to create recipes that can be shared with other people. It will also allow us to edit recipes that we have contributed to the site.

Adding recipes to a library

As we find good recipes, we will want to be able to locate them again. We need to support adding them to a library. We may also grow tired of them so we need the ability to remove them as well.

Rating recipes

Much as we rate music to better identify our tastes, we should do this with beer too. Our app will provide users the ability to rate recipes on a scale of one to five.

Commenting on recipes

We not only want to share recipes, but to solicit feedback on what makes good beer and how to make our beer better. To allow this type of feedback, we want to allow constructive comments about the recipes on our site.

Anonymous browsing, authenticated contributing

We want our recipes hosted within our mobile web app to be available to the world, but if a user wants to contribute to the site we want to know who the user is. Likewise, we don't want users editing the recipes contributed by other users. Seems like we need to add some authentication and authorization to our mobile app.

Now that we know what our app should do, let's get started by creating our ASP.NET MVC 4 solution.

The BrewHow solution

To build the BrewHow mobile app, we are going to use Visual Studio Express 2012 for Web. If you don't have a version of Visual Studio capable of building ASP.NET MVC 4 projects, Visual Studio Express 2012 for Web is freely available at http://www.microsoft.com/visualstudio/eng/downloads.

> We will constantly refer to Visual Studio or Visual Studio 2012. These are references to any version of Visual Studio 2012 or Visual Studio 2010 SP1 that is capable of building ASP.NET MVC 4 apps.

Creating the project

We will start with creating a new solution in Visual Studio 2012. Start by launching Visual Studio. Click on the **FILE** menu and then click on **New Project...**. You may also press *Ctrl + Shift +N*.

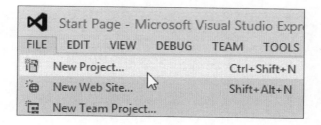

Visual Studio will then prompt you with a dialog box asking you for the type of solution you want to create. We will be creating a new ASP.NET MVC 4 Web application.

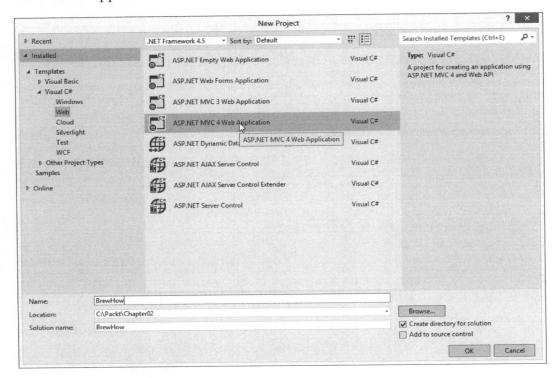

Select the **ASP.NET MVC 4 Web Application** icon and provide a name and location for the new project in the **Name** and **Location** text boxes respectively. In this book, we will be referencing the BrewHow project in the Packt directory located on the C:, but you may name it anything you like and put it wherever you want to. When you have decided on a name and location, click on **OK**.

Visual Studio will now prompt you to choose your project template.

Choosing our template

Visual Studio 2012 ships with six ASP.NET MVC 4 project templates.

The Empty template

The Empty template isn't as empty as you might think. The project template is not empty, instead it contains the minimal content required to make it an MVC project. There are no scripts or content and the `Models`, `Controllers`, and `App_Data` folders are empty.

The Basic template

The Basic template is essentially the new version of the MVC 3 Empty template. This template adds the `Content` and `Scripts` folder to the Empty template and includes additional assembly references that are required for some of the new features of MVC 4.

The Internet Application template

This template will be the template from which most sites will be created. This template includes everything present in the Basic template but adds an `Account` and `Home` controller to the structure to enable authentication against the traditional ASP.NET SQL Server Membership structure and, new to MVC 4, third-party authentication providers such as Microsoft, Google, and Facebook through the DotNetOpenAuth library.

The Intranet Application template

The Intranet Application template is a variation of the Internet Application template. It has been altered to support Windows authentication as the authentication mechanism.

The Mobile Application template

If you are sure that almost all of your traffic will be from mobile devices, you will want to create your application from the Mobile Application template. This template adds support for jQuery Mobile to the Internet Application but removes the DotNetOpenAuth library support in favor of traditional forms authentication.

The Web API template

New to ASP.NET MVC 4 is the Web API. The Web API provides an easy way to develop RESTful HTTP services and APIs that understand XML and JSON content types. This project template provides the base for constructing new services utilizing the Web API.

We will create our sample application from the Internet template. We do this for a couple of reasons. First, most of the applications that we implement and support on a day-to-day basis require us to target both desktop browsers as well as mobile browsers. Second, by developing from the Internet template, we can learn more about what is necessary to support the mobile web from the perspective of ASP.NET MVC 4 as well as a general application development perspective.

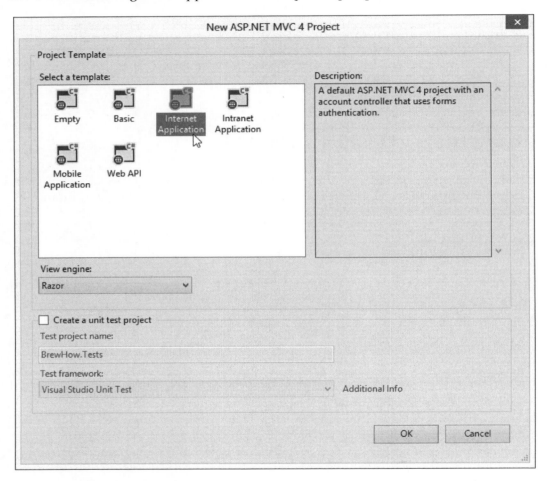

Select **Internet Application** from the template options and click on the button labeled **OK**.

Congratulations! You have just created your first ASP.NET MVC 4 project.

Project changes in MVC 4

In addition to new framework features, ASP.NET MVC 4 projects have also undergone some important changes that you should note if you have worked with ASP.NET MVC in the past.

NuGet

If you are unfamiliar with NuGet, NuGet is a .NET platform package management system. Its goal is to simplify the management of third-party libraries, tools, and scripts within .NET projects. It is now a first-class member of Visual Studio 2012 and the MVC project templates.

If you examine the project we just created, you will notice there is a `packages.config` file at the bottom of the solution.

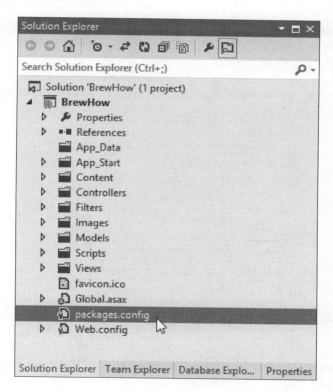

This file is a NuGet package list and contains a list of all the external dependencies to the project. For the Internet Application template, the file includes references to DotNetOpenAuth, Entity Framework, jQuery, knockoutjs, non-core Microsoft libraries, Modernizr, Netwonsoft's JSON library, and WebGrease.

Global.asax

In prior versions of MVC, all of the application bootstrap code was located in the
Global.asax code-behind. New in MVC 4, you will notice that the class within
the Global.asax file contains only a single method named Application_Start.
Have a look at the following piece of code:

```
protected void Application_Start()
{
  AreaRegistration.RegisterAllAreas();
  WebApiConfig.Register(GlobalConfiguration.Configuration);
  FilterConfig.RegisterGlobalFilters(GlobalFilters.Filters);
  RouteConfig.RegisterRoutes(RouteTable.Routes);
  BundleConfig.RegisterBundles(BundleTable.Bundles);
  AuthConfig.RegisterAuth();
}
```

This method invokes several other classes with which you may be unfamiliar.
While it is true that some new functionality regarding bundling and the Web API
are reflected in the class names, these names also identify the functionality that has
been present in prior versions such as area registration and routing. These new
classes encapsulate the traditional configuration information you might expect
to see here and the classes exist in the project's App_Start folder.

This new organization of code provides for better separation of functionality
and makes the Global.asax code-behind a lot easier to read and digest.

Now that we've seen some of the structural changes that have taken place inside
the new MVC 4 project templates, let's examine how the output of the new project
templates looks by launching the project from within Visual Studio 2012.

Launching the BrewHow app

To launch the application, simply press *Ctrl + F5* to start the app without running the debugger.

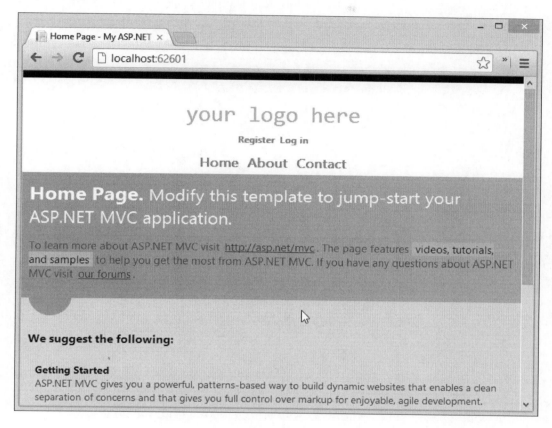

You will notice that the default theme for MVC applications has been retooled. Not only does the initial application look better, but also it is structured in such a way that it supports responsive design.

Responsive design

Responsive design means an app has been designed to attempt to present itself properly within any browser window and to continually respond to changes in the size of the browser window or in the content that the page, itself, is displaying.

Notice how the content of the browser window has reorganized itself to work within a smaller browser window. All of the content is still logically grouped and is available to the user and there is no horizontal scroll bar present indicating that while the content may have collapsed it still will display within the window.

This compressed view does allow you to get an idea of how the site will appear on a mobile device, but if you really want to know how it will look, then you should view the app in an emulator.

Configuring and launching an emulator

It would be pretty useful for us to launch our app from within Visual Studio 2012 and have an emulator, or multiple emulators, open up the landing page. Fortunately for us, Visual Studio 2012 supports the simultaneous launching of multiple browsers when attempting to run or debug an app.

Choose and use an emulator

Hopefully you have installed one of the emulators listed in the first chapter. If not, let me emphasize again that unless you are testing the app on physical hardware (preferred) or on an emulator. It is disservice to users because it's buggy and also to you as it tarnishes your reputation.

To configure Visual Studio to launch multiple browsers simultaneously, we first need to add an empty HTML page to our solution. The empty HTML page will add no functionality and exists only to gain us access to the context menu that will allow us to set the default browser/browsers for our app.

To add a new HTML page file to the project, right-click on the **BrewHow** project to bring up the project context menu. From the menu, select **Add** and then select **HTML Page**.

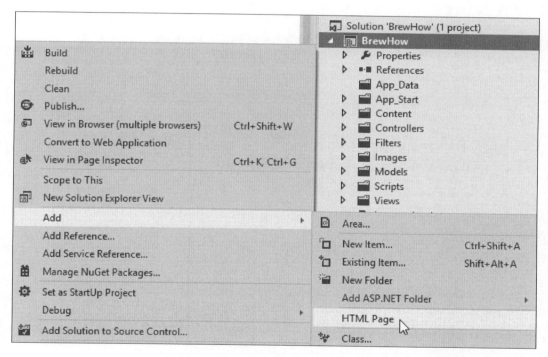

You will be presented with a dialog box asking you to specify a name for the item. Name the file anything you'd like (the sample project filename is `browser.html`) and then click on the button labeled **OK**.

Right-click on the HTML page you just added to the project and select **Browse With...** from the context menu.

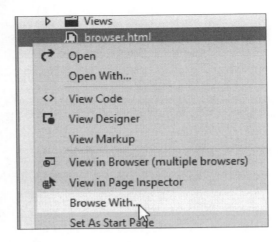

This will bring up the Visual Studio 2012 **Browse With** dialog box. This dialog box allows us to set the default browser with which we will view our app when launching it from within Visual Studio.

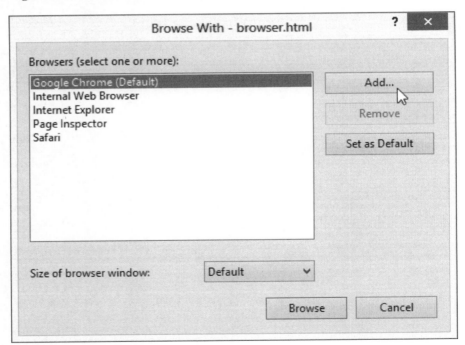

We are going to use Google Chrome and the Opera Mobile emulator as our default browsers for the BrewHow project.

 Though we're configuring Opera Mobile to launch, these instructions can be used with any emulator or desktop browser.

Since Opera Mobile isn't a browser that's typically registered with Visual Studio, we first need to tell Visual Studio where it can be found. Click on the **Add...** button on the **Browse With** dialog box to begin registering the browser.

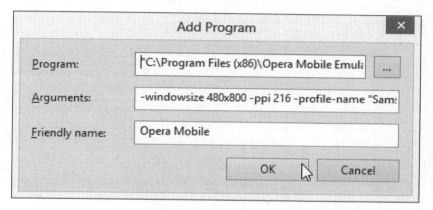

Assuming you have installed the Opera Mobile emulator in the default location, enter the following values into the dialog box to register an emulator for Opera Mobile running on a Samsung Galaxy S II and then click on **OK**.

Field	Description
Program	`C:\Program Files (x86)\Opera Mobile Emulator\OperaMobileEmu.exe`
Arguments	`-windowsize 480x800 -ppi 216 -profile-name "Samsung Galaxy S II"`
Friendly name	`Opera Mobile`

You should now see **Opera Mobile** displayed in the **Browse With** dialog box.

Hold down the *Ctrl* key, click on both **Google Chrome** and **Opera Mobile**, click on the button labeled **Set as Default** and then close the dialog box.

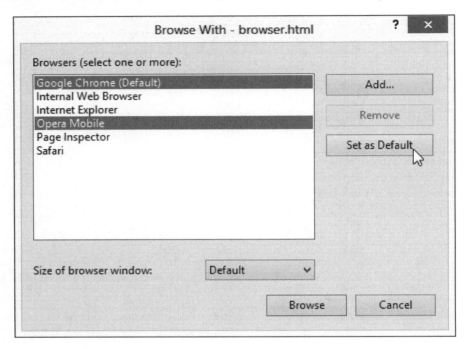

If you were successful, you should notice that the text beside the **Start Debugging** button in Visual Studio now says **Multiple Browsers**.

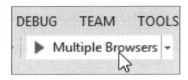

Press *Ctrl + F5* to launch the app without debugging and Visual Studio will open the BrewHow app in both Chrome and the Opera Mobile emulator.

Summary

You should now have a good enough understanding of the homebrewing domain to apply it to the sample application. We also learned about the changes that have occurred in Visual Studio 2012's MVC 4 project templates and project structure and have now properly configured your environment to begin developing BrewHow, our mobile homebrew recipe-sharing app.

In the next chapter, we will do a detailed examination of the code generated by the template and how that code relates to the MVC design pattern. We will also create our first controller using this knowledge.

Introducing ASP.NET MVC 4 _3_

ASP.NET MVC 4 is the latest version of Microsoft's Model-View-Controller (MVC) framework for the web. The MVC pattern is not specific to this framework. It was first introduced as a feature of the Smalltalk language in the 1970s and has seen much success in client/server, desktop, mobile, and web development. It is a software design pattern that helps to enforce a separation of concerns between data and the interaction with data.

In this chapter, we are going to examine the MVC pattern and how it is implemented within the ASP.NET MVC framework. We will then begin by applying that knowledge to the BrewHow app. At the end of this chapter, our application will be returning sample recipes to any user making a request.

The Model-View-Controller pattern

Each component of the MVC pattern fills a very specific purpose in separating data within an application from user interaction with the data. The following is a very brief introduction to the components of the MVC design pattern.

The controller

In the MVC pattern, the controller acts as a delegator. It submits modifications to the model on behalf of some external interaction (typically a user), and retrieves data for a view as the result of a notification or direct request via user interaction.

The view

Views handle the presentation of the data to some external entity. If a view contains logic, that logic is limited to the presentation of the data it received from the controller as the result of an interaction with the model.

The model

The model is the encapsulation of application-specific data, and the means by which to store, retrieve, and maintain the integrity of that data. The model may or may not mimic the structure in which the actual data is stored or presented.

The MVC pattern and ASP.NET MVC 4

The implementation of the MVC pattern in ASP.NET MVC 4 largely follows a **convention-over-configuration** paradigm. Simply stated, if you put something in the right place and/or name it the right way, it simply works. That is not to say that we cannot configure the framework to ignore or alter these conventions. It is the flexibility and adaptability of ASP.NET MVC 4 along with its adherence to web standards that has driven its rapid adoption.

 If you have no exposure to ASP.NET or ASP.NET MVC, please note that each of the components of the MVC pattern, as they relate to ASP.NET MVC 4, is often presented in a separate chapter of its own.

The following is a very condensed high-level overview of the MVC pattern in ASP.NET MVC 4.

Controllers in ASP.NET MVC

In ASP.NET MVC 4, controllers respond to HTTP requests and determine the action to take based upon the content of the incoming request.

Controllers in ASP.NET MVC 4 are located in a project folder named, appropriately, `Controllers`. The Internet Application project we selected for BrewHow contains two controllers in the `Controllers` folder: `AccountController` and `HomeController`.

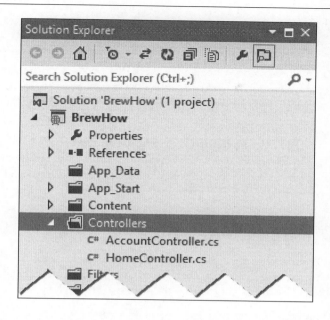

If you examine the code in the `HomeController.cs` file, you will notice that the
`HomeController` class extends the `Controller` class.

```
public class HomeController : Controller
{
    /* Class methods... */
}
```

> **Downloading the example code**
>
> You can download the example code files for all Packt books you have
> purchased from your account at `http://www.packtpub.com`. If you
> purchased this book elsewhere, you can visit `http://www.packtpub.`
> `com/support` and register to have the files e-mailed directly to you.

The `Controller` class and the `ControllerBase` class, from which the `Controller`
class derives, contain methods and properties used to process and respond to HTTP
requests. Almost all interaction that occurs while retrieving data from a request or
returning data in response to a request will be through the methods and properties
exposed by the `Controller` inheritance chain.

If you have no prior experience with ASP.NET MVC, you might assume that controllers in the project are identified by either placement in the `Controllers` folder or by extending the `Controller` class. In actuality, the runtime uses class name to identify controllers in the default MVC framework configuration; controllers must have a `Controller` suffix. For example, there might be a controller for recipes, and the class representing this controller would be named `RecipeController`.

> As we discussed briefly, every part of the ASP.NET MVC framework is extensible and configurable. You are free to provide some other convention to the framework that it can use to identify controllers.

Creating the Recipe controller

Let's create a new controller to return recipes to our users. In the **Solution Explorer**, right-click on the **Controllers** folder in the BrewHow project, select **Add**, and then select the **Controller** menu item. You may also press *Ctrl + M, Ctrl + C*.

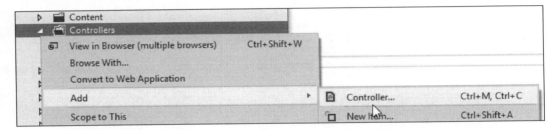

In the **Add Controller** dialog, name the controller `RecipeController`, select the **Empty MVC controller** template from the **Template** drop-down menu, and then click on the **Add** button.

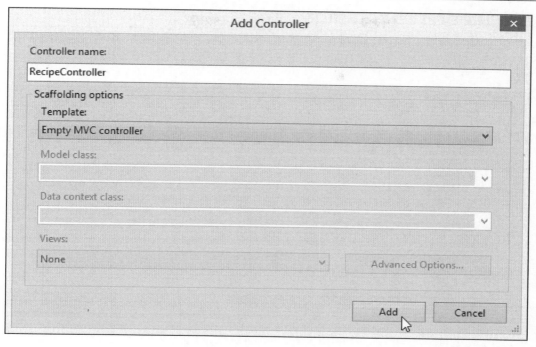

Congratulations! You have created your first controller in the BrewHow application. The code should look similar to the following:

```
public class RecipeController : Controller
{
    public ActionResult Index()
    {
        return View();
    }
}
```

Notice that this code is very similar to the code in HomeController. The RecipeController inherits the Controller class and, like HomeController, contains an Index method that returns ActionResult. The class is also properly named with a Controller suffix, so the runtime will be able to identify it as a controller.

I'm sure you're ready to examine the output of this controller, but before we can do that we need to understand a little about how the controller is invoked in the first place.

Introduction to routing

At application startup, a series of formatted strings (similar to formatted strings you would use in String.Format) along with name, default values, constraints, and/or types are registered with the runtime. This combination of name, formatted string, values, constraints, and types is termed a **route**. The runtime uses routes to determine which controller and action should be invoked to handle a request. In our BrewHow project, routes are defined and registered with the runtime in the RouteConfig.cs file in the App_Start folder.

The default route for our app is registered with the runtime as shown below.

```
routes.MapRoute(
    name: "Default",
    url: "{controller}/{action}/{id}",
    defaults: new
    {
        controller = "Home",
        action = "Index",
        id = UrlParameter.Optional
    });
```

The formatted string for our default route looks very similar to a URL you might type within the browser. The only notable difference is that each segment of the URL — the portion of the URL between the slashes (/) — is surrounded with curly braces ({}).

Our default route contains segments to identify a controller, an action (method), and an optional ID.

When our app receives a request, the runtime looks at the URL requested and attempts to map it to any formatted string that has been registered via the MapRoute method. If the incoming URL contains segments that can be mapped into the segments of the formatted string URL, the runtime determines that a match has been found.

Two segments, controller and action, have special meaning, and determine the controller to be instantiated and method (action) to be invoked on the controller. The other segments may be mapped to parameters on the method itself. All segments are placed in a route dictionary using the name of the segment within the curly braces as the key, and the mapped portion of the URL as the value.

To help clarify that with an example, assume a request is made to our app for the URL /do/something. The runtime would consult the route table, which is the collection of all routes registered by the application, and find a match on our Default route. It would then begin to map the segments of the URL request to the formatted string URL. The value do would be placed in the route dictionary under the key controller and the value of something would be under the key action. The runtime would then attempt to invoke the Something method of the DoController, appending the Controller suffix to the controller name.

If you examine our Default route a little further, you will see the words within the curly braces correspond to the names of values passed via the defaults parameter of MapRoute. This is, in fact, what makes this a default route. If no controller has been identified by a route, then the runtime will use HomeController. If it can find no action, the Index method on the identified controller will be used. The welcome page we viewed in *Chapter 2*, *Homebrew and You*, was invoked because the requested URL of / (slash) mapped to our Default route, and hence, invoked the Index method of HomeController.

Routing is a very complex topic. Incoming routes can be ignored, may contain specific values or constraints as part of their mapping, and may include optional parameters. And never forget, the order in which routes are registered is important, very important. Routing is so complex that entire tools have been built around debugging routing issues. This introduction covers only the information needed to understand the content of this book until we get to *Chapter 7*, *Separating Functionality Using Routes and Areas*.

Action methods

An action method (action for short) is a special method in an ASP.NET MVC controller that does the heavy lifting. The code within action methods handles business decisions based upon the data passed to it, interacts with the model on behalf of the request, and tells the runtime which view should be processed in the response to the client.

In the initial request to our application, we identified that the HomeController class was being invoked and instructed to execute the Index action when we examined how routing worked.

For our Recipe controller, this method is pretty straightforward.

```
public ActionResult Index()
{
    return View();
}
```

There is no model interaction and no business decision to be made within our action method. All that the action does is use the `View` method of the base `Controller` class to return the default view. The `View` method is one of several methods in the base `Controller` class that return an `ActionResult`.

ActionResults

An `ActionResult` is a special return type used by action methods. `ActionResult` allows you to render a view to the response, redirect the requestor to another resource (a controller, view, image, and others), translate data into JSON for AJAX method calls, and pretty much anything else you can imagine.

The base `Controller` class provides methods that return most of the `ActionResult` derived classes you need, so you should rarely need to instantiate a class derived from `ActionResult`. The following table illustrates the helper methods within the base `Controller` class that return an `ActionResult`:

Controller ActionResult Helper	Returns	Use
Content	ContentResult	Returns content in response to a request on a controller
File	FileContentResult FileStreamResult FilePathResult	Returns the contents of a file in response to a request on a controller
JavaScript	JavaScriptResult	Returns JavaScript in response to a request on a controller
Json	JsonResult	Returns the JSON representation of an object, typically a model or view model, in response to a request on a controller

Controller ActionResult Helper	Returns	Use
PartialView	PartialViewResult	Returns a rendered partial view result in response to a request on a controller
Redirect	RedirectResponse	Instructs the requestor to retrieve the requested resource from another location
RedirectPermanent	RedirectResponse	Instructs the requestor to retrieve the requested resource from another location, and that the resource has been permanently moved
RedirectToAction	RedirectToRouteResult	Behaves the same as RedirectResponse but uses the route table to create the redirect location returned to the requestor
RedirectToActionPermanent	RedirectToRouteResult	This is identical to RedirectToAction, but informs the requestor that the resource has been moved permanently
RedirectToRoute	RedirectToRouteResult	Takes route parameters, values that map to URL segments in the route table, to construct a redirect URL to return to the requestor

Controller ActionResult Helper	Returns	Use
RedirectToRoutePermanent	RedirectToRouteResult	Behaves the same as RedirectToRoute but informs the requestor that the resource has been moved permanently
View	ViewResult	Returns a rendered view result in response to a request on a controller

Invoking the Recipe controller

Applying what we've learned about routing, accessing /Recipe should invoke the Index action method of our new RecipeController using the Default route. Launch the app in the browser, append /Recipe to the URL, and press *Enter*.

This is probably not the result you were expecting. The error exists because there is no view available for the Index action of RecipeController.

Views in ASP.NET MVC

In ASP.NET MVC and the MVC pattern in general, the view handles the presentation of the data as the result of a request sent to a controller. By default, views are stored in the Views folder.

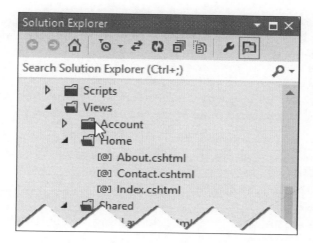

Within the Views folder of the project there are folders corresponding to each controller. Note that in the Home folder there are views corresponding to each action method in the HomeController class. This is by design, and is one of the other ASP.NET MVC's convention-over-configuration features.

Whenever the runtime is looking for the view to correlate back to an action, it will first look for a view whose name matches the action being invoked. It will try and locate that view in a folder whose name matches the controller being invoked. For our initial request of /Home/Index, the runtime will look for the view Views/Home/Index.cshtml.

There is a pretty substantial search order that the runtime goes through to determine the default view. You can see that search order if you examine the error screen presented when trying to invoke the RecipeController without first creating the view for the action.

Razor

Razor is the default **View Engine**, part of the runtime that parses, processes, and executes any code within a view, in ASP.NET MVC 4. The Razor View Engine has a very terse syntax designed to limit keystrokes and increase readability of your views.

Note that I said syntax and not language. Razor is intended to be easily incorporated into your existing skill set and allow you to focus on the current task. All you really need to know to use Razor successfully is the location of the @ character on your keyboard.

The .cshtml is an extension that identifies a view as a Razor View Engine view written in C#. If the language in which the view is written is Visual Basic, the extension will be .vbhtml. If you elect to use the Web Form View Engine, your views will have a .aspx extension associated with them, but you will be unable to follow along with the samples in this book. All of the views used by the BrewHow app are parsed and processed by the Razor View Engine.

The @ character

The @ character is the key to understanding the Razor syntax. It is the symbol used to denote blocks of code, comments, expressions, and inline code. More precisely, the @ character instructs the View Engine to begin treating the content of a view as code that must be parsed, processed, and executed.

Code blocks

If you want to place a block of code within a Razor view, simply prefix the block of code using @.

```
@{
    string foo = "bar";
}
```

Code blocks are the portions of code between the curly braces ({}).

Expressions

Expressions are portions of code whose evaluation results in a value being returned. Expressions can be a method invocation.

```
@foo.Bar()
```

They can also be used to retrieve the value of a property.

```
@user.FirstName.
```

Expressions can be embedded directly into the output HTML.

```
<h1>Hello, @user.FirstName</h1>
```

By default, the result of any Razor expression evaluation is HTML encoded. This means that any special characters having meaning to the client are escaped as part of the output processing. This functionality also serves as a security mechanism, preventing accidental (or malicious) additions of executable code being sent to a requestor.

If you need to expose the raw value of a property or method, you may do so using the `Raw` HTML helper extension method.

```
@Html.Raw(beVeryCarefulDoingThis)
```

HTML encoding helps prevent Cross-Site Scripting (XSS) attacks by instructing the browser to render the output as data. It is critical that you encode any and all data you return to the client. There are several other attacks possible on websites, which are well beyond the scope of this book, and I urge you to develop defensive coding practices and become knowledgeable about the potential threats your application may face.

Inline code

As mentioned earlier, the Razor View Engine is smart enough to infer when an actionable piece of code has terminated and processing should stop. This is exceptionally handy when placing inline code in your views.

```
@if (userIsAuthenticated) {
    <span>Hello, @username</span>
} else {
    <a href='#'>Please login</a>
}
```

If the content you want to display to the user within inline code has no wrapping tag such as span or div, you can wrap the content in `<text>` tags.

```
@if (jobIsDone) {
    <text>profit!</text>
}
```

Note that merely mentioning the placement of code directly within your view may result in discussions similar to those about the location of your opening curly brace. If you are a practicing member of the Church of Inline Code it may be best that you follow a "Don't Ask, Don't Tell" policy.

Comments

If you are wise and comment your code, Razor supports it.

```
@* Your comment goes here. *@
```

Comments, like anything else, need to be maintained. If you modify your code, modify your comments.

There are several other things that can be done with Razor such as creating delegates, but we will address them as we encounter them in our application.

Shared views

When we examined the views of `HomeController`, we learned that the views for a controller are placed in a folder that shares the same name. Views are only readily available to the controller owning that folder. If we want to make a view easily accessible to more than one controller, we need to mark that view as shared by placing the view in the `Shared` folder underneath the `Views` folder.

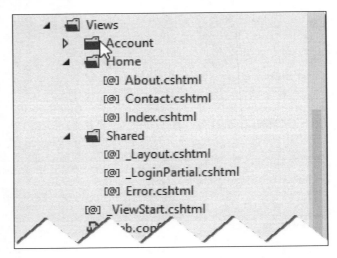

If the runtime cannot find the appropriate view in the executing controller's view folder, the next place it will look is the Shared folder. Our current app has three views located in the Shared folder.

_LoginPartial.cshtml is a partial view that contains our login control. This control is embedded in several of our views and displays the login form for users who are unauthenticated. Its consumption by several of the views merits it a position in the Shared folder.

The view Error.cshtml is the global error page. It is returned by action methods when something unforeseen has happened. Since any action can return this view, it has been placed in the Shared folder.

The third view, _Layout.cshtml, is a special type of shared view known as a layout.

Layouts

A layout is a template for the content of your view. Layouts typically contain scripts, navigation, headers, footers, or other elements you deem necessary on more than one page of your site. If you have worked with ASP.NET in the past, you are likely familiar with master pages. A layout is the master page of the ASP.NET MVC world.

You can specify the layout for a page using the Layout property of the view.

```
@{
    Layout = "~/Views/Shared/_Layout.cshtml"
}
```

When a view is loaded, the layout is executed and the content of the view is placed where the call to @RenderBody() is.

The _ViewStart file

If you have several views using the same layout, specifying the layout in each and every view may get a little repetitive. To keep things DRY (Don't Repeat Yourself), you can specify the default layout for all views of the site in _ViewStart.cshtml.

_ViewStart.cshtml is located at the root of the Views folder. It is used to store code common to all views within the app, not just to specify the layout. When each view is loaded, _ViewStart.cshtml is invoked. It acts like a base class for the views and any code within it becomes part of the constructor for every view in the site.

You will note that both _LoginPartial.cshtml and _Layout.cshtml start with an underscore. The underscore is another convention indicating that the views are not to be requested directly.

Partial views

Partial views allow you to design portions of your view as reusable components. These are very similar to controls in ASP.NET Web Forms development.

Partial views may be returned directly from a controller using the PartialView method, or directly returning a PartialReviewResult return type. They may also be embedded directly into a view using the RenderPartial, Partial, RenderAction, or Action HTML helper methods.

HTML helpers

Much of the code you will see in our views has methods prefixed with Html. These methods are HtmlHelper extension methods (HTML helpers for short) intended to provide you a quick way to perform some action or embed some information into the output of your view. Typically, these methods have a return type of string. HTML helpers assist in standardizing the rendering of content presented in views such as forms or links.

Html.RenderPartial and Html.Partial

The RenderPartial HTML helper processes the partial view and writes the result directly to the response stream. The result is as if the code of the partial view were placed directly into the calling view.

```
@Html.RenderPartial("_MyPartialView", someData)
```

The Partial HTML helper does the same processing of the view as the RenderPartial helper, but the output of the processing is returned as a string. The _LoginPartial.cshtml in our project is rendered within the _Layout.cshtml layout using the Partial HTML helper.

```
@Html.Partial("_LoginPartial")
```

If you are returning a large amount of data in a partial view, RenderPartial will be slightly more efficient than Partial due to its direct interaction with the response stream.

Html.RenderAction and Html.Action

The `RenderAction` HTML helper differs from `RenderPartial`, in that it actually invokes a controller's action method and embeds that content within the view. This functionality is extremely useful as it provides a way to execute business logic or other code specific to a view in the controller responsible for returning the view to the requestor.

Let's say we decided we wanted to show a tag cloud of the most viewed styles of beer on our BrewHow site on every page.

You have two options: you could make every action of the site retrieve from the database or cache the current values to display in the tag, or you could have a controller action solely responsible for retrieving the values for the tag cloud and invoke that action in every view using the `RenderAction` or `Action` method.

The differences between `RenderAction` and `Action` are the same as those between `RenderPartial` and `Partial`. `RenderAction` will write the output of the processing directly to the response stream. `Action` will return the output of the processing as a `string`.

Display templates

Display templates are type-specific partial views. They exist in a folder named `DisplayTemplates`. This folder may exist inside a controller's `View` folder if the display template is specific to a controller, or it may exist under the `Shared` folder if it is to be used by the entire application.

Each of the display templates must be named for its type. A display template for a `Beer` class that could be used everywhere in the application would be named `Beer.cshtml` and placed in `~/Shared/Views/DisplayTemplates`.

We can also create display templates for base types like strings or integers.

Display templates may be added to a view using either `Display`, `DisplayFor`, or `DisplayForModel` HTML helper methods.

Html.Display

The `Display` HTML helper takes a single string parameter. The string represents the property name of the current model or a value in the `ViewData` dictionary to be rendered.

Assume that the model passed to our view is defined as follows:

```
public class Recipe
{
    public string RecipeName { get; set; }
    /* Other properties here… */
}
```

If we want to invoke a display template for the `RecipeName` property, we put the following code into our view:

```
@Html.Display("RecipeName")
```

The runtime will try and locate a display template for the string type and use any identified template to render the `RecipeName` property.

Html.DisplayFor

`DisplayFor` is the expression-based version of `Display`. It takes as its argument the current model for the view and processes the display template for the specified property on the model.

```
@Html.DisplayFor(model => model.RecipeName)
```

We will examine how the view knows the model type when we populate our views later in this chapter.

Html.DisplayForModel

If we want to invoke the display template chain for an entire model, we simply use the `DisplayForModel` helper method.

```
@Html.DisplayForModel()
```

Editor templates

Editor templates are the read/write version of display templates. Their implementation and usage are identical to display templates.

Editor templates are stored in a folder named `EditorTemplates`. This folder may exist in the same location as the `DisplayTemplates` folder.

Editor templates, like display templates, are invoked using one of three HTML helper methods: `Editor`, `EditorFor`, or `EditorForModel`.

We will utilize display and editor templates as we refine our BrewHow app.

Creating our Recipe view

Having taken the long way around, we can get back to the task at hand. We now know we need to create a view in the `~/Views/Recipe` folder named `Index.cshtml` if we want the `/Recipe` URL to succeed. We could manually create the folder structure in the solution (the `Recipe` folder does not currently exist), and then create a new partial view, but why not allow Visual Studio to do the heavy lifting for us.

Open the `RecipeController.cs` file in **Solution Explorer** and right-click anywhere within the `Index` action method. You will see a menu item labeled **Add View...**.

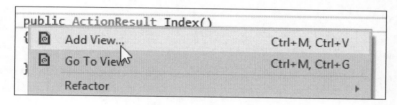

Clicking on **Add View...** or pressing *Ctrl + M, Ctrl + V* will display the **Add View** dialog. Accept the default values by simply clicking on the **Add** button.

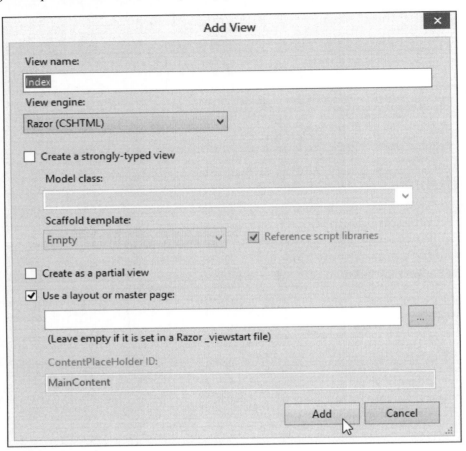

If you return to **Solution Explorer**, you will now see the view directory structure and the `Index.cshtml` view for `RecipeController`.

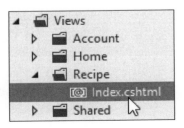

Launch the app by pressing *Ctrl + F5* and append `/Recipe` to the URL in the browser's address bar as before. You should now see a page very similar to the following screenshot:

Making Recipe default

We should set the `/Recipe` controller's `Index` action to be the default action for the app, given our app is all about sharing recipes.

Open the `RouteConfig.cs` file in the `App_Start` folder and modify the values for the `defaults` parameter to default to the `RecipeController`. Remember that the runtime will append `Controller` to the controller name when looking for the class to handle a request.

```
routes.MapRoute(
    name: "Default",
    url: "{controller}/{action}/{id}",
    defaults: new
    {
        controller = "Recipe",
        action = "Index",
        id = UrlParameter.Optional
    });
```

Press *Ctrl* + *F5* to build and launch the app.

Our `RecipeController`'s `Index` action and view now handle presenting the default landing page to the user. The only thing left is to modify our layout so users are redirected to `/Recipe/Index` instead of `/Home/Index` when clicking on the Home navigation link or the logo text itself.

```
<p class="site-title">
    @Html.ActionLink("your logo here",
        "Index",
        "Recipe")
</p>
<!-- Other stuff happens -->
<li>
    @Html.ActionLink("Home",
        "Index",
        "Recipe")
</li>
```

Returning a model to the view

We have successfully processed the view and returned it to the client. Now we need to return some data from `RecipeController`'s `Index` action. This data represents the model portion of the MVC pattern, and ASP.NET MVC supports several ways to return to the view any data gathered by the controller.

Using ViewData

The `ViewData` property of the `ControllerBase` class (the parent of the `Controller` class) is a "magic strings" mechanism for passing data from a controller to a view. It is more or less a dictionary. Almost all interaction with it occurs through a key/value syntax courtesy of its `IDictionary<string,object>` interface implementation.

```
ViewData["MyMagicProperty"] = "Magic String Win!"
```

Any value put into the `ViewData` dictionary is retrievable in the view using the `ViewData` property of the `WebViewPage` base class.

```
@ViewData["MyMagicProperty"]
```

All other methods of sending a model to a view from within the `Controller` and `ControllerBase` classes are wrappers and abstractions of the `ViewData` dictionary.

While you may (or may not) view magic strings as an appropriate mechanism for data exchange, all other methods of returning data to a view leverage `ViewData` internally.

Using ViewBag

`ViewBag` is a wrapper around the `ViewData` dictionary enabling support for dynamic properties and types on the `ViewData` dictionary.

If we examine the `HomeController` class's `Index` action, we'll see it's using the `ViewBag` property to send a message back to the view.

```
public ActionResult Index()
{
    ViewBag.Message = "Modify this template to jump-start your ASP.NET
MVC application.";

    return View();
}
```

Message is not a declared member of the ViewBag property. The ViewBag property's support for dynamic typing, also referred to as duck typing, allows assignment of values to properties not declared on the object. The mere act of assigning values to these properties adds them to the object.

The ViewBag data can be accessed from within the view using the ViewBag property of the WebViewPage base class. The Index view for HomeController has the following code:

```
<hgroup class="title">
    <h1> @ViewBag.Title. </h1>
    <h2> @ViewBag.Message </h2>
</hgroup>
```

This is displayed to the user as part of the content of the page.

Any use of ViewBag should be well documented. Due to their dynamic nature, the compiler has no way to validate references to dynamic types. Attempts to access properties or methods that do not exist, or that are defined with different types or arguments will not be caught at compile time. Instead, these errors will be captured at runtime and will cause your app to crash.

Using TempData

If you need to persist data for the view between redirects or sequential requests, then you may want to consider using TempData. TempData is another wrapper around the ViewData dictionary, but data placed in TempData is intentionally short-lived; anything stored in TempData will persist for exactly two requests: the current request and the next subsequent request for the same user.

Placing data in the TempData dictionary should be done sparingly as the implementation can result in unexpected behavior.

Assume that a user of our app has two tabs open to compare two recipes. A request originates from one of the tabs inserting data into TempData for consumption. A second request to the app is then triggered from the another open tab. The second request will force the values put in TempData by the first request to expire whether or not the intended recipient has retrieved and operated on the values.

The TempData dictionary is accessible through the TempData properties of ControllerBase and WebViewPage.

```
TempData["UserNotification"] = "Hope you get this message."
```

```
@TempData["UserNotification"]
```

The three methods presented thus far provide means to submit loosely coupled data to a view from a controller. While you certainly could send a full model to the view through these mechanisms, the framework provides a strongly typed method for moving data between the controller and view.

Strongly typed models

If you want to pass a strongly typed model from a controller to a view, you can do this in one of two ways. You can do this directly by setting the value of the Model property on the ViewData dictionary (OK, so it's a little more than a dictionary), or you can pass the model to the view through one of the ActionResult methods on the Controller class.

Setting the property directly can be done as follows:

```
ViewData.Model = myModel;
```

You will likely not set the value directly very often, but will instead use one of the ActionResult methods.

```
return View(myModel);
```

This is much more concise and if you examine the code in the `Controller` class you will see it's actually setting `ViewData.Model` on your behalf.

```
protected internal virtual ViewResult View
    (string viewName, string masterName, object model)
{
    if (model != null)
    {
        ViewData.Model = model;
    }
    /* Other code removed */
}
```

Take the initiative

The code above is taken directly from the RTM version of ASP.NET MVC 4. Microsoft's entire web stack is available under an open source license at aspnetwebstack.microsoft.com. You are urged to take the time and explore the code to learn what is actually being done by the framework.

For the view to operate on this model in a strongly typed fashion, it must be informed of the type of model to expect. In Razor views, this is done with the `@model` keyword.

```
@model BrewHow.Web.Model.MyModel
```

Returning a Recipe list

Let's put into practice everything we've learned. When a user of our app lands on the recipe page, we will present them with a list of recipes.

Creating the model

We need to define a model to represent a recipe within our app. For now, that model will contain four properties: name, style, original gravity, and final gravity.

> The gravity of a liquid is a measurement of its density compared to water, with water having a gravity of 1.0. Measuring the gravity of beer is done to determine how much sugar exists as a percentage of the liquid. Two measurements are taken when brewing beer. The original gravity is taken to measure the amount of sugar in the wort before yeast is added. The final gravity is taken to measure the gravity of the liquid at the end of fermentation. The difference between the two measurements can be used to determine how much of the sugar within the unfermented wort was converted into alcohol during fermentation. The formula for determining the amount of alcohol by volume is 132.715*(original gravity - final gravity).

In **Solution Explorer**, right-click on the **Models** folder, select **Add**, and then click on **Class...**.

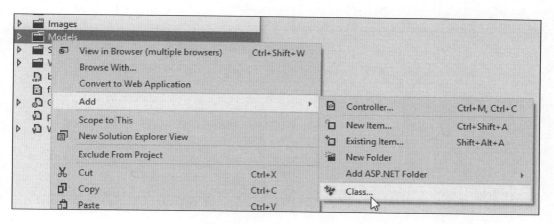

Select **Class** as the type of item to add in the **Add New Item** dialog if it is not already selected. Name the class `Recipe`, and click on **Add** to create the class.

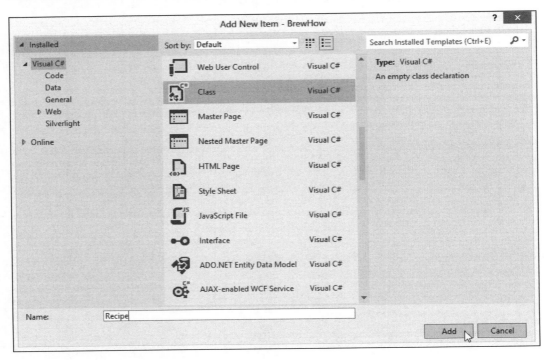

Open the new `Recipe.cs` file, and replace the `Recipe` class definition with the following:

```
public class Recipe
{
    public string Name { get; set; }
    public string Style { get; set; }
    public float OriginalGravity { get; set; }
    public float FinalGravity { get; set; }
}
```

Save and close the file.

Returning the model

Open the `RecipeController` class, and replace the `Index` action with the following code:

```
public ActionResult Index()
{
    var recipeListModel = new List<Recipe>
    {
        new Recipe { Name = "Sweaty Brown Ale", Style = "Brown Ale",
OriginalGravity = 1.05f, FinalGravity = 1.01f },
        new Recipe { Name = "Festive Milk Stout", Style="Sweet/Milk
Stout", OriginalGravity = 1.058f, FinalGravity = 1.015f },
        new Recipe { Name = "Andy's Heffy", Style = "Heffeweisen",
OriginalGravity = 1.045f, FinalGravity = 1.012f }
    }
    return View(recipeListModel);
}
```

The new `Index` action is pretty straightforward. The new code creates a populated list and assigns it to the `recipeListModel` variable. The populated list is sent to the `Index` view as a strongly typed model through the `View` method (remember, the view has the same name as the action unless otherwise specified).

```
return View(recipeListModel);
```

For the code to compile, you will need to add a `using` statement to the top of the file to reference the new `Recipe` model defined in `BrewHow.Models`.

```
using BrewHow.Models;
```

Displaying the model

The final step is to inform the view of the incoming model and provide the view the means to display the model.

Open up the `Index.cshtml` view in the `~/Views/Recipe` folder and add the following line at the top of the view.

```
@model IEnumerable<BrewHow.Models.Recipe>
```

This declares the model we are passing to the view is an enumeration of recipes. It is now strongly typed.

Place your cursor at the bottom of the `Index.cshtml` view and paste the following code. You won't be judged for flinching at the use of tables even though they are being used appropriately to display tabular data. We are just trying to get the model to display right now.

```
<table>
    <tr >
        <th>
            @Html.DisplayNameFor(model => model.Name)
        </th>
        <th>
            @Html.DisplayNameFor(model => model.Style)
        </th>
        <th>
            @Html.DisplayNameFor(model => model.OriginalGravity)
        </th>
        <th>
            @Html.DisplayNameFor(model => model.FinalGravity)
        </th>
    </tr >

@foreach (var item in Model) {
    <tr >
        <td>
            @Html.DisplayFor(modelItem => item.Name)
        </td>
        <td>
            @Html.DisplayFor(modelItem => item.Style)
        </td>
        <td>
            @Html.DisplayFor(modelItem => item.OriginalGravity)
        </td>
```

```
    <td>
        @Html.DisplayFor(modelItem => item.FinalGravity)
    </td>
</tr >
}

</table>
```

The markup you pasted into the view lays out a table to list each entry in the model collection passed to the view. Do take note of how little the Razor syntax interferes with the markup of the view.

The first row of the table contains the headers for the recipe list. During the processing of the view within the `foreach` loop, the view engine iterates over each item in the collection passed to it and outputs a row for the table using the display template for the type. Since we have not defined display templates, the values of the properties will simply be output as strings.

You have successfully created a model, populated the model in the controller, passed the populated model from the controller to the view, and displayed the populated model to the user. Press *Ctrl + F5* on the keyboard to start the app and admire your work.

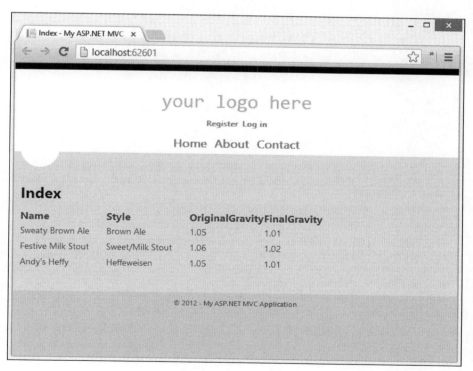

Summary

Congratulations! This chapter was a whirlwind of information, but we now have a basic understanding of the MVC pattern and how it relates to ASP.NET MVC 4. We learned about controllers and action methods and how to create them. We created a model, passed the model from the controller to the view, and wrote code that displayed that model. With the basics known, it's time for us to look at bigger and better things.

In the next chapter, we leverage the functionality of Entity Framework 5.0 to create a persistence layer for our application and return the information stored in the database. This persistence layer will be used as the basis for our models moving forward.

4

Modeling BrewHow in EF5

If you're developing a new application, Microsoft would very much like you to use **Entity Framework 5.0 (EF5)**. Entity Framework is Microsoft's officially supported **Object-Relational Mapping (ORM)** tool, finally coming on its own after a much maligned introduction with .NET 3.5 SP1.

As with any ORM, Entity Framework is designed to separate the domain model of an application from the actual storage mechanism. This allows the developer to focus on the actual problem they're trying to solve and spend less time worrying about the tables and columns underneath the model.

Having a framework provide the underlying storage mechanism does have its own set of issues. As almost any DBA will tell you, ORMs will often generate substandard storage models and Entity Framework is not excluded from this issue. However, Entity Framework allows you to customize the translation between the domain and database to match almost any conceivable underlying data store, allowing you and your DBA to work in relative harmony.

In this chapter, we will create the persistence layer for the BrewHow app using Entity Framework 5. We will explore migrations and how we can use them to apply and remove changes to the database. Additionally, we will look at some of the conventions and configurations used by Entity Framework 5.0 to tailor our model to a database mapping we or our DBA prefer.

What's new in Entity Framework 5.0?

Version 5.0 of the Entity Framework is a fairly major update to Microsoft's ORM. While there are several improvements and additions, we will only briefly examine the improvements as they relate to the use of EF5 in the development of our BrewHow app.

Performance enhancements

Under the hood, Microsoft has squeezed every ounce of performance it can out of the framework. One of the key performance enhancements is the automatic use of compiled queries—a query in which the LINQ to Entities expression tree has been translated into pure SQL. To accomplish this, upon first invocation the EF5, the framework configures all of the components the query needs, caches certain components of the query, and stores them locally in the memory so that any subsequent invocations do not need to be translated or have resources loaded. This greatly increases performance of a warmed-up application.

LocalDB support

LocalDB is now supported within the EF5 Code First development model. In fact, it is the default server used within Visual Studio 2012.

If you are unfamiliar with LocalDB, it is a new version of SQL Server targeted at developers. It is intended to fit between SQL Server Express and SQL Server Compact. You may be asking yourself, "Isn't that what SQL Server Express is for?" Although Microsoft's original intention was to have SQL Server Express as the database standard for developers, as the SQL Server line improved it became harder to maintain the low-overhead, small-footprint requirements of developers because of the requirements forced on SQL Server Express by its fully licensed siblings. To rectify this, Microsoft created LocalDB, a repackage of the same SQL Server executable as Express and other versions of SQL Server but without the large footprint and configuration of the SQL Server line. The repackage allows us as developers to maintain SQL Server compatibility in our development without having to install and configure SQL Server Express or one of the enterprise variants.

LocalDB differs from SQL Server Compact, in that it is a separate process (SQL Server Compact is an in-proc DLL) and provides support for stored procedures and extended data-types where SQL Server Compact does not.

Enumeration support

EF5 has finally received support for enumerations, a feature that has been requested since the earliest versions of Entity Framework. Framework support for enumerations is provided by mapping enumeration values to and from an integer value in the database. If you require a lookup table, want to add or alter values without recompiling, or are the type of person that doesn't want magic integers in their database, you will still need to use classes mapped to a lookup table to represent enumerated values.

There is one important caveat around enumeration support; it is only available if you are targeting version 4.5 of the .NET Framework. If you are targeting Version 4.0, you will receive an error message about the framework being unable to map the enumeration property. If, however, you are targeting Version 4.5 or higher of the .NET Framework, enumerations are one of those nice little "it just works" features we as developers love.

The BrewHow model

The Entity Framework supports three distinct ways to model our data: **Database First**, **Model First**, and **Code First**.

- Database First is used when the database already exists and provides support to derive a model from the existing database schema

- The Model First approach provides support to visually model our data and, from the model, generate the database

- Code First allows us to generate our database schema from a model we define in code

Since we are developing a new app, the Database First method of modeling our data doesn't really apply. The Model First approach, introduced in Visual Studio 2010, could be used for the BrewHow app, but we will instead opt for the more agile approach of Code First.

The Code First approach will also allow us to update the schema in a (largely) non-destructive manner using migrations. This is important since we will adjust the model to better map our domain as we continually enhance our app. Additionally, it's just cool and we like new shiny toys, right? So let's get EF5 enabled and start using it in our app.

Modeling data

Using the Code First feature of EF5, classes will dictate the database schema used to model our domain. We will start with three classes: `Recipe`, `Review`, and `Style`. Each of these classes will be added to the `Models` folder of our BrewHow app.

Recipe

The `Recipe` class contains all of the information about our recipe. This is a slightly modified version of the class presented in the previous chapter.

```
public class Recipe
{
    public int RecipeId { get; set; }
    public string Name { get; set; }
    public Style Style { get; set; }
    public float OriginalGravity { get; set; }
    public float FinalGravity { get; set; }
    public string GrainBill { get; set; }
    public string Instructions { get; set; }
}
```

Review

The `Review` class contains information related to the review of a recipe.

```
public class Review
{
    public int ReviewId { get; set; }
    public int Rating { get; set; }
    public string Comment { get; set; }
}
```

Style

The `Style` class will allow us to associate a style to a particular beer recipe. Examples of beer styles are India Pale Ale, Milk/Sweet Stout, Pilsner, and Porter.

```
public class Style
{
    public int StyleId { get; set; }
    public Category Category { get; set; }
    public string Name { get; set; }
}
```

Category

The `Category` class is an enumeration that will be used to define a beer as ale or lager. We use an enumeration because these values are not going to change.

```
public enum Category
{
    Ale,
    Lager
}
```

The BrewHow context

We now have the classes that represent our model. We need a way to map these classes to a persistent store. To do this, we will create a class named `BrewHowContext` that extends the `DbContext` class.

`DbContext` is a combination of repository and unit-of-work patterns. It provides the glue to map the Code First model to the database. It also provides change tracking, allowing you to make several edits to an entity or several entities in a context, committing them to the database in bulk.

`DbContext` isn't magic, however. It needs to have some idea of the entities that exist for a model, the entities for which it's responsible. `DbContext` uses a special collection class to map entities to tables within the database. This class is `DbSet<T>`.

The `DbSet<T>` class is a special class within the Entity Framework used to represent a set of typed objects upon which you can perform **CRUD (Create, Retrieve, Update, and Delete)** operations. These operations may be performed using LINQ as `DbSet<T>` implements the `IQueryable` interface.

Create `BrewHowContext` in the `Models` folder of our app. You will need to add `System.Data.EntityFramework` to the `using` statements in `BrewHowContext.cs`.

```
public class BrewHowContext : DbContext
{
    public DbSet<Recipe> Recipes { get; set; }
    public DbSet<Review> Reviews { get; set; }
    public DbSet<Style> Styles { get; set; }
}
```

 You cannot directly construct the `DbSet<T>` class. Only the `DbContext` class may create new instances of `DbSet<T>`.

Generating our database

To generate our database we simply need to run our application, but if we try and run it right now we will get a compilation error. The error occurs because we changed the definition of the `Recipe` class. Locate the `RecipeController` class in the `Controllers` folder and replace the `Index` action method with the following:

```
public ActionResult Index()
{
    List<Recipe> recipes = null;

    using (var context = new BrewHowContext())
    {
        recipes = (from recipe in context.Recipes
                   select recipe).ToList();
    }

    return View(recipes);
}
```

Our application should now compile and run. Press *Ctrl* + *F5* to launch our application.

Of course, there's nothing to really see. Our table headings are there but there's not much else. All we've really done is created the database—an empty database, but a database nonetheless.

To view our database and the tables within, click on the **View All Files** icon on the **Solution Explorer** toolbar.

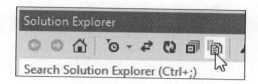

Expand the App_Data folder and double-click on the file named BrewHow.Models. BrewHowContext.mdf.

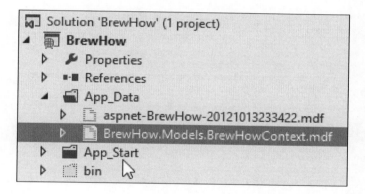

Our new database is now open in the **Database Explorer** window.

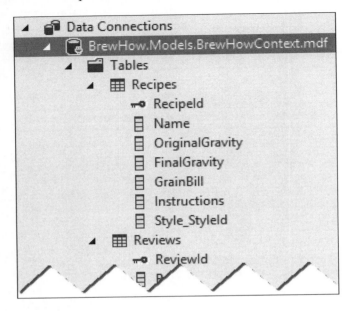

You will notice as you examine the structure of each table that Entity Framework was smart enough to identify the keys for the tables. This is a convention-over-configuration feature. Any property of type `int` or `Guid` ending with `Id` and having the same name as the class containing it will be used as the primary key for the table.

Altering the model

As we continue to examine our new database, there are some things that we need to change.

Currently, `Review` classes are not associated with `Recipe` classes. This appears to be a major oversight on our part. We need to provide a way to navigate to `Review` classes from a `Recipe` class.

The relationship between `Style` and `Recipe` also needs modification. We can represent the one-to-many relationship between `Style` and `Recipe` and between `Recipe` and `Review` by creating properties of type `ICollection<T>`.

As for conventions, having a foreign key of Style_StyleId in the Recipe class seems a bit redundant. The convention in Entity Framework is to look for foreign key properties in the format [EntityName][EntityKeyName]. In this case, it was looking for a property named StyleStyleId. As the property did not exist, it created a foreign key named Style_StyleId to satisfy the foreign key relationship identified by the Style property of the Recipe class.

Adding relationships

The following code shows the modified Review and Recipe classes:

```
public class Recipe
{
    public int RecipeId { get; set; }
    public string Name { get; set; }
    public Style Style { get; set; }
    public decimal OriginalGravity { get; set; }
    public decimal FinalGravity { get; set; }
    public string GrainBill { get; set; }
    public string Instructions { get; set; }

    public virtual ICollection<Review> Reviews { get; set; }
}

public class Style
{
    public int StyleId { get; set; }
    public Category Category { get; set; }
    public string Name { get; set; }

    public virtual ICollection<Recipe> Recipes { get; set; }
}
```

Overriding conventions

To override conventions, we can override the OnModelCreating method of DbContext in the BrewHowContext class. Entity Framework will invoke this method when the first instance of BrewHowContext is created and pass it an instance of DbModelBuilder.

DbModelBuilder provides us support to fluently map the entities of our model to the database in which they're persisted. With DbModelBuilder we can change the column name for a property or the keys used for a relationship. We can even change the name of the table to which an entity is mapped.

The following is the code to modify the model mapping for the `Recipe` to `Review` relationship and the `Style` to `Recipe` relationship.

```
protected override void OnModelCreating(DbModelBuilder modelBuilder)
{
    // Add a foreign key to Recipe from Review
    // to account for the new relationship.
    modelBuilder.Entity<Recipe>()
        .HasMany(r => r.Reviews)
        .WithRequired()
        .Map(m => m.MapKey("RecipeId"));

    // Adjust the relationship between Style
    // and Recipe to fix the key name.
    modelBuilder.Entity<Recipe>()
        .HasRequired(s => s.Style)
        .WithMany(s => s.Recipes)
        .Map(m => m.MapKey("StyleId"));

    base.OnModelCreating(modelBuilder);
}
```

Running our app now results in an error message telling us that our context has changed. This is because of the changes we made to our model. The model now no longer matches the model persisted in the database.

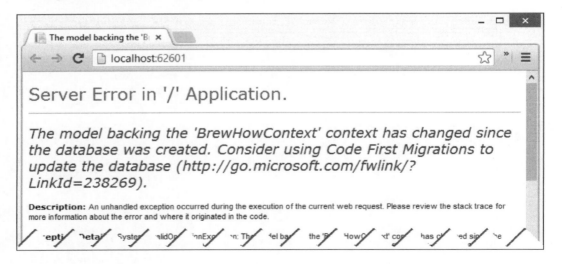

Fortunately, EF5 provides a mechanism to alter our database to match our adjusted model. That mechanism is migrations.

Enabling migrations

Using migrations in EF5 will require us to use the **Package Manager Console**. To open the **Package Manager Console**, click on the **Tools** menu, click on **Library Package Manager**, and then click on **Package Manager Console**.

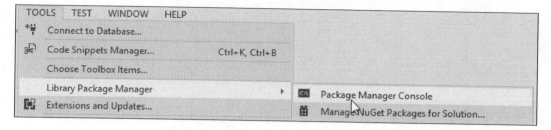

In the console, type `Enable-Migrations -ContextTypeName BrewHow.Models.BrewHowContext` and hit *Enter*.

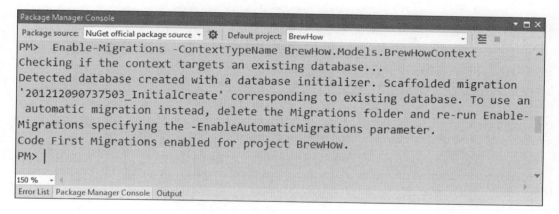

 Normally, you can type `Enable-Migrations` in the **Package Manager Console** without specifying the `-ContextTypeName` parameter. However, we based our app off of the `Internet Application` template and it also has created a `Context` class. When multiple `Context` classes exist within a project, you must specify the name of the `Context` class for which you want to enable migrations.

Enabling migrations results in a new `Migrations` folder added to the solution. This folder contains two files controlling schema and configuration.

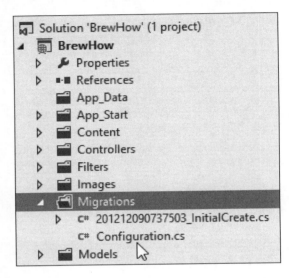

The InitialCreate migration

The initial migration is named `InitialCreate`. It was generated for us because Entity Framework's migrations need a baseline to work. As our database was initialized before we enabled migrations, the framework reverse-engineered the `InitialCreate` migration from the database.

```
public partial class InitialCreate : DbMigration
{
    public override void Up()
    {
        CreateTable(
            "dbo.Recipes",
            c => new
                {
                    RecipeId = c.Int(nullable: false, identity: true),
                    Name = c.String(),
                    OriginalGravity = c.Decimal(nullable: false,
precision: 18, scale: 2),
                    FinalGravity = c.Decimal(nullable: false,
precision: 18, scale: 2),
                    GrainBill = c.String(),
```

```
                    Instructions = c.String(),
                    Style_StyleId = c.Int(),
                })
            .PrimaryKey(t => t.RecipeId)
            .ForeignKey("dbo.Styles", t => t.Style_StyleId)
            .Index(t => t.Style_StyleId);

        CreateTable(
            "dbo.Styles",
            c => new
                {
                    StyleId = c.Int(nullable: false, identity: true),
                    Category = c.Int(nullable: false),
                    Name = c.String(),
                })
            .PrimaryKey(t => t.StyleId);

        CreateTable(
            "dbo.Reviews",
            c => new
                {
                    ReviewId = c.Int(nullable: false, identity: true),
                    Rating = c.Int(nullable: false),
                    Comment = c.String(),
                })
            .PrimaryKey(t => t.ReviewId);

    }

    public override void Down()
    {
        DropIndex("dbo.Recipes", new[] { "Style_StyleId" });
        DropForeignKey("dbo.Recipes", "Style_StyleId", "dbo.Styles");
        DropTable("dbo.Reviews");
        DropTable("dbo.Styles");
        DropTable("dbo.Recipes");
    }
}
```

By examining the code in the InitialCreate class, we can see the generated code has two methods: Up and Down. Each method is using the fluent API. Entity Framework uses the Up method to apply a migration to the database. The Down method is used to undo a migration.

The Configuration class

The `Configuration` class provides us a means to control the behavior of our migrations.

```
internal sealed class Configuration : DbMigrationsConfiguration<BrewH
ow.Models.BrewHowContext>
{
    public Configuration()
    {
        AutomaticMigrationsEnabled = false;
    }

    protected override void Seed(BrewHow.Models.BrewHowContext
context)
    {
        /* … */
    }
}
```

Through this class we can configure things such as enabling automatic loss of data through a migration or how long a command may be executed before timeout. The two uses you see presented in the code are the two most common uses of this class: automatic migration support and seed data.

Adding seed data

The `Seed` method of the `Configuration` class is used to insert sample data during the process of a migration. Because we want to have a little data available when we launch the application, let's replace the `Seed` method with the following code (you will need to add `BrewHow.Models` to the `using` statements).

```
protected override void Seed(BrewHow.Models.BrewHowContext context)
{
    var brownAle = new Style
    {
        Name = "Brown Ale",
        Category = Models.Category.Ale
    };

    var milkStout = new Style
    {
        Name = "Sweet/Milk Stout",
        Category = Models.Category.Ale
```

```
    };
    var heffeweisen = new Style
    {
        Name = "Heffeweisen",
        Category = Models.Category.Ale
    };

    context.Styles.AddOrUpdate (
        style => style.Name,
        brownAle,
        milkStout,
        heffeweisen
    );

    context.Recipes.AddOrUpdate(
        recipe => recipe.Name,
        new Recipe
        {
            Name = "Sweaty Brown Ale",
            Style = brownAle,
            OriginalGravity = 1.05M, FinalGravity = 1.01M
        },
        new Recipe
        {
            Name = "Festive Milk Stout",
            Style = milkStout,
            OriginalGravity = 1.058M,
            FinalGravity = 1.015M
        },
        new Recipe
        {
            Name = "Andy's Heffy",
            Style = heffeweisen,
            OriginalGravity = 1.045M,
            FinalGravity = 1.012M
        }
    );
}
```

This code adds new entities to our `BrewHowContext` class' `DbSet`. These entities will be committed to storage following the execution of the `Seed` method.

It is very important to note that this method will be executed every time we apply a migration. This means we must keep the `Seed` method in sync with any changes we make to the model.

Adding a migration

We're almost there. We need to add a new migration that will reflect the changes we've made. We use the `Add-Migration` command in the **Package Manager Console** to do this.

`Add-Migration` will be invoked with a single argument: the name of the migration. As the biggest change we made was the foreign key reference to `Recipe` from `Review`, we will call it `Reviews`. In the **Package Manager Console**, type `Add-Migration Reviews` and hit *Enter*.

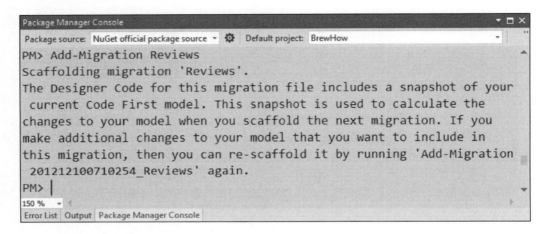

Open the new file in the `Migrations` folder of our project. You will find a new migration class named `Reviews`.

```
public partial class Reviews : DbMigration
{
    public override void Up()
    {
        /* Fluent Migrations Up */
    }

    public override void Down()
    {
        /* Fluent Migrations Down */
    }
}
```

We again see that we have support for migrating from the prior model to this model via the `Up` method, or we can migrate from this model to the prior model via the `Down` method.

There is one key difference between the Reviews migration and the InitialCreate migration created for us from the database: the Reviews migration has not been applied. This allows us to make some final tweaks to the migration before it is applied. Let's get rid of the cascading deletes for our foreign keys. Update the two AddForeignKey method calls to set the named parameter cascadeDelete to false and save the file.

```
AddForeignKey(
    "dbo.Recipes",
    "StyleId",
    "dbo.Styles",
    "StyleId",
    cascadeDelete: false);

AddForeignKey(
    "dbo.Reviews",
    "RecipeId",
    "dbo.Recipes",
    "RecipeId",
    cascadeDelete: false);
```

All that is left is for us to apply the migration.

Applying migrations

Applying the migration is really just a matter of applying the Up or Down method of a migration to the database. In the **Package Manager Console**, type Update-Database and hit *Enter*.

```
this migration, then you can re-scaffold it by running 'Add-Migration
 201212100710254_Reviews' again.
PM> Update-Database
Specify the '-Verbose' flag to view the SQL statements being applied
to the target database.
Applying code-based migrations: [201212100710254_Reviews].
Applying code-based migration: 201212100710254_Reviews.
Running Seed method.
PM>
```

The Update-Database command, when executed with no arguments, applies the Up method of any unapplied migrations.

Getting help on migration commands

Help is available for all of the migration commands. Simply type help and then the command for which you want help in the Package Manager Console and hit *Enter* (for example, help Update-Database). Take some time and investigate these commands as you can use them to generate SQL scripts, target specific migrations, and many other useful things.

To see the output of our work, open up the BrewHow database in the **Database Explorer**.

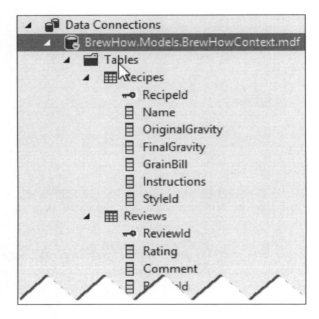

We can see that the mapping we created in OnModelCreating was successfully applied. We successfully renamed the Style_StyleId foreign key to StyleId and the Reviews table now has a foreign key named RecipeId that references the Recipes table.

We can look in the database to make sure that our `Seed` method was executed and behaved as we thought it would. To view the content of our `Recipes` table, right-click on the `Recipes` table and select **Show Table Data** from the context menu.

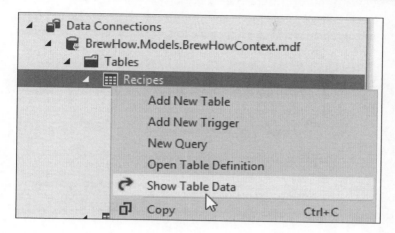

Our sample data is indeed there.

	RecipeId	Name	OriginalGravity	FinalGravity	GrainBill	Instructions	StyleId
▶	1	Sweaty Brown ...	1.05	1.01	NULL	NULL	1
	2	Festive Milk Sto...	1.05	1.01	NULL	NULL	2
	3	Andy's Heffy	1.04	1.01	NULL	NULL	3
*	NULL	NULL	NULL	NULL	NULL	NULL	NULL

Consuming the model

When we altered our `RecipeController` class at the start of the chapter, we replaced the code within the `Index` action method to use the new `Recipe` model and `BrewHowContext`. If you press *Ctrl + F5* to launch the app, you will see we are indeed consuming data from the database via the `BrewHowContext`.

This is impressive, but there are a couple of issues with our implementation. For starters, note the order of the recipes. There isn't one. It may appear that the data is in the order it was inserted into the database. That's more or less true right now, but there are three pretty big problems with this:

- We provide no date to show when an item was inserted into the list.
- Seeing a list of recipes sorted by the date they were entered (oldest first) provides little value to the user.
- SQL Server can, and will, change the order in which the data is returned. This is all but guaranteed.

It's also important to note that the home page loads and displays every recipe from the database every time. The impact of this is minimal for small datasets and small numbers of users, but if we have hundreds or thousands of recipes in our database and several hundred users — let's be modest here — our app performance is going to suffer.

The solutions to these problems are pretty straightforward. We can begin by providing a default sort order for the recipes. If we order by the name of the recipe, users should be able to find what they're looking for rather easily—at least while there's only a few recipes in our database. We can leave changing the sort order as a problem to solve later.

As for breaking up the recipes on our home page into manageable chunks, we need to provide support for pagination.

Pagination

Allowing users to page through the recipes is a tried-and-true method of breaking up data retrieval and presentation into digestible pieces.

Pagination options

Techniques such as forever scrolling can be used to load the next page of data when the user nears the bottom of the page. Other options include a button allowing users to retrieve the next page of data and append it to the current view. The pager, however, is a time-tested option still employed by the majority of the Web. Feel free to experiment.

To support paging, we need a class that can return a paged result to the view. This class needs to make available not only the list of items for the page—in this case, the recipes—but must also make available the current page and the total number of pages to support pagination controls. Following is the PagedResult class:

```
public class PagedResult<T> : List<T>, IPagedResult
{
    private const int PageSize = 10;

    public PagedResult(IQueryable<T> query, int page)
    {
        this.Page = page;
        this.TotalPages = (int) Math.Ceiling(
            query.Count() / (double)PageSize);

        this.AddRange(query
            .Skip(page * PageSize)
            .Take(PageSize));
    }
}
```

```
        public int Page { get; private set; }
        public int TotalPages { get; private set; }
    }
```

The `PagedResult` class extends the generic List class to provide lists of recipes or anything else to the view. The class itself also implements an interface named `IPagedResult`.

The `IPagedResult` interface exists to allow us to create a generic paging control on any page. The interface itself is pretty straightforward, containing only the `Page` and `TotalPages` properties.

```
    public interface IPagedResult
    {
        int Page { get; }
        int TotalPages { get; }
    }
```

Any model passed to a view that implements `IPagedResult` has the information necessary to provide paging information. We can build a control that takes an implementation of `IPagedResult` as its model. The code to our pagination control, `PagingPartial`, is shown as follows:

```
@model BrewHow.Models.IPagedResult

<div id="pager">

@if (Model.Page > 0)
{
    @Html.RouteLink("<< Prev", new
    {
        page = Model.Page - 1,
        controller = ViewContext.RouteData.Values["controller"],
        action = ViewContext.RouteData.Values["action"]
    },
    new
    {
        id = "paging-prev"
    });
}
<span>Page @(Model.Page + 1) of @Model.TotalPages</span>
@if (Model.Page +1 != Model.TotalPages)
```

```
{
    @Html.RouteLink("Next >>", new
    {
        page = Model.Page + 1,
        controller = ViewContext.RouteData.Values["controller"],
        action = ViewContext.RouteData.Values["action"]
    },
    new
    {
        id = "paging-next"
    });
}
</div>
```

The `PagingPartial` partial view shows a link to view the previous page of data if not already on the first page, a link to view the next page of data if not already on the last page, and displays the current page number and total page count.

To construct the links to the previous and next pages, the control uses the `RouteLink` HTML Helper. `RouteLink` can construct a link based on a named route or any routing values. We will discuss routing more in a later chapter, but note that we are passing in values for controller and action to be used constructing the route. These are the same variables we discussed in our default route in *Chapter 3, Introducing ASP.NET MVC 4*.

Loading the `PagingPartial` control on the `RecipeController` class's `Index` view is straightforward.

```
@{ Html.RenderPartial("PagingPartial", Model); }
```

All that's really left to do is modify the `Index` action to take a page number as a parameter and return a `PagedResult` object as the model for the view.

```
public ActionResult Index(int page = 0)
{
    PagedResult<Recipe> recipes = null;

    using (var context = new BrewHowContext())
    {
        recipes = new PagedResult<Recipe>(
            context.Recipes.OrderBy(r => r.Name),
            page);
    }

    return View(recipes);
}
```

You will note that we are applying our default order, recipe name, to the recipes retrieved from `BrewHowContext`. If we set the page size in the `PagedResult` class to contain only one recipe, the output looks similar to the following:

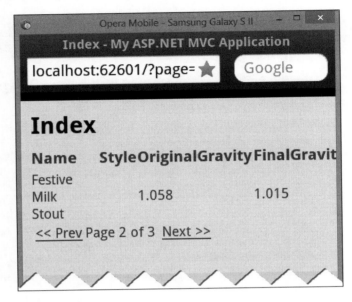

Make sure to set the page size to something a little more reasonable before publishing your work.

Summary

This chapter provided a very brief introduction to Entity Framework. You were presented with information on creating a domain model and using Entity Framework to map that model to a database. You also learned how to change the mapping of the model and seed the database with sample data.

In the upcoming chapters, we will revisit EF5 as we make adjustments to our model to support new requirements' implementation.

In the next chapter, we will look at **Domain-Driven Design** and how we can leverage some of its principles to help us write more maintainable code as well as the effect of those principles on how we structure our code. We will then modify our app to adhere to those principles.

5

The BrewHow Domain and Domain-driven Design

When we began discussing the BrewHow app, we went through a rather lengthy description of both beer and the brewing process. Though I admittedly love to talk about beer to anyone willing to listen, and occasionally those who aren't, I presented the information to help you understand the concepts relevant to beer and its production. Why is knowing how to make good beer important to writing the BrewHow app?

I will answer the question with another question. If someone were to ask you to write an app to determine the air-speed velocity of an unladen swallow, could you do it? Were you to go it alone, you would need more than software development skills. You would need a good understanding of aerodynamics and kinematics. Given that's not likely the case—and kudos to you, dear reader, if it is—you would need to consult with a domain expert.

This same principle applies to designing software; not just software about beer or swallows (African, European, or otherwise), but any software in any domain. If you do not understand the domain, you cannot write software to support it.

Domain-driven Design (DDD), a phrase originated by Eric Evans, is a development approach that places the domain and its abstracted model at the forefront. In this chapter, we will be learning about the principle concepts and patterns of DDD. We will then take that knowledge and apply it to our BrewHow app.

Tenets of DDD

A detailed discussion of DDD can, and in fact does, merit an entire book. Since we are developing a small app here, we will focus on the pieces of DDD relevant to our development efforts.

Domain model

The Domain Model is just as its name implies. It is a model of the domain. Unfortunately, the term is also ambiguous. If someone talks about a model, most developers immediately think about the underlying storage of an app. That is not the case here.

Oversimplified, a domain model is the translation of the problem space into a common language. It can be used to define common terms to apply to entities, values, collections, properties, actions, events, or any other item in the problem domain. If done properly, a domain model will be free of technical guidance or implementation. The clarification provided by a domain model makes it an excellent tool to assist in communication across all levels of an organization.

Entities

Entities are pieces of a domain model that are uniquely distinguishable within the domain. Their uniqueness is not the collection of attributes that comprise the object but, rather, their continued existence throughout the lifetime of the application.

Within our app, a recipe is an example of an entity. While one instance of a recipe may share the same attributes as many other recipes, it is uniquely identifiable within the application and will be throughout its lifetime.

Value objects

Value objects are objects that cannot exist alone. They exist only within the context of other objects. Unlike entities, value objects are not uniquely identifiable. The other characteristic of a value object is it is immutable—the value of a value object cannot change.

Gravity would be an example of a value object in our app. While we currently represent original gravity and final gravity as float values, we could represent them much more meaningfully as a type. The gravity type would have no identifying characteristics and would be meaningless outside the context of a recipe entity, the very definition of a value object.

Aggregates

Aggregates are collections of objects under the control of a single parent object. You can think of them as an object graph or tree. The parent of an aggregate is called the aggregate root. Access to any child object in the aggregate is obtained through the aggregate root.

When we created the model for BrewHow in *Chapter 4, Modeling BrewHow in EF5*, we constructed an aggregate consisting of `Style`, `Recipe`, and a collection of `Reviews`. Within this aggregate, the `Recipe` class is the aggregate root. `Reviews` cannot exist without `Recipe` and, likewise, if there are no `Recipes` associated with `Style`, `Style` lacks purpose within our domain.

Factories

When aggregates or entities become too complex for simple construction, factories are leveraged for their creation. They provide a means to encapsulate the bootstrapping required for the object and to enforce any rules around the creation of the entity or aggregate.

Factories are free of ties to infrastructure and deal solely with the creation of entities or aggregates.

Repositories

Unlike factories that deal with the creation of aggregates and entities, repositories are used for aggregate and entity persistence and retrieval. They provide a means for a client of the repository to retrieve a reference to an entity or aggregate by its identifying characteristics or for a client to persist a new aggregate or entity to storage.

Repositories should provide a simple interface to the client that is free of any information that would identify the underlying infrastructure used for storage. Put another way, repositories exist to map the entities of a domain from the domain model to the data model. They are the boundary between the domain model and its persistence.

Services

While most of the domain logic within DDD exists within the entities themselves, there are times when certain domain rules or decisions don't necessarily belong to one object or another. One common example used is the transfer of funds between two accounts. To which entity would you assign the responsibility of moving those funds?

Services are meant to serve this need. They encapsulate domain logic that may be shared between multiple aggregates or entities.

Learn More about DDD

As stated in the introduction, Domain-driven Design is a subject unto itself. There are several resources available should you wish to learn more about it, but I would recommend starting with *InfoQ's Domain Driven Design Quickly* and, from there, either read *Domain-Driven Design* and *Tackling Complexity in the Heart of Software* by *Eric Evan* or *Applying Domain-Driven Design and Patterns* by *Jimmy Nillson*, with examples in C# and .NET.

BrewHow design

Since Eric Evans' seminal work on DDD, there have arisen many variations and adaptations of the patterns and practices within DDD. Today, there are as many implementations proclaiming to be DDD as there are practitioners of DDD. We will focus on adhering to the tenants described previously as we design our app. Variants will be noted as they are created.

During this chapter, all code related to our domain will be placed within a `Domain` folder in the project. The `Domain` folder will contain subfolders for each code grouping.

BrewHow entities

The entities within the BrewHow domain model almost mirror the data model at this point. We have domain entities for the `Category`, `Recipe`, `Review`, and `Style` data models named `CategoryEntity`, `RecipeEntity`, `ReviewEntity`, and `StyleEntity` respectively. These entities are responsible for business rules and logic specific to their role in the domain.

BrewHow repositories

Our current model has three entities we need to worry about persisting and retrieving: recipes, reviews, and styles. Given the recipe is the aggregate root, a sound case could be made for having a single repository for the recipe aggregate. We, however, will be varying from that approach.

While management of aggregate roots works well for connected systems (systems in which state is maintained) or for roots of small aggregates, fitting a full implementation into a book of this size without introducing poor coding practices and increased maintenance cost is not possible. To keep things simple, we will adopt a DDD variant where we break apart the domain model on large collections. Each break will provide a reference point to continue navigating the domain model through to related entities.

As an example, I can use `StyleId` from a `Style` entity to retrieve all `Recipes` of that style with a second request. This second request is deliberate and removes the need for us to worry about the management of eager versus lazy loading of `Recipes` belonging to the particular `Style`. The same rules apply when navigating from `Recipe` to `Reviews` of the `Recipe` entity.

> The variant we are employing is similar in implementation to two other DDD patterns that are out of the scope of this book: **Bounded Contexts** and **Command Query Responsibility Segregation (CQRS)**. If you are curious about these patterns, I suggest you check out the works of Eric Evans (yes, him again) on Bounded Contexts and Greg Young on CQRS.

Our domain model can be broken down as follows:

- A `Style` entity has multiple `Recipes` and a single `Category`
- A `Recipe` entity has a single `Style` and multiple `Reviews`
- A `Review` entity belongs to a single `Recipe`

Based on this breakdown, we need three repositories within our app: `StyleRepository`, `RecipeRepository`, and `ReviewRepository`.

The following `RecipeRepository` class illustrates how the boundary between domain entity and data model is managed:

```
public class RecipeRepository : RepositoryBase
{
  public IQueryable<RecipeEntity> GetRecipes()
  {
    /* ... */
  }

  public IQueryable<RecipeEntity>
    GetRecipesByStyle(string styleName)
    {
      /* ... */
    }

  public RecipeEntity GetRecipe(int recipeId)
  {
    /* ... */
  }

  public void Save(RecipeEntity recipe)
  {
    /* ... */
  }

  // Consult the code accompanying this book for the
  // full listing of this class.
}
```

In previous chapters, we were operating directly on the models of the BrewHowContext. By putting a repository in place, we can operate directly on the entities of the domain. The repository is responsible for marshaling the models — often called **POCOs (Plain Old CLR Objects)** — to and from the domain entities.

> We could maintain this boundary using the POCOs we created for a data model were we to choose to do so. That said, were we to use the POCOs as our domain entities, we would introduce an anti-pattern known as the aenemic domain model and increase the likelihood of inadvertently leaking data persistence information into other portions of our app.

The marshaling from POCOs by the repository is another variant of pure DDD. Typically this is the domain of a factory, but our entities are fairly simple to construct at this point and the introduction of factories to our app might be a little more than necessary.

Consuming the domain

From the repositories, we can now consume the entities of the domain model and their encapsulated logic within our controllers.

In the previous chapter, we were returning POCOs from our BrewHowContext directly to the view. Since we have abstracted away the BrewHowContext class within the repositories, we need to alter our RecipeController to use RecipeRepository for retrieval and persistence of recipe entities. We also want to map those recipe entities to a class the view itself can use. This will prevent us from inadvertently allowing execution of code against a domain entity from the view. This view-specific class is called a view model.

Recipe view model

The view model for a view designed to display a recipe is straightforward. It is really a field-to-field mapping of the RecipeEntity class to a POCO class:

```
public class RecipeDisplayViewModel
{
  [Key]
  public int RecipeId { get; set; }

  [Display(Name = "Name")]
  public string Name { get; set; }

  [Display(Name = "Style")]
  public string Style { get; set; }

  [Display(Name = "Category")]
  public string Category { get; set; }

  [Display(Name = "Original Gravity")]
  [DisplayFormat(DataFormatString = "{0:0.00##}")]
  public float OriginalGravity { get; set; }
```

```
    [Display(Name = "Final Gravity")]
    [DisplayFormat(DataFormatString = "{0:0.00##}")]
    public float FinalGravity { get; set; }

    [Display(Name = "Grain Bill")]
    [DataType(DataType.MultilineText)]
    public string GrainBill { get; set; }

    [Display(Name = "Instructions")]
    [DataType(DataType.MultilineText)]
    public string Instructions { get; set; }

    [Display(Name = "ABV")]
    [DisplayFormat(DataFormatString = "{0:0.00}")]
    public float PercentAlcoholByVolume { get; set; }
}
```

You may have noticed the view model class is heavily decorated with attributes. Those attributes are part of the Data Annotations library found in `System. ComponentModel.DataAnnotations` and are discussed in the next section.

You may have also noticed the name of the class is `RecipeDisplayViewModel`. The class is only for displaying of recipes to the consumer. We have a separate view model class to allow for the editing or creation of new recipes:

```
public class RecipeEditViewModel
{
    [Key]
    public int RecipeId { get; set; }

    [Display(Name = "Style")]
    public int StyleId { get; set; }

    [Display(Name = "Name")]
    public string Name { get; set; }

    [Display(Name = "Original Gravity")]
    [DisplayFormat(DataFormatString = "{0:0.00##}")]
    public float OriginalGravity { get; set; }

    [Display(Name = "Final Gravity")]
    [DisplayFormat(DataFormatString = "{0:0.00##}")]
    public float FinalGravity { get; set; }

    [Display(Name = "Grain Bill")]
    [DataType(DataType.MultilineText)]
    public string GrainBill { get; set; }
```

```
[Display(Name = "Instructions")]
[DataType(DataType.MultilineText)]
public string Instructions { get; set; }

public SelectList StyleList { get; set; }
}
```

The difference between the read-only version and the read/write version of the view model exist because we don't want to present, as modifiable, a derived property such as the percentage of alcohol by volume. Likewise, when displaying read-only information, we do not want to return model data to the view that is only useful when attempting to create or edit an entity.

 Since the Index action of RecipeController will be returning a list of RecipeDisplayViewModels to the view, IPagedResult has been modified slightly and moved to the ViewModels folder. Consult the code accompanying this book if you are curious about these changes.

Now, let's discuss all the attributes applied to the view models' properties.

Data annotations

Data annotations are used to provide hints to the runtime, or consumers of attributed classes and properties, about their behavior. These hints may help the runtime validate information being assigned to a property such as the RangeAttribute data annotation. Attributes like DisplayAttribute used in our view model classes provide hints to the UI about how a particular property should be captioned—the Html.DisplayFor helper uses this attribute.

One particularly useful attribute is DataTypeAttribute. In *Chapter 3, Introducing ASP.NET MVC 4*, we learned about display templates and editor templates. The DisplayFor and EditorFor helpers will actually use the DataTypeAttribute of a property should it exist. In our view model classes, we are using the DataTypeAttribute and specifying that GrainBill and Instructions properties should be treated as multiline text. Now, whenever DisplayFor is invoked on these properties, the runtime will render a textarea control in the view in lieu of the standard text input used for string values.

Of course for GrainBill and Instructions properties to be rendered as textarea elements within the view, we need to first provide the view with the view models.

Recipe controller

Our controllers should be retrieving entities from the repository and returning them to the view. Since our repository operates on entities and our view operates on view models, one of the jobs of our controller is to perform this translation.

The `RecipeController` class needs to be modified to consume the `RecipeRepository` method, retrieve and persist the `RecipeEntity` objects from the repository, and provide a mapping between those entities and the view models returned to the views. A portion of the modified `RecipeController` class now appears in the code as follows:

```
public class RecipeController : Controller
{
  private RecipeRepository _recipeRepository =
    new RecipeRepository();

  public ActionResult Index(int page = 0)
  {
    var model =
      new PagedResult<RecipeEntity, RecipeDisplayViewModel>(
      _recipeRepository.GetRecipes(),
       page,
      ToDisplayModel);

    return View(model);
  }

  public ActionResult Details(int id)
  {
    /* ... */
  }

  public ActionResult Create()
  {
    /* ... */
  }

  public ActionResult Create(RecipeEditViewModel recipe)
  {
    /* ... */
  }
```

```
public ActionResult Edit(int id)
{
  /* ... */
}


public ActionResult Edit(RecipeEditViewModel recipe)
{
  /* ... */
}

private RecipeDisplayViewModel ToDisplayModel(RecipeEntity
entity)
{
  if (entity == null)
  {
    throw new ArgumentNullException(
      "entity",
      "Cannot convert null to a view model.");
  }

  return new RecipeDisplayViewModel
  {
    RecipeId = entity.RecipeId,
    Name = entity.Name,
    Category = entity.Style.Category.ToString(),
    Style = entity.Style.Name,
    OriginalGravity = entity.OriginalGravity,
    FinalGravity = entity.FinalGravity,
    PercentAlcoholByVolume = entity.PercentAlcoholByVolume,
    GrainBill = entity.GrainBill,
    Instructions = entity.Instructions,
  };
}

// Consult the code accompanying this book
// for the full listing of this class.
}
```

You will notice that we've filled out some additional actions. The Details, Create, and Edit actions allow us to retrieve the details of a specific recipe, to create a new recipe, or to edit an existing recipe respectively. Two of these actions, Create and Edit, have overloaded method signatures and each signature has different attributes applied to them.

The action methods decorated with [HttpPost] will respond only to requests that occur over HTTP POST. The action methods without an attribute implicitly respond to HTTP requests made using the HTTP GET verb. These actions, though named the same, serve two separate purposes.

GET versus POST

The undecorated actions, those without [HttpPost], operate on the HTTP GET verb and handle the presentation of the Create and Edit views. They only serve to provide an interface through which our users may create or edit recipes.

The actions responding to the HTTP POST verb are the actions used to create or modify entities. These actions have a parameter that corresponds to the edit version of our RecipeEntity's view model. To convert the contents of the HTTP POST received by the runtime into an object that we consume as a parameter to the action method, the controller leverages the MVC runtime's model binding infrastructure. Information should only ever be modified in response to an HTTP POST.

Model binding

Model binding is the means by which the runtime maps query string or POST parameters to action method properties. When an action method is invoked, the model binder examines the contents of the incoming request and tries to determine if it needs to map values to simple or complex properties—complex properties are in the form of [parent].[property]. The model binder then, recursively, begins constructing models to be passed back to the action method should it support receiving them.

To illustrate, assume a view contains a form to invoke some action. The form itself contains an input field with the name MyProperty:

```
<input type="text" name="MyProperty" />
```

When the user clicks submit, the runtime will look at the action being invoked and try and marshal the values in the body of the POST request into the parameters of the action. If the action takes a parameter named MyProperty, the model binder will pass whatever value the input had at the time of submission to the action parameter MyProperty. If the action takes a complex type and the complex type has a property named MyProperty, then the model binder will construct the complex type (if it can) and set its MyProperty property to the value submitted from the form.

The model binding is extensible, allowing you to create new binders for custom types. If it can't bind to your particular parameter, you can give it a little help.

Recipe views

The views now need to be modified to accept a view model as opposed to the POCOs of the data model. To create these views, we simply leverage the same scaffolding provided by Visual Studio that we used in *Chapter 3, Introducing ASP.NET MVC 4*. Right-click anywhere within the action method to bring up our context menu and then click on **Add View...**.

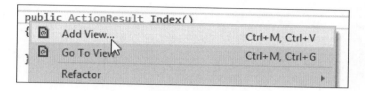

This time, however, we will create a strongly typed view and select the view model as our model class. If you are following along, make sure to select the appropriate Scaffold template in the **Add View** dialog. The following image shows the appropriate settings for creating the Edit view:

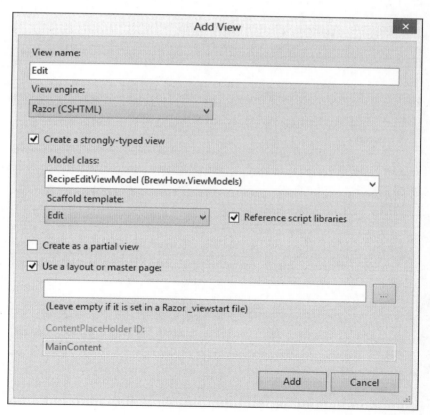

Following is the code for our Edit view. The highlighted portion of the code illustrates how we are consuming the StyleList property of our RecipeEditViewModel:

```
@model BrewHow.ViewModels.RecipeEditViewModel

@{
  ViewBag.Title = "Edit";
}

<h2>Edit</h2>

@using (Html.BeginForm()) {
  @Html.ValidationSummary(true)

  <fieldset>
    <legend>RecipeEditViewModel</legend>

    <div class="editor-label">
      @Html.LabelFor(model => model.Name)
    </div>
    <div class="editor-field">
      @Html.EditorFor(model => model.Name)
      @Html.ValidationMessageFor(model => model.Name)
    </div>

    <div class="editor-label">
      @Html.LabelFor(model => model.StyleId)
    </div>
    <div class="editor-field">
      @Html.DropDownListFor(model => model.StyleId,
        Model.StyleList)
    </div>
    <!--See accompanying code for the full listing -->
    <p>
      <input type="submit" value="Save" />
    </p>
  </fieldset>
}

<div>
  @Html.ActionLink("Back to List", "Index")
</div>
```

```
@section Scripts {
  @Scripts.Render("~/bundles/jqueryval")
}
```

When we invoke the view, the runtime displays the inputs for the `Instruction` and `GrainBill` properties as multiline inputs just as our `DataTypeAttribute` suggested.

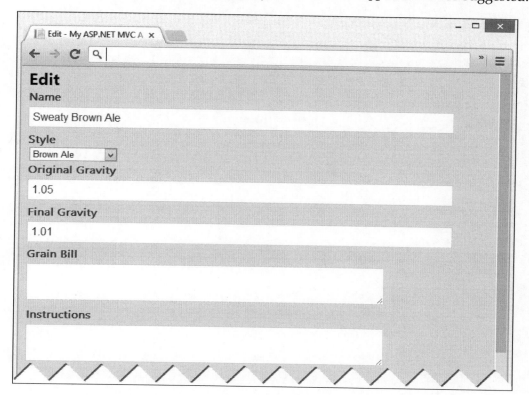

Summary

You now have a basic understanding of DDD and we have applied that understanding to our app. Our app now enforces boundaries between persistence, logic, and display. We have identified and implemented entities that correspond to our domain model. The domain model is persisted and restored through the entities exposed by our repositories. Each entity within our model can contain logic specific to it and, should the need arise, we will implement services to handle interaction across entities and factories to construct complex entities. Our controllers provide the glue between the entities of our domain model and the presentation of the domain model to the user where they can, should they so choose, act upon it.

In the next chapter we will structure our app to use Inversion of Control and Dependency Injection. We will also look at designing code that adheres to the SOLID principles. Leveraging these patterns will provide us with a more maintainable code base.

6
Writing Maintainable Code

Spaghetti code. Big Ball of Mud. If you've been writing code for at least a couple of years, you are likely to know these terms. You have certainly seen or perhaps contributed to a project so unmaintainable that you placed bets on the day it would collapse under its own weight. However, if you stepped back and dug a little deeper into the history of the project, you would likely discover that it began with honorable intentions.

Nobody sets out to write bad code. Nobody sets out to write unmaintainable code. Whether it's the urgency to get a project complete on time, proof-of-concept code that unexplainably made it to production, or some other external force of business, sometimes we just end up writing unmaintainable code.

In this chapter, we will discuss ways in which we can design our classes and structure our app to make it more maintainable and, by proxy, make it more testable by exploring the SOLID principles of class design. These principles, if adhered to, do not guarantee that we won't create a project the next generation of developers will complain about. They do, however, make it much harder. Once we have examined these principles, we will apply them to BrewHow.

The SOLID principles

The SOLID principles are a collection of five object-oriented principles of class design. The principles themselves, which were put into the **SOLID** acronym by Robert Martin, are acronyms within the acronym: **SRP**, **OCP**, **LSP**, **ISP**, and **DIP**. We will be leveraging each of these principles in our class design moving forward.

Single Responsibility Principle

Single Responsibility Principle (SRP) can loosely be translated as "do one thing and do it well." If you find yourself describing the functionality of a class or method by saying it does A "and" B, you've likely violated this principle. Consider our controllers.

One could argue that our app's `RecipeController` class violates SRP, as it currently retrieves data on behalf of the user, translates the data to a format appropriate for the view, and either returns the user the requested view or reroutes them to the appropriate one. That's a lot of work going on. However, if we state that the intent of our application's `RecipeController` class is to retrieve data for a view based on user input, we can lose the "and" and it doesn't sound quite so bad — that is, after all, what a controller is supposed to do.

Perhaps a better example would be to consider a class responsible for managing users. This hypothetical class simply creates, retrieves, modifies, and deletes users.

```
public class UserManager
{
    public void CreateUser(User user) { /* … */ }
    public void GetUser(UserId userId) { /* … */ }
    public void UpdateUser(User user) { /* … */ }
    public void DeleteUser(User user) { /* … */ }
}
```

Having a single class to manage users would adhere to SRP. If, however, someone decided to construct e-mails and send them to new users within the class's `create` method, the class would now be in violation of SRP. It is now responsible for maintaining users and communicating with them.

Robert Martin, therefore, sums it up better by saying if there is more than one reason for a class to change, it has violated SRP.

Open Closed Principle

Open Closed Principle (OCP) states that software components "should be open for extension, but closed for modification." Simply put, if a class needs to have its behavior altered, that behavior should be altered through object-oriented design techniques like inheritance or composition.

Assume you have a method named `Transfer` that is designed to transfer funds between two separate accounts. At the time the class was written, there were rules around how much money could be transferred from a single account on any given day, and the amount depended on the account type.

```
public void Transfer(Account fromAccount, Account toAccount)
{
  switch (fromAccount.Type)
  {
    case AccountType.Checking:
      if (fromAccount.DailyAmountTransferred < 500)
      {
        // Transfer funds.
      }
      break;
    case AccountType.Savings:
      if (fromAccount.DailyAmountTransferred < 300)
      {
        // Transfer funds.
      }
  }
  // Other logic.
}
```

What would happen if a new account type of MoneyMarket were added or, simply, the daily limits were changed? As the code is written, either of these changes would necessitate the Transfer method be modified to support the extension. It would be better if the Transfer method were ignorant of both the type and limit of accounts.

To make the Transfer method ignorant, we need to make our Account class a little more intelligent. If we add properties to the Account class to provide to the Transfer method the daily amount transferred from the account as well as the transfer limit, the Transfer method could support any account type existing now or in the future.

```
public void Transfer(Account fromAccount, Account toAccount)
{
  if (fromAccount.DailyAmountTransferred <
    fromAccount.DailyAmountAllowed)
  {
    // Transfer funds.
  }
}
```

This code would be far more maintainable and would adhere to OCP. Transfer is open for extension but closed for modification.

Strict adherence to OCP generally implies both the source code and the binary output are closed to modification. While this is practical and desirable for larger enterprise applications, for our purposes we are going to apply it to source code only.

Liskov Substitution Principle

Liskov Substitution Principle (LSP) states that if two objects, A and B, are subtypes of object Z, then any method or class that operates on an object of type Z can operate on objects of type A or type B without changes to the behavior of the application.

Assume that the classes `Train` and `Motorcycle` are both subtypes of the class `Vehicle`. Let's assume that we also have a class named `Navigate` that operates on a `Vehicle` class that is passed into it. What happens if an instance of the `Navigate` class is sent an instance of type `Train`, and it instructs the instance of type `Train` to turn left? This certainly alters the behavior of the application, and I cannot imagine it ending well for the train.

Interface Segregation Principle

Have you ever found yourself implementing an `interface` or `abstract` class and throwing `NotImplementedException` exceptions on a majority of the methods defined? It is quite likely that the interface you implemented violated **Interface Segregation Principle (ISP)**.

ISP states an interface — in this context, a contract by which any implementation should abide — should be small and specific. You may recall a brief mention of CQRS in *Chapter 5, The BrewHow Domain and Domain-Driven Design*. In CQRS, commands against a data store are separated from queries designed to retrieve data from the same data store. Within CQRS, it would be perfectly reasonable and desired to have two interfaces implemented by our repository: one for submitting data to the data store and one for retrieving that data.

If you want a specific example of what many believe to be a clear violation of this principle, you might want to look at the older ASP.NET membership APIs.

```
public abstract class MembershipProvider : ProviderBase
{
    public abstract bool ChangePassword(/* ... */)
```

```
    public abstract bool
        ChangePasswordQuestionAndAnswer(/* ... */)
    public abstract MembershipUser CreateUser(/* ... */)
    public abstract bool DeleteUser(/* ... */)
    public abstract MembershipUserCollection
        FindUsersByEmail(/* ... */)
    public abstract MembershipUserCollection
        FindUsersByName(/* ... */)
    public abstract MembershipUserCollection
        GetAllUsers(/* ... */)
    public abstract int GetNumberOfUsersOnline();
    public abstract string GetPassword(/* ... */)
    public abstract MembershipUser GetUser(/* ... */)
    public abstract MembershipUser GetUser(/* ... */)
    public abstract string GetUserNameByEmail(/* ... */)
    public abstract string ResetPassword(/* ... */)
    public abstract bool UnlockUser(/* ... */)
    public abstract void UpdateUser(/* ... */)
    public abstract bool ValidateUser(/* ... */)

    public abstract string ApplicationName { get; set; }
    public abstract bool EnablePasswordReset { get; }
    public abstract bool EnablePasswordRetrieval { get; }
    public abstract int MaxInvalidPasswordAttempts { get; }
    public abstract int MinRequiredNonAlphanumericCharacters
        { get; }
    public abstract int MinRequiredPasswordLength { get; }
    public abstract int PasswordAttemptWindow { get; }
    public abstract MembershipPasswordFormat PasswordFormat
        { get; }
    public abstract string PasswordStrengthRegularExpression
        { get; }
    public abstract bool RequiresQuestionAndAnswer { get; }
    public abstract bool RequiresUniqueEmail { get; }
}
```

While attempting to describe this contract, it might be simpler to talk about what is not included as opposed to what is.

Dependency Inversion Principle

The formal definition of **Dependency Inversion Principle (DIP)** posits high-level logic within an application that should not depend on a specific implementation of low-level logic. Instead, high-level logic should rely only on abstractions when dealing with low-level logic and vice-versa.

A simple way to define DIP is to say that you should always code to interfaces and never to a concrete implementation of an interface.

Assume we are writing a newsreader app that serves up articles from "Joe's House-o-News". We might have a method within the app that looks something like the following:

```
public Article[] GetArticles()
{
   JoesHouseONewsService newsService = new JoesHouseONewsService();
   /* random service logic to filter the articles */
   return newsService.Articles;
}
```

There's nothing obviously wrong with this code other than the fact that we've assumed Joe's House-o-News is going to be in business two weeks from now. Realizing after some deep thought that the odds are against poor Joe, we decide to change our app to provide articles to our users from their Feedly reading list. This requires us to crack open the `reader` class and change it to pull articles from a new source.

Had we coded to an `interface` in our `GetArticles` method instead of a particular news service, it would have been unnecessary for us to modify the method. Of course, you can't instantiate an interface, so we would also have to introduce a `Factory` as we discussed in *Chapter 5, The BrewHow Domain and Domain-Driven Design*:

```
public Article[] GetArticles()
{
   INewsService newsService = NewsServiceFactory.Create();
   /* Same random service logic. */
   return newsService.Articles;
}
```

Our method no longer has to be changed whenever we make changes to our news provider. We could even extend the app to now support consumption of news from multiple sources.

SOLIDifying BrewHow

Let's apply what we now know about the SOLID class design to our app. Given that abstractions are important in SOLID design, we will begin by adding abstractions for our repositories.

Adding interfaces

In .NET, we create an abstraction through an `interface` and provide a concrete implementation of an abstraction through a `class`, so our first step should be providing interfaces for our classes.

Open Visual Studio and add new files, namely `IRecipeRepository`, `IStyleRepository`, and `IReviewRepository` in the `Repositories` folder of our project to hold the interface for each repository in the app. The extracted interfaces for `IRecipeRepository` is as follows:

```
public interface IRecipeRepository
{
    IQueryable<RecipeEntity> GetRecipes();

    IQueryable<RecipeEntity>
        GetRecipesByStyle(string styleName);

    RecipeEntity GetRecipe(int recipeId);

    void Save(RecipeEntity recipe);
}
```

These interfaces are narrow in scope and adhere to ISP. While they will also be vital in adhering to the other tenants of SOLID design, they are not of any inherent value. They must first have a concrete implementation in the form of a class.

The next step is for the repository classes to implement the interfaces. Open up the repository classes and add the appropriate `interface` to the `class` definition. The `Recipe` repository declaration are as follows:

```
public class RecipeRepository : IRecipeRepository
```

The `Style` repository declaration is as follows:

```
public class StyleRepository : IStyleRepository
```

Our class implementation and our interface abstraction have now been separated, but we need to go one step further by placing the implementation and the abstraction in separate namespaces. We do this to simplify our adherence to DIP, as any inclusion of a specific implementation must now be deliberate by including the implementation in a `using` statement.

The abstractions will remain a part of the domain, but the implementation-specific details of these domain-level abstractions are part of our infrastructure.

Enterprise Development

If we were developing an enterprise-caliber application, we would separate the implementation not only into a new namespace but also into a new assembly as well. This would allow us to exchange technology-specific implementations of an interface at the application level. We would accomplish this through an IoC container, as we will discuss momentarily.

Infrastructure

Infrastructure refers to actual classes or specific implementations of which the application and only the application is aware. We need to create a new folder structure in our project into which we will place the implementation of our domain-level repositories.

Within Visual Studio, create a new folder named `Infrastructure` within the project. Within the new `Infrastructure` folder, create another folder named `Repositories` and move the implementation of the repository interfaces into this folder. Make sure you change the namespace for each of the repository implementations to `BrewHow.Infrastructure.Repositories` from `BrewHow.Domain.Repositories`.

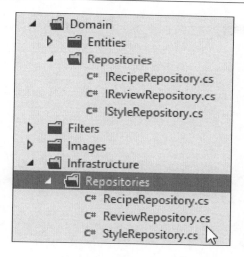

As we moved the implementation and now need to reference abstractions, our controllers need to be modified such that the repository member variables are typed to the interface and not the repository class. This will allow us to complete our move to dependency inversion.

In the definition of DIP provided earlier in the chapter, we were using factories for dependency inversion. Another method for us to accomplish dependency inversion is to inject the dependencies into the class. This method of injecting dependencies into a class is aptly named **Dependency Injection (DI)**.

Dependency Injection

Dependency Injection is a pattern by which the dependencies of a class are provided to the class, the class does not need to go and identify them. The most common form of DI is **Constructor Injection (CI)**. CI requires that a class declare all dependencies upon which it relies as parameters to the constructor. This technique ensures that an instance of a class cannot be created unless all dependencies upon which it relies are available to it at the time of creation.

CI is problematic in the ASP.NET MVC world because controllers are required to have a parameter-less constructor in the standard implementation. To get around this constraint, a common solution is to overload the constructor to provide both a constructor for CI and a parameter-less constructor that injects those dependencies into the overload as follows:

```
private IRecipeRepository _recipeRepository = null;
private IStyleRepository _styleRepository = null;
```

```
public RecipeController()
    : this( new RecipeRepository()
    , new StyleRepository())
{
}

public RecipeController(
    IRecipeRepository recipeRepository,
    IStyleRepository styleRepository)
{
    this._recipeRepository = recipeRepository;
    this._styleRepository = styleRepository;
}
```

We have now modified our controllers to rely on the abstractions and have inverted our dependencies. Should we need to alter the implementation of the repository classes to use different technology or, more likely, provide implementations that return mock data for testing, we no longer have to alter the code within the `RecipeController` class. And provided all implementations of the repository interfaces do not alter the expected behavior of the repository, these abstractions help us adhere to LSP.

We've accomplished a lot, but we still have a few issues with our design. Primarily, we haven't solved the base problem of our controllers knowing where to look for their dependencies. This means that if we change the default implementation of the repositories, we have to open up each controller that creates class instances in its parameter-less constructor and change the type of class being instantiated. We need some other way to resolve these dependencies and for that, we will leverage a pattern known as a **service locator**.

The service locator is often considered an anti-pattern due to some very unique problems it introduces to a codebase. Without being specific, the scenarios under which problems arise are typically associated with the development of frameworks and not applications. Having said that, should you decide to make use of the service locator pattern in your future development efforts, I suggest you research first.

Service locator

A service locator is exactly what the name implies. It provides a means for code, upon request, to locate an implementation of a particular abstraction. The calling code has no idea how the abstraction is implemented or what the abstraction's dependencies might be. It simply knows to make a request for an abstraction.

The locator itself is typically configured at the application level. The configuration may be a fluent configuration expressed in code, or it may load the configuration from an external configuration file. The service locator we are going to create is going to use the **Managed Extensibility Framework (MEF)** to inspect our assembly, locate specific implementations, and export them for consumption to the service locator.

Managed Extensibility Framework

As we are going to use MEF, we should know a little about it. MEF is designed to provide extensibility to applications through the use of components known as parts — pieces of code that adhere to a contract. These parts are registered within a catalog. Each catalog, in turn, is added to one or multiple composition containers from which an application may request parts that implement a specific contract. These parts may be composited together to form other parts and they share the lifetime of their container — a part isn't disposed until the composition container from which it was created is disposed.

All of this composition should sound familiar. We are, ourselves, composing classes within our app through a series of dependency injections. Our current controllers are responsible for disposing the repositories injected into them. Each controller and its repositories are living as a single unit — a part composited from other parts.

Shipping with the .NET Framework 4.5 is MEF 2.0. MEF 2.0 provides several improvements over the initial release including multiple scope levels for composition and generic type support. Of most immediate interest to us, however, is the ability for convention-based configuration.

Microsoft, in 2011, developed a NuGet package designed specifically for using MEF within MVC. This package was, however, experimental and at the time of writing only supports object composition within MVC. While that's enough for what we are doing, MEF 2.0 supports everything we need and ships with the .NET 4.5 Framework. As such, it is being leveraged here.

Convention-based configuration

Prior to version 2.0, MEF required code to be decorated with `Import` and `Export` attributes. The `Import` attributes would define dependencies a particular piece of code needed, while an `Export` attribute would define the type of part for which a particular piece of code could be used. This convention-based configuration is centralized within the `RegistrationBuilder` class, and it is around this class that we will build our MEF Service Locator.

MEF Service Locator

In the `App_Start` folder, create a new class named `ServiceLocatorConfig` and place the following code within the class:

```
public class ServiceLocatorConfig
{
  private static CompositionContainer _container = null ;

  public static void RegisterTypes()
    {
      RegistrationBuilder rb = new RegistrationBuilder ();

      rb
        .ForTypesDerivedFrom<IRecipeRepository >()
        .Export<IRecipeRepository>()
        .SetCreationPolicy(CreationPolicy.NonShared);

      rb
        .ForTypesDerivedFrom<IStyleRepository>()
        .Export<IStyleRepository >()
        .SetCreationPolicy(CreationPolicy.NonShared);

    ServiceLocatorConfig._container =
      new CompositionContainer(
        new AssemblyCatalog(
                  Assembly.GetExecutingAssembly(),
                  rb
          )
        );
  }

  public static CompositionContainer Container
  {
    get { return ServiceLocatorConfig._container; }
  }
}
```

The class itself is pretty sparse. As I said, we are heavily leveraging the `RegistrationBuilder` class and as you can see I wasn't understating this. As we will continue to leverage this class, let's talk about what it is doing by examining the following code:

```
RegistrationBuilder rb = new RegistrationBuilder ();
rb
    .ForTypesDerivedFrom<IRecipeRepository >()
    .Export<IRecipeRepository>()
    .SetCreationPolicy(CreationPolicy.NonShared);
```

First, we construct an instance of the `RegistrationBuilder` class. We then tell the `RegistrationBuilder` instance the types of classes we want to export for consumption, and whether or not we want those classes shared.

The highlighted portion of code tells the registration builder to export a type of `IRecipeRepository` for all types derived from `IRecipeRepository`. Note that we are not exporting a type of `RecipeRepository` using the `Export` method. This distinction is important. If we were to change the export from `Export<IRecipeRepository>()` to simply `Export()` or the equivalent `Export<RecipeRepository>()`, we would export the actual class implementing the interface: `RecipeRepository`. We would then need to request from the locator the actual implementation and would not be separating our implementation from our abstraction.

In addition to exporting the `IRecipeRepository` interface for all parts implementing it, we create a new instance for each request by setting the creation policy to `NonShared`.

We briefly discussed the `Import` and `Export` attributes for declaring dependencies and the ability to fulfill those dependencies at the beginning of this chapter. MEF allows parts to specify whether or not they can be shared to fulfill the dependency declarations of other classes. Likewise, components can declare that their dependencies must be shared or unique to them. MEF will not provide a dependency to a component unless the part matches both the expected type and supported creation policy. MEF supports creation policies of `NonShared`, `Shared`, and `Any`.

We then need to construct a `CompositionContainer` and tell it where our exports are.

```
ServiceLocatorConfig._container =
  new CompositionContainer(
    new AssemblyCatalog(
            Assembly.GetExecutingAssembly(),
            rb
    )
  );
```

This code creates a new `CompositionContainer` and assigns it to the `_container` member variable. The `CompositionContainer` class is one of several classes that extend the `ExportProvider` class within MEF. These classes provide an interface through which consumers can retrieve exported types.

The `CompositionContainer` class is supplied with an instance of a `ComposablePartCatalog`, in this case an instance of `AssemblyCatalog`, as a parameter. When asked for an implementation of a particular interface, the `CompositionContainer` class will consult any registered `ComposablePartCatalogs` to determine if they can return an implementation. The catalog itself knows to search `RegistrationBuilder` for any types it is permitted to export. Our `AssemblyCatalog` will scour the currently executing assembly for the types defined in `RegistrationBuilder`, and will export them if they are found and declared for export.

 MEF supports exporting types from more than just the currently executing assembly. For instance, you can export all the types from all assemblies within a directory by using `DirectoryCatalog` instead of `AssemblyCatalog` that we are currently using.

Using the MEF Service Locator

Now that we've created our service locator, we need to hook it up. We will start by adding the highlighted code to the `Application_Start` method in our `Global.asax.cs` file:

```
protected void Application_Start()
{
    ServiceLocatorConfig.RegisterTypes();
    AreaRegistration.RegisterAllAreas();
    WebApiConfig.Register(GlobalConfiguration.Configuration);
    FilterConfig.RegisterGlobalFilters(GlobalFilters.Filters);
    RouteConfig.RegisterRoutes(RouteTable.Routes);
    BundleConfig.RegisterBundles(BundleTable.Bundles);
    AuthConfig.RegisterAuth();
}
```

And finally, we'll adjust the controllers to use the new service locator class. Delete the constructor for the `Recipe` controller containing parameters for the `Recipe` and `Style` repositories and replace the parameter-less constructor with the following one:

```
public RecipeController()
{
    this._recipeRepository = ServiceLocatorConfig
    .Container
        .GetExportedValue<IRecipeRepository>();

    this._styleRepository = ServiceLocatorConfig
    .Container
        .GetExportedValue<IStyleRepository>();
}
```

The new `RecipeController` class now has no dependencies on any class from the `Infrastructure` namespace. We need some way to abstract this even further. Ideally, we'd like to return to Constructor Injection so that our class cannot be constructed without having all dependencies resolved, but we need a way to overcome the requirement that a controller have a parameter-less constructor. Fortunately for us, Microsoft has provided a way for us to do this, the **Dependency Resolver**.

Dependency Resolver

The ASP.NET MVC Framework provides an extensibility point for dependency resolution via the `System.Web.Mvc.DependencyResolver` class. This class has a static method, `SetResolver`, accepting as a parameter an instance of `System.Web.Mvc.IDependencyResolver`.

Internally, the MVC Framework heavily leverages the `DependencyResolver` class. Of particular interest to us is the fact the default implementation of `IControllerFactory` and `DefaultControllerFactory`—the portion of the MVC framework responsible for instantiating controllers—uses the registered implementation of `IDependencyResolver` to attempt to find a concrete implementation for a particular controller. If an implementation is found, `DefaultControllerFactory` will attempt to further satisfy the dependencies of the controller using the registered implementation of `IDependencyResolver`.

This functionality allows us to return to our preferred Constructor Injection method of DI with our controllers, provided we register both the controller classes and the classes on which the controller classes depend with an implementation of `IDependencyResolver` and then supply the resolver to the framework.

We can also take this a step further and define dependencies for our dependencies. For example, we can require that the `RecipeRepository` have injected into it a class that implements some `IDbContext` interface. This would allow us to test the logic that will occur within the `RecipeRepository` when converting entities to and from models, or to provide mock data to the application for partial integration tests.

The MefDependencyResolver class

The MefDependencyResolver class implements the IDependencyResolver interface and implements the two methods GetService and GetServices. These methods allow a requestor to find a single service or multiple services of a specific type that have been registered with the resolver.

```csharp
public class MefDependencyResolver : IDependencyResolver
{
    private ExportProvider _parentContainer;
    private const string RequestContainerKey = "ServiceLocatorConfig.
RequestContainer";

    public MefDependencyResolver(ExportProvider parentContainer)
    {
        this._parentContainer = parentContainer;
    }

    public object GetService(Type serviceType)
    {
        var export = this
            .RequestContainer
            .GetExports(serviceType, null, null)
            .SingleOrDefault();

        if (export != null)
        {
            return export.Value;
        }

        return null;
    }

    public IEnumerable<object> GetServices(Type serviceType)
    {
        var exports = this
            .RequestContainer
            .GetExports(serviceType, null, null);

        foreach (var export in exports)
        {
            yield return export.Value;
        }
    }
```

```
public void Dispose()
{
    using (RequestContainer as IDisposable) { }
}


ExportProvider RequestContainer
{
    get
    {
        ExportProvider requestContainer =
            HttpContext
            .Current
            .Items[RequestContainerKey] as ExportProvider;

        if (requestContainer == null)
        {
            requestContainer =
                new CompositionContainer(
                    this._parentContainer);
            HttpContext
                .Current
                .Items[RequestContainerKey]
            = requestContainer;
        }

        return requestContainer;
    }
}
}
```

Our `MefDependencyResolver` receives an `ExportProvider` as a constructor argument, allowing us to pass our `CompositionContainer` class to the constructor but not prohibiting us from changing the type of `ExportProvider` in the future.

When MEF was introduced, we discussed how a part will live until the composition container from which it is created is disposed. As a new composition container is created for every request to the container—our parts have a creation policy of `NonShared`—this could be problematic, as every request to our app will create a controller and two repositories. To address this, we need to scope the composition container to the current HTTP request. Our Dependency Resolver does this through the `RequestContainer` property.

When asked for a specific implementation of a type, the implementations of `GetService` and `GetServices` simply forward the request to the `RequestContainer` property. This property looks at the current HTTP request cache to see if an instance of a container already exists. If it doesn't, a new `CompositionContainer` class is created as a child of the global composition container and added to the cache. The `GetService` and `GetServices` methods then look through the `RequestContainer` property's exports to find the requested part.

The child container put into the HTTP request cache is able to locate and create parts because it inherits the entire catalog collection assigned to its parent. And as it's assigned to the request cache, we can dispose of the child catalog at the completion of the request to dispose of any parts it created.

```
protected void Application_EndRequest()
{
    using (DependencyResolver.Current as IDisposable) { }
}
```

Completing the conversion

To complete our conversion to a truly SOLID codebase, we need to provide abstractions for our `DbContext` class, declare dependencies in our classes as constructor parameters, register these dependencies with our resolver, and then register our resolver with the framework.

IBrewHowContext

Our first step, then, is to provide an interface for our `BrewHowContext` that is currently extending the `DbContext` class. The following is the definition for our `IBrewHowContext` interface:

```
public interface IBrewHowContext
{
    IDbSet<Recipe> Recipes { get; set; }
    IDbSet<Review> Reviews { get; set; }
    IDbSet<Style> Styles { get; set; }

    int SaveChanges();
}
```

Note that our interface has changed the return type of the `Recipes`, `Reviews`, and `Styles` properties to be `IDbSet<T>` collections and not `DbSet<T>` collections. Because the `DbSet` class exposes no public constructor, if we choose to provide mock data to our repository implementations, we cannot return `DbSet` collections. We therefore had to adjust the definition to be of `IDbSet`.

The definition of our `BrewHowContext` class should now look as follows:

```
public class BrewHowContext : DbContext, IBrewHowContext
```

To separate the implementation from the abstraction, we now need to move the `BrewHowContext` class into the `Repositories` folder in the `Infrastructure` folder in our project and adjust the namespace to `BrewHow.Infrastructure.Repositories`. This move will require us to adjust the constructor for `BrewHowContext`.

```
public BrewHowContext()
    : base("BrewHow.Models.BrewHowContext")
{
}
```

Entity Framework uses, as convention, the fully qualified name of the context as the name of the database to which it connects. As we altered the fully qualified name by changing the namespace, this constructor modification was necessary if we wanted to keep our existing sample data.

Repositories

The repositories should now be modified to have the context provided to them via Constructor Injection. This change is a little more impactful to the codebase. Previously, each method constructed a `BrewHowContext` within a `using` statement. As the context will be provided to the constructor, we will need to touch each method and remove the creation of `BrewHowContext`. The code for `RecipeRepository` illustrates the difference.

```
public class RecipeRepository
    : RepositoryBase, IRecipeRepository
{
    private IBrewHowContext _context;

    public RecipeRepository(IBrewHowContext context)
    {
        this._context = context;
    }
```

```
    /* Other methods omitted for space */
}
```

Registering dependencies

We have created a whole new set of dependencies. First, we've reverted to injecting dependencies into our controllers' constructors. Those dependencies, the repositories, now have their dependencies supplied to their constructor in the form of an IBrewHowContext. We need to register each of these dependencies with the CompositionContainer class used by our MefDependencyResolver, and then register our resolver with the MVC runtime.

Our new ServiceLocatorConfig class is as follows:

```
public class ServiceLocatorConfig
{
    private static CompositionContainer _container = null;

    public static void RegisterTypes()
    {
        RegistrationBuilder rb = new RegistrationBuilder();

        RegisterDbContexts(rb);
        RegisterRepositories(rb);
        RegisterControllers(rb);

        ServiceLocatorConfig._container = new CompositionContainer(
            new AssemblyCatalog(
                Assembly.GetExecutingAssembly(),
                rb
            )
        );

        var resolver = new MefDependencyResolver(ServiceLocatorConf
ig._container);

        DependencyResolver.SetResolver(resolver);
    }

    private static void RegisterDbContexts(RegistrationBuilder rb)
    {
        rb.ForTypesDerivedFrom<IBrewHowContext>()
```

```
                    .Export<IBrewHowContext>()
                    .SetCreationPolicy(CreationPolicy.NonShared);
        }


        private static void RegisterRepositories(RegistrationBuilder rb)
        {
            rb.ForTypesDerivedFrom<IRecipeRepository>()
                .Export<IRecipeRepository>()
                .SetCreationPolicy(CreationPolicy.NonShared);

            rb.ForTypesDerivedFrom<IStyleRepository>()
                .Export<IStyleRepository>()
                .SetCreationPolicy(CreationPolicy.NonShared);
        }


        private static void RegisterControllers(RegistrationBuilder rb)
        {
            rb.ForTypesDerivedFrom<Controller>()
                .Export()
                .SetCreationPolicy(CreationPolicy.NonShared);
        }
    }
```

The static methods and, in fact, the entire static approach to this class are unnecessary. It was put in place to be consistent with the other classes within the App_Start folder. Feel free to change these methods and class to be instance-based if the use of the static keyword makes your eyes twitch.

You can see that our controllers, our repositories, and our context are now all registered with the RegistrationBuilder instance. The RegistrationBuilder instance, in turn, provides the exports to the CompositionContainer class through AssemblyCatalog. We then construct a new MefDependencyResolver, providing an instance of CompositionContainer to the constructor. Finally, our MefDependencyResolver is registered with the ASP.NET MVC runtime by calling the static SetResolver method on the DependencyResolver class.

Launch the app to validate it still functions, declare success, and go grab a homebrew. You have learned a lot and it's time to celebrate.

Summary

We now have a SOLIDly designed app. All concrete implementations of our abstractions are being provided to the app at runtime through `DependencyResolver`, and the loose coupling we have obtained in our app by adhering to the SOLID principles of class design now makes it more maintainable and more testable. We have also learned a bit about Dependency Injection and MEF.

In the next chapter, we are going to look at providing more functionality to our BrewHow app by allowing users to add reviews of our recipes and to view recipes by style. This new functionality will require us to look at the MVC Framework's routing mechanism and support for areas.

7
Separating Functionality Using Routes and Areas

Think about all of the URLs that begin with facebook.com or twitter.com. Think about the MSDN section of Microsoft's site. Imagine if you had to maintain controllers and actions to handle every single piece of content returned from those sites. It's pretty safe to say the task is beyond daunting, it's pretty much impossible.

While we would be exceptionally fortunate to have to deal with those problems in something we create, odds are we will never have to concern ourselves with scalability and functionality on that scale. That doesn't mean our app will never cross some maintenance threshold. When it does, we may decide we need to separate it into different logical divisions. We may choose to do so because our app has become too big or too complex to have every controller sitting within the Controllers folder. Sometimes it's just wanting the URLs of our app to be simple, meaningful, and RESTful.

In this chapter, we are going to work on separating our application into logical divisions. These divisions, architecturally, will enforce a separation of concerns. For our users, these divisions will result in meaningful and predictable URLs. To accomplish this, we will leverage two features of the ASP.NET MVC 4 framework: routes and areas.

Routes

In *Chapter 3, Introducing ASP.NET MVC 4*, we learned that the ASP.NET MVC 4 framework makes the determination of which controller should handle an incoming request by looking at the routes added to our route table. In actuality, it uses the route table for more than matching incoming routes. It also uses the route table to determine how to generate URLs using the HTML helpers `ActionLink` and `RouteLink`. When determining how to route an incoming request or generate a link, the runtime selects the first matching route from the route table.

Currently, our `RouteConfig` class registers a single route named `Default`:

```
routes.MapRoute(
  name: "Default",
  url: "{controller}/{action}/{id}",
  defaults: new {
  controller = "Recipe",
  action = "Index",
  id = UrlParameter.Optional
  }
);
```

This route is sufficient for most apps where users are simply creating objects and then retrieving them by id. However, one of our requirements is the ability to allow users of our app to filter the type of recipe by style. It would be nice for the filtered list of recipes to have a URL of `/Recipe/{style}`, something meaningful and legible to the user.

As our app currently functions, if we invoke our app with a URL in the format of `/Recipe/{style}` the `Default` route would result in a 404 error unless the style name happened to coincide with the name of an action within the controller; even then, it would likely cause our app to throw an error. What we need to do is register a new route to support the `/Recipe/{style}` format and provide a mechanism by which the user can invoke the new route.

Locating by style

Our default route is a simple three-segment route with two default values and one optional value. Any request made of our app between 0 and 3 segments will map to this route. Assuming this route is the first route registered in the route table, it will always be chosen for any URL having 3 or fewer segments. The new style route we want to register has two segments, so it may appear that registering our style route before the default route is the solution we need to take.

It's true that registering our `Recipe/{style}` route before the default route would solve the problem in most instances, but it's not a foolproof solution. Consider the URL `/Recipe/Details?id=3`. It's not in the format normally expected, but it is still a very valid URL. The URL consists of 2 segments and begins with `Recipe`. We would expect this URL to show the details for a recipe having an `id` of `3`, but if we register the style route before our default route the runtime will try to show all recipes with a style of `Details`, which is not what we want.

What we need is the ability to register our style route first, but only have it selected if the `{style}` segment is indeed a style. To do this, we can apply a constraint to the route.

Routing constraints

Placing constraints on a route allows us to reduce the ambiguity involved in the selection of a route by the runtime. To assist us, the ASP.NET MVC framework provides us with the `IRouteConstraint` interface:

```
public interface IRouteConstraint
{
   bool Match(
      HttpContextBase httpContext,
      Route route,
      string parameterName,
      RouteValueDictionary values,
      RouteDirection routeDirection);
}
```

When a route is registered with the runtime, we can provide the route table with a collection of constraints, each implementing the `IRouteConstraint` interface. When a route is being evaluated for a match, the runtime will not only attempt to match the request against the route's URL, but it will also make sure that the request passes all of the constraints set upon it using the `Match` method of each registered constraint.

We should set the constraint on our style route to check if the style passed in exists. If the style does not exist, then the request is either intended for an action as identified by the `Default` route or the request is invalid.

Our `RecipeStyleConstraint` constraint is presented below:

```
public bool Match(HttpContextBase httpContext,
  Route route,
  string parameterName,
  RouteValueDictionary values,
  RouteDirection routeDirection)
{
  if (!values.ContainsKey(parameterName))
    {
      return false;
    }

  var styleRepository = DependencyResolver
    .Current
    .GetService(typeof(IStyleRepository))
    as IStyleRepository;

  string styleName =
    (string)values[parameterName];

  var style = styleRepository
    .GetStyles()
    .FirstOrDefault(s =>
    s.Name == styleName
    );

  return style != null;
}
```

The next step is to register the route in the route table. Our style route, `BeerByStyle`, should restrict the {style} segment to match the rules set in our new `RecipeStyleConstraint` class:

```
routes.MapRoute(
  name: "BeerByStyle",
  url: "Recipe/{style}",
  defaults: new {
    controller = "Recipe",
    action = "Style"
  },
  constraints: new {
    style = new RecipeStyleConstraint()
  }
);
```

The `BeerByStyle` route is registered before the `Default` route to ensure it is selected first. It also identifies that any request mapped to our route should invoke the `Style` action on `RecipeController`. This is a new action method that reuses the `Index` view currently used by the `Index` method. The `Index` view is reused because the content is no different between the `Index` and `Style` actions. Only the context has changed:

```
public ActionResult Style(string style, int page = 0)
{
  var model = new PagedResult<RecipeEntity,
    RecipeDisplayViewModel>(
    _recipeRepository.GetRecipesByStyleSlug(style),
    page,
    ToDisplayModel);

  var styleEntity = _styleRepository.GetStyleBySlug(style);

  if (style != null)
  {
    ViewBag.Title = styleEntity.Name + " Recipes";
  }

  return View("Index", model);
}
```

This change in context is addressed in the `Style` action by adding a property to the `ViewBag`. The property is used as the header on the `Index` view if it is present, otherwise the `Index` view will set the header to simply read `Recipes`:

```
@model BrewHow
  .ViewModels
  .ITypedPagedResult<BrewHow
  .ViewModels
  .RecipeDisplayViewModel>
@{
  ViewBag.Title = ViewBag.Title ?? "Recipes";
}
<h2>@ViewBag.Title</h2>
```

All that's left to do to support location by style is to provide a means for the user to actually invoke the functionality.

Style interaction

For the user to use the new functionality we've created, we need to do a few things. First, we need to modify the `Index` view for `RecipeController` to make the style name an actual link. This will allow the user to see other recipes having the same style of a recipe they may like.

We also need to provide users with a direct mechanism to find a style and, from the style, view all recipes of that style. This will require us to create a new controller and view.

Recipe list modification

The list of recipes currently displays the style of the recipe among other pieces of information. We need to modify the recipe list to convert the name of the style to an actual link that will invoke our new route.

So far, our invocation of the `ActionLink` HTML helper has been pretty vanilla. We provide the `ActionLink` helper with the text for the link and a controller action. We also pass the `id` of the entity we're currently viewing into the route data dictionary in the form of an anonymous type as follows:

```
@Html.ActionLink(
   item.Name,
   "Details",
   new { id=item.RecipeId })
```

For us to invoke the `Style` action of our `Recipe` controller we need to pass the style's `Name` property to the route data dictionary. In an effort to distinguish the route to `RecipeController`'s `Style` action from a route to the style controller we are about to create, we also want to pass the name of the controller into the HTML helper.

Replacing `Html.DisplayFor` (`modelItem` => `item.Style`) in the `RecipeController` class's `Index` view with the following code will convert the style name to a link:

```
@Html.ActionLink(
   Html.DisplayFor(modelItem => item.Style)
     .ToHtmlString(),
   "Style",
   "Recipe",
   new { style = item.Style },
   null)
```

Now, requests to `/Recipe/Heffeweisen` appropriately map to our `Style` action. The action filters the recipe list and returns the results to the user.

Style Controller and view

Creating the `StyleController` class is no different than any controller we've created. It is a class that exists within the `Controllers` folder of our project and extends the `Controller` class.

`StyleController` has a single `Index` action that retrieves a list of `StyleEntity` objects from the implementation of `IStyleRepository` injected into the constructor. The implementation of the `Index` action should be nothing new at this point:

```
public ActionResult Index(int page = 0)
{
  var model = new PagedResult<StyleEntity, StyleDisplayViewModel>(
    _styleRepository.GetStyles(),
    page,
    ToDisplayModel);

  return View(model);
}
```

The view to which the `Index` action returns data is also nothing new. It's a paginated list view to display to the users all beer styles within the app. Each row in the list shows the name of the style, the category to which the style belongs, and a link to view all recipes associated with the style:

```
@model IEnumerable<BrewHow.ViewModels.StyleDisplayViewModel>
@{
  ViewBag.Title = "Styles";
}
<h2>@ViewBag.Title</h2>
<table>
  <tr>
    <th>
      @Html
      .DisplayNameFor(
        model => model.Name)
    </th>
  <th>
      @Html
      .DisplayNameFor(
        model => model.Category)
    </th>
    <th></th>
  </tr>

  @foreach (var item in Model) {
  /* ... */
  }
</table>
```

While we're making all of these adjustments to the navigation of the site, go ahead and open the layout file for our app and add a link to the `Style` controller and remove the **About** and **Contact Us** links. Also change the copyright at the bottom and the logo text at the top of the page. The style list with navigation adjustments is shown in the following screenshot:

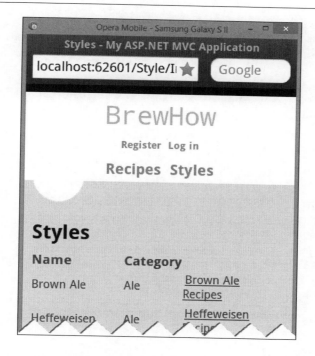

Our solution is not without problems. For instance, requests to `/Recipe/Brown Ale` redirect our users to Google if they are using Opera (or the emulator in this case). This occurs because Opera and several mobile browsers (and some desktop browsers) treat URLs containing spaces as requests for search results. To solve this, we need to change our strategy a bit. We want our URLs to be human readable, but we also want them to uniquely identify the content to which they resolve. What we need is a slug.

Slugging BrewHow

Slugs are human-readable identifiers that may be used either alone or in conjunction with another piece of identifiable information to uniquely identify a resource. Not only are slugs beneficial to the user by helping them uniquely identify the content their browser is currently displaying (`/Recipe/Heffeweisen` is far more informative than `/Recipe/1`), slugs play a huge role in how search engines treat your site and are a common **Search Engine Optimization (SEO)** technique.

Given slugs can solve our existing URL issue around spaces in the style names and they can provide us some SEO benefit, we need to adjust our models, entities, view models, and URLs to support slugs.

Model slugs

We want add support for slugging to the style and recipe entities, models, and view models in our application. The first step in accomplishing this is modifying the Recipe and Style data model classes to support slugging. This is as simple as adding a Slug property to each model. And, as we learned, modifications to the model will require us to apply migrations to the database.

Stage the database

We need to modify the database to support the new Slug properties added to the Recipe and Style models. We can do this by opening up the Package Manager Console and executing Add-Migration Slugs. This will generate our Slugs migration class in the project's Migration folder with Up and Down methods to add and remove the Slug property respectively.

The new properties will need values applied to them when the database is seeded. We can do this using the Seed method of our Configuration class since it will be executed when these new changes are applied:

```
protected override void Seed(BrewHowContext context)
{
  var brownAle = new Style
  {
    Name = "Brown Ale",
    Category = Category.Ale,
    Slug = "brown-ale"
  };

  /* ... */

  context.Styles.AddOrUpdate(
    style => style.Name,
    brownAle,
    /* ... */
  );

  context.Recipes.AddOrUpdate(
    recipe => recipe.Name,
    new Recipe
    {
      Name = "Sweaty Brown Ale",
      Style = brownAle,
```

```
        OriginalGravity = 1.05f,
        FinalGravity = 1.01f,
        Slug = "sweaty-brown-ale"
      },
    /* ... */
  );
}
```

 While we are able to make these adjustments to the data using the Seed method of our Configuration class, there are times when this might not be possible, if, for instance, you are running migrations on a production database. When this occurs, you can use the Sql method of the DbMigration class to directly execute SQL against the database as part of the migration process.

All that's left to commit the change to the model is to run the Update-Database command in the Package Manager Console.

Modifying entities

The domain level entities need to be adjusted to support the retrieval and setting of slugs as well as any rules or logic imposed upon the property. Since we currently provide no mechanism to create or edit styles, the adjustment to the StyleEntity class is as simple as adding a Slug property to the definition. Adding a Slug property to the RecipeEntity class is a bit different.

A **URL**, by definition, is a **Uniform Resource Locator**. URLs uniquely identify the location of a resource on the Internet for all eternity. Since we will be making the slug part of the URL, our slugs cannot change. The implication being the Slug property for a RecipeEntity class is set once and only once. Thus, our RecipeEntity class needs logic put into the Slug property to only allow Slug to be set one time:

```
public string Slug
{
  get
  {
    if (string.IsNullOrEmpty(this._slug))
    {
      if (string.IsNullOrEmpty(this.Name))
      {
        return string.Empty;
      }
```

```
        this._slug = Regex.Replace(
          this
          Name
          ToLower()
          .Trim(),
          "[^a-z0-9-]",
          "-");
      }

    return this._slug;
    }

  set
  {
    if (!string.IsNullOrEmpty(this._slug))
    {
      throw new InvalidOperationException(
        "The slug for the recipe has already been set.");
    }

    this._slug = value;
    }
  }
}
```

Our slug in the RecipeEntity class is generated upon the first retrieval and can only be assigned if no value already exists. If it is generated, the Name property will be used as the seed value for the Slug property. Any other set is an invalid operation.

DDD in Action

Separating our domain entities from our data model is what allows us to enforce domain rules separately from storage and presentation. The mapping from model to entity still occurs within the repository, but the repository is not responsible for knowing the rules being applied to the entity. It is merely a means to transfer the domain to persistent storage. Likewise, our views and controllers know nothing of the rules around the domain entities. They simply marshal them between the repository and the user.

Retrieval by slug

If we're going to be retrieving styles via their slug, we should to modify the
`BrewByStyle` route to take a slug as opposed to the name of the style. We need to
modify the repository interface `IStyleRepository` to provide a method to support
the functionality. This method can then be implemented by the `StyleRepository`
class being injected into `RecipeController` and being used via the dependency
resolution in `RecipeStyleConstraint`:

```
public StyleEntity GetStyleBySlug(string slug)
{
  return this
    .StyleEntities
    .FirstOrDefault(
    s => s.Slug == slug);
}
```

We also need to make adjustments to the `Default` route to accept an optional slug.
The slug here has no effect on data retrieval or storage. It simply serves to make the
URL more legible:

```
routes.MapRoute(
  name: "Default",
  url: "{controller}/{action}/{id}/{slug}",
  defaults: new {
    controller = "Recipe",
    action = "Index",
    id = UrlParameter.Optional,
    slug = UrlParameter.Optional
  }
);
```

Finally, our views and view models should also have access to the `Slug` property.
The work here is pretty straight forward. Create `Slug` properties on the view models
for recipes and styles and then alter any generated links to pass the slug back to the
controllers. Adding a slug to generated URLs is as simple as adding a slug key into
to the `routeValues` parameter of the `ActionLink` and `RouteLink` HTML helpers:

```
@Html.ActionLink(item.Name, "Details", new
{
  id=item.RecipeId,
  slug=item.Slug
})
```

The full extent of these changes can be viewed by looking at the code accompanying this book. The result of these changes can be viewed in the following screenshot showing the details of a recipe with the slug included in the URL:

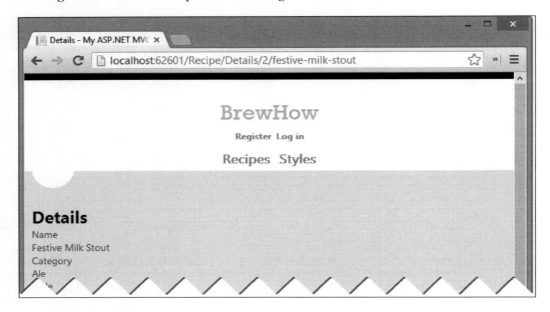

Areas

While we can use routes to create friendly and meaningful URLs, routing isn't the best tool when it comes to grouping functionality. When we need to group functionality into a different logical container, whether it's to reduce the number of controllers or action methods or to create a location to place code to handle crosscutting concerns, areas are what you want.

While our app focuses on the collection of recipes, we also want to provide a social component for our users allowing them to review recipes submitted by others. Given reviews bring with them their own set of management needs, it makes sense for us to separate this functionality into an area.

Creating the review area

To add an area to our project, simply right-click on the project and navigate to **Add | Area...** from the context menu.

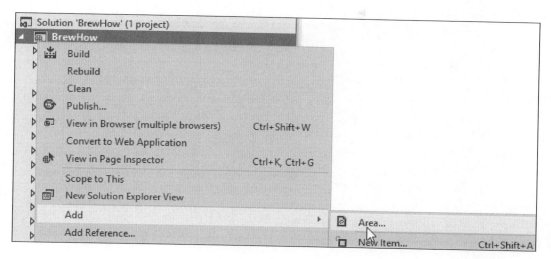

When presented with the **Add Area** dialog, enter `Review` in the textbox labeled **Area name:** and click on the **Add** button.

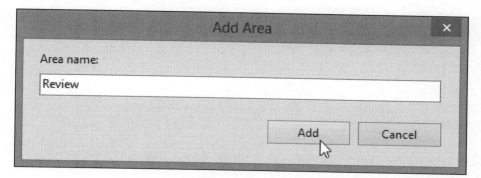

Areas within an MVC project are all contained within an `Areas` folder. For each area contained within the project, there exists a folder structure that largely mirrors the structure of the MVC project root.

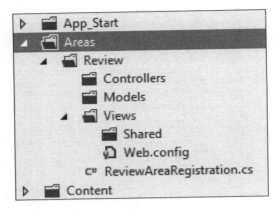

Our `Review` area contains a file named `ReviewAreaRegistration.cs`. This file is an area registration file and it is used to inform the framework of the area's existence.

Registering the Review area

The `ReviewAreaRegistration.cs` file in our `Review` area extends a special class named `AreaRegistration`. It contains one method to register the area with the app and one property to identify the area by name:

```
public class ReviewAreaRegistration : AreaRegistration
{
  public override string AreaName
  {
    get
    {
      return "Review";
    }
  }

  public override void RegisterArea(AreaRegistrationContext
    context)
  {
    context.MapRoute(
    "Review_default",
    "Review/{controller}/{action}/{id}",
```

```
    new {
      action = "Index",
      id = UrlParameter.Optional
    });
  }
}
```

The app is made aware of this area and all other areas within the app by invoking the `AreaRegistration.RegisterAllAreas` method. We do this in our `Global.asax.cs` file:

```
protected void Application_Start()
{
  ServiceLocatorConfig.RegisterTypes();
  AreaRegistration.RegisterAllAreas();
  WebApiConfig.Register(GlobalConfiguration.Configuration);
  FilterConfig.RegisterGlobalFilters(GlobalFilters.Filters);
  RouteConfig.RegisterRoutes(RouteTable.Routes);
  BundleConfig.RegisterBundles(BundleTable.Bundles);
  AuthConfig.RegisterAuth();
}
```

 You're not crazy. We didn't actually put this code here, it was part of the application template we chose when we created the BrewHow app solution. Areas aren't automatically registered with the app unless you use a template that is aware of them, and then they are automatically registered.

When invoked, the `RegisterAllAreas` method searches the app assembly for all classes that inherit `AreaRegistration`. It then calls the `RegisterArea` method of each class it found. Within our `RegisterArea` method, we register any routes that the runtime should use to map incoming requests to the controllers in our `Review` area.

If you examine the route in our `RegisterArea` method displayed earlier, you will see that all requests having a root of `Review/` can be mapped to our area and any part of the request that follows will be mapped into a controller, action, and ID. Go ahead and add a slug as part of the route for the review area. You can consult the accompanying code if you need assistance.

The Recipe review controller

Our review area needs a controller to handle requests to list and create reviews. To add the controller, simply right-click on the `Controller` folder in the `Review` area and add a controller named `RecipeController`.

In the **Add Controller** dialog, make sure to select the **Empty MVC controller** template and then click on **Add**. We will return to fill out our `RecipeController` class once we have created the view models.

Recipe review view models

The view models are a prerequisite to both our `RecipeController` action methods and the views to which they send data. Create a folder to hold our view models by right-clicking on the `Review` area folder and create a new folder named `ViewModels`. Within this folder, create two new classes named `ReviewEditViewModel` and `ReviewListViewModel`. These classes are identical except for their name. The code for these classes is as follows:

```
public class ReviewEditViewModel
{
  public int Rating { get; set; }
  public string Comment { get; set; }
}

public class ReviewListViewModel
{
  public int Rating { get; set; }
  public string Comment { get; set; }
}
```

Recipe review action methods

Now that the view models exist, we can fill out our `RecipeController` class. The `RecipeController` class will have three actions.

The first action, `Index`, contains the code to retrieve all of the reviews for the recipe identified by the `id` parameter.

The other two action methods allow us to create reviews for a recipe; the action method decorated with `HttpGet` returns the view on which the user enters the review while the action method decorated with `HttpPost` invokes the repository to persist the review and redirects the user back to the details of the recipe:

```
public class RecipeController : Controller
{
  public ActionResult Index(int id)
  {
    /* ... */
  }

  [HttpGet]
  public ActionResult Create(int id)
  {
    /* ... */
  }

  [HttpPost]
  public ActionResult Create(
    int id,
    ReviewEditViewModel reviewEditViewModel)
  {
    /* ... */
  }
}
```

It should be pointed out that our new `RecipeController` is using an instance of `IReviewRepository` but no class that implements that interface is registered with our dependency resolver. To remedy this, open up the `ServiceLocatorConfig.cs` file in the `App_Start` folder and add the `IReviewRepository` interface to the exports:

```
private static void RegisterRepositories(RegistrationBuilder rb)
{
  rb.ForTypesDerivedFrom<IRecipeRepository>()
  .Export<IRecipeRepository>()
  .SetCreationPolicy(CreationPolicy.NonShared);

  rb.ForTypesDerivedFrom<IStyleRepository>()
  .Export<IStyleRepository>()
  .SetCreationPolicy(CreationPolicy.NonShared);

  rb.ForTypesDerivedFrom<IReviewRepository>()
  .Export<IReviewRepository>()
  .SetCreationPolicy(CreationPolicy.NonShared);
}
```

We have now created our controller, the view models upon which it operates, and the action methods that will allow us to create and retrieve reviews. The last step is to create our views.

Creating the views

We are going to use the Visual Studio scaffolding to create the views for our action methods. We first need to build our application to make Visual Studio aware of our view models. Do this by pressing *Ctrl + Shift + B* or by selecting **Build Solution** from the **Build** menu.

After the build has completed, right-click anywhere within the Index action and select **Add View** from the context menu. Since we want to create a strongly typed view for listing reviews for a recipe, check the checkbox labeled **Create a strongly-typed view**, set the **Model** class to be ReviewListViewModel, and select **List** in the **Scaffold template**. As this view is going to be placed beneath the details of a recipe, also check the checkbox labeled **Create as a partial view**. When you have completed these steps, validate that the dialog box looks similar to the following screenshot and then click on **Add**.

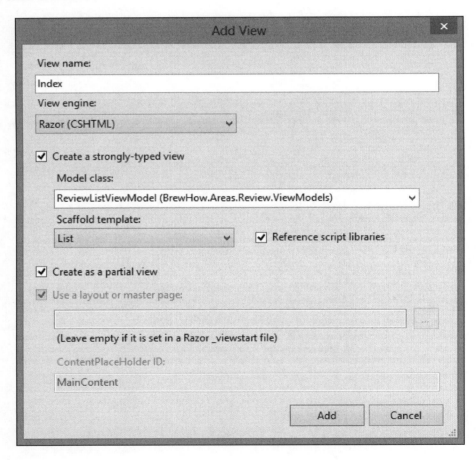

Repeat the same steps for the `Create` action method selecting **ReviewEditViewModel** as the **Model class** and **Create** for the **Scaffold template**. Make sure this view is not created as a partial view.

Open up the `Index.cshtml` view for our `RecipeController` in the `Review` area and replace the code with the following:

```
@model
  IEnumerable<BrewHow.Areas.Review.ViewModels.ReviewListViewModel>

<table>
  <tr>
    <th>
      @Html.DisplayNameFor(model => model.Rating)
    </th>
    <th>
      @Html.DisplayNameFor(model => model.Comment)
    </th>
  </tr>

  @foreach (var item in Model) {
    <tr>
      <td>
        @Html.DisplayFor(modelItem => item.Rating)
      </td>
      <td>
        @Html.DisplayFor(modelItem => item.Comment)
      </td>
    </tr>
  }

</table>
<p>
  @Html.ActionLink("Create New",
    "Create",
    new {
      area = "Review",
      id = ViewBag.RecipeId
    }
  )
</p>
```

The `Index` view now lists all of the reviews for a given recipe. It also provides a mechanism to create a new review through the use of the highlighted `ActionLink` call. In the `ActionLink` call, we provide additional values to the route data dictionary so when the runtime constructs the URL it has enough information to create a link to the appropriate `Create` action method.

The final step for displaying the review list is adding it to the detail view in our root `RecipeController`. Open up the `Details.ascx` file and add the following line to the bottom:

```
@{Html.RenderAction(
  "Index",
  "Recipe",
  new {
  area = "Review",
  id = Model.RecipeId,
  slug = Model.Slug
  });
}
```

Area route values

Notice our `RenderAction`, like the `ActionLink` code highlighted before it, is also passing a few extra routing values to the route data dictionary. The area of a route is passed through the route data dictionary just like the values for controller and action. In the `ActionLink` and `RenderAction` links, the runtime will use the area of the current request when constructing a route unless otherwise instructed. This leads to some unwanted behavior in certain scenarios.

In this particular scenario, we are instructing the runtime to render the links and actions for the view of our recipe controller using the `Review` area. This forces the selection of a route within the `Review` area and not in any other area of our application.

Our layout page also contains links that render a view associated with a controller named `RecipeController`. These links are in the top navigation banner:

```
@Html.ActionLink("Recipes", "Index", "Recipe")
```

When in the default area of our app, these links render as `/Recipes/Index`. When in the `Review` area, the value of area in the route data dictionary is `Review` and the preceding are evaluated to be `/Review/Recipes/Index`. This isn't what we want. We want these routes to always evaluate to our recipe list. If we supply the area to the route data dictionary, we can solve this problem:

```
@Html.ActionLink(
  "Recipes",
  "Index",
  "Recipe",
  new { area = "" },
  null)
```

While it would be nice to say we're done at this point, the runtime has a differing opinion. If we were to launch our app right now, we'd still be presented with a nice exception:

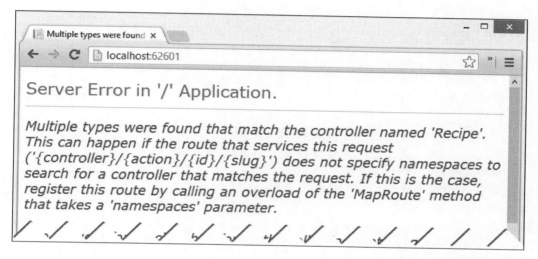

The summary of this screen is this: When determining the controller to be executed as part of a request, the runtime doesn't actually evaluate the entire namespace unless explicitly told to do so. Because our app contains two controllers named `RecipeController`, the runtime has no way to distinguish between `RecipeController` in the root of our app and `RecipeController` in our `Review` area. We need to provide it a hint.

Routing namespaces

We can restrict the namespace in which the routing engine searches for a controller when our routes are declared in the `MapRoute` method. We currently declare routes in two places, the `ReviewAreaRegistration` class in our `Review` area and the `RouteConfig` class in `App_Start`.

To restrict the namespace, we simply need to add a `namespaces` parameter both to `ReviewAreaRegistration` and to `RouteConfig`. The value for the new parameter in `RouteConfig` is shown in the following code:

```
routes.MapRoute(
  name: "BeerByStyle",
  url: "Recipe/{style}",
  defaults: new { controller = "Recipe", action = "Style" },
  constraints: new { style = new RecipeStyleConstraint() },
  namespaces: new [] { "BrewHow.Controllers" }
);
```

As for our `ReviewAreaRegistration` class, it is modified as follows:

```
context.MapRoute(
  name: "Review_default",
  url: "Review/{controller}/{action}/{id}/{slug}",
  defaults: new {
    action = "Index",
    id = UrlParameter.Optional,
    slug=UrlParameter.Optional },
  namespaces: new[] {
    "BrewHow.Areas.Review.Controllers"}
);
```

Now if we launch our app, we will be greeted with our familiar list of recipes. Clicking on the details of a recipe will present us with a screen showing the new list of reviews beneath:

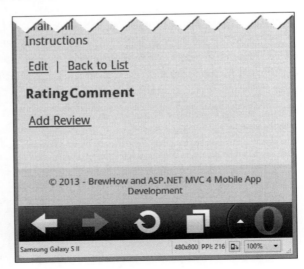

If we click on the **Create New** link, we will be taken to the `Create` view returned by our new `RecipeController` in our `Review` area:

And, if we click on the **Create** button, we will be returned to the `Detail` view for the recipe that will now show our review:

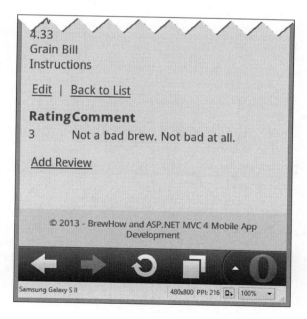

Summary

We began our work in this chapter by adding a route to the route table. This new route provided our users with a meaningful and predictable URL allowing them to filter the recipes contributed to our app by other users based upon style. We also learned the creation of these meaningful URLs helps optimize our site for search engines.

Our application was also divided into areas. These areas separate the concerns for managing recipes and reviews and will serve to make our app much more maintainable in the future.

In the next chapter we will continue to improve upon our application by adding user input validation to our controllers and views.

8
Validating User Input

Never trust data provided to your app by an outside source. How many times have you heard this? Yet, time and again, we learn of new and exciting ways for hackers to penetrate applications, operating systems, and even entire networks. While it is true most common languages protect you from stalwart exploits such as buffer overrun attacks, the new breed of connected web apps has brought with it a new breed of exploits.

In this chapter, we will take a look at using the data validation attributes found in the `System.ComponentModel.DataAnnotations` namespace to validate data submitted to our app. We will then look at the tools provided to us by the ASP. NET MVC 4 framework used to help prevent **Cross-Site Request Forgery (CSRF)** and **Cross-Site Scripting (XSS)** attacks.

At the end of this chapter you really need to remember only one rule— its the one already stated but bears repeating, that is never, never, never, ever trust data provided to our app by an outside source.

Data validation

Why might we want to validate our data? Well, for starters, our app may need to identify some fields to the user as required. We might also want to inform the user that they entered an invalid number for the original gravity of a recipe, or that they entered text and not a number at all. The feedback to the user not only protects our app from capturing invalid or malicious data, it also provides a better user experience by notifying the user an error has occured before an attempt is made to persist the data.

Our data validation will be accomplished by leveraging the data annotation attributes.

Data annotations

The data annotations, defined in `System.ComponentModel.DataAnnotations`, have already been leveraged to some extent in our app on the view models to provide display and formatting hints to the view renderer. You can see this in the following piece of code:

```
[Display(Name = "Original Gravity")]
[DisplayFormat(DataFormatString = "{0:0.00##}")]
public float OriginalGravity { get; set; }
```

We will now look at using the data annotation validation attributes to further define our data model and our view models.

And here is the first challenge with our architectural structure. We have separated our data model from our domain entities. Those domain entities are separated from the view model. Since the data annotations are attributes, it appears that we need to apply the attributes to the data model, the entities, and the view models making sure we keep them in sync. Fortunately for us, that's not the case.

MetadataType attribute

The `MetadataType` attribute, a data annotation attribute itself, allows us to specify attributes for properties of a class in an external class, sometimes referred to as a buddy class. These buddy classes contain properties of identical name and type as those in the actual class (or classes) to which they will be applied.

This may seem a bit confusing, so let's look at a version of our `BrewHow.Models.Recipe` class that uses the `MetadataType` attribute to identify a buddy class.

```
[MetadataType(typeof(RecipeValidationMetadata))]
public class Recipe
```

Within the `RecipeValidationMetadata` class, we define all of the restrictions, ranges, and requirements of the properties of the `Recipe` class that are shared with the `Recipe*ViewModel` classes:

```
public class RecipeValidationMetadata
{
    [Required]
    [StringLength(128)]
    public string Name { get; set; }
```

```
    [Required]
    [Range(1.0f, 2.0f)]
    public float OriginalGravity { get; set; }

    [Required]
    [Range(1.0f, 2.0f)]
    public float FinalGravity { get; set; }

    [Required]
    public string GrainBill { get; set; }

    [Required]
    public string Instructions { get; set; }
}
```

In our validation buddy class, we have marked all of the properties as required and have set ranges and lengths where appropriate. These properties share the name and type of the properties defined in Recipe. These validations can also be applied to our RecipeEditViewModel class using the same MetadataType attribute as follows:

```
[MetadataType(typeof(RecipeValidationMetadata))]
public class RecipeEditViewModel
```

Updating the database

The entity framework will use the metadata values to better define the fields in our database. We need to run Add-Migration to generate the migration script, but for this migration we will actually need to edit the Up method. As part of the metadata, we made the Instructions and GrainBill properties required. This sets the corresponding fields in the database to not allow null values. Placing the following code at the start of the Up method will ensure the migration will succeed for any data already in the database:

```
Sql("update dbo.Recipes set GrainBill = 'No grain bill.' where
    GrainBill is null");
Sql("update dbo.Recipes set Instructions = 'No instructions.'
    where Instructions is null");
```

The Seed method of our configuration needs to be updated as well. Always remember the Seed method runs after every migration is applied unless we instruct it otherwise. In each of the Recipe classes in the Seed method, make sure to add values for the Instructions and GrainBill properties.

We can now run `Update-Database` to apply our constraints. The EF Migrations process will pick up the validation attributes from the `RecipeValidationMetadata` class applied to our migration and apply them to our database schema.

We can validate these changes by looking at the table definition in our database as follows:

	Name	Data Type	Allow Nulls
⚷	RecipeId	int	☐
	Name	nvarchar(128)	☐
	OriginalGravity	real	☐
	FinalGravity	real	☐
	GrainBill	nvarchar(MAX)	☐
	Instructions	nvarchar(MAX)	☐
	StyleId	int	☑
	Slug	nvarchar(MAX)	☑

Validating the validations

If we launch the app and try and submit some invalid data when creating a recipe, you will see that the MVC framework was kind enough to validate our data in the browser using JavaScript and jQuery and inform the user of the validation errors. If we opted to change the error messages presented to the user, we could modify the data annotation attributes to display the appropriate error message. For now, the default messages are acceptable.

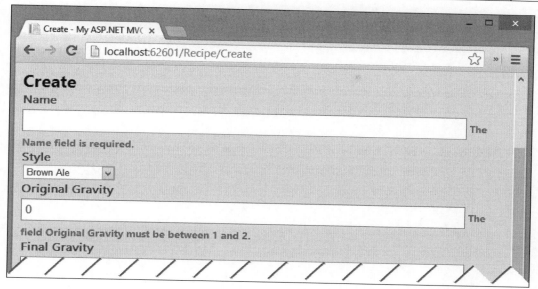

To understand how this is working, you can look at the Create.cshtml view in the RecipeController's View folder. At the very bottom of the view you will find the following markup:

```
@section Scripts {
  @Scripts.Render("~/bundles/jqueryval")
}
```

This bundle adds the jQuery unobtrusive validation libraries to the page. When our page is rendered, the validation attributes we placed on the view model are translated into jQuery validation markup by the EditorFor HTML helper. On form submission, the fields are validated against those attributes.

Note that the only validations that are occurring are client side. For the instances where the user may have disabled JavaScript or where someone is trying to find an exploit by circumventing our views, we want to validate the data once we have received it on the server and send it back to the client if there are validation errors.

Server validation

Validation on the server is fairly straightforward. We are already using the MVC Model Binder to map the content of an HTTP POST into our view models. When the Model Binder does this, it sets up a ModelStateDictionary object for each model it attempts to bind and logs any errors that occur into the dictionary. The dictionary is exposed to our controller via the ModelState property.

When our action method is invoked and we want to validate that the input to the action method is valid, we can invoke the `IsValid` property on the `ModelStateDictionary` to determine if we should proceed to hand the data off to the domain or if we should return the input to the user to fix any errors or omissions:

```
public ActionResult Create(RecipeEditViewModel recipe)
{
  try
  {
    if (ModelState.IsValid)
    {
      this._recipeRepository.Save(
      ToEntity(recipe));

      return RedirectToAction("Index");
    }
  }
  catch
  {
  }

  return View(recipe);
}
```

 Our current server-side validation is tied closely to the Controller. For enterprise-scale validation scenarios, we would abstract the validation and the mapper used to translate to and from Domain Entities and View Models to better facilitate testing and code reuse.

We are now protected from errant information entering our system via user input, but we are still exposed to other malicious forms of input against which we must protect our users and ourselves.

Cross-Site Request Forgery (CSRF)

A Cross-Site Request Forgery is an attack in which a user's browser is clandestinely directed to retrieve information or perform an action on a site without that user's knowledge. In these types of attacks, the user is presumed to have access to the targeted site. It is perhaps better explained with an example.

Let's assume a member of Local Bank and Trust of Bedford Falls just visited the bank's website in their browser. The user logged in, performed some actions, and never explicitly logged out leaving the authentication cookie in their browser's cache. Later, while surfing the seedy side of the Web, they visit a site of questionable repute.

On this site, someone has placed a script file that submits a funds transfer request to the website of Local Bank and Trust of Bedford Falls' website via an AJAX invocation. This script has no visible action the user can see. However, the user is still technically logged into the bank site and this script is successful in executing a funds transfer from the user's account. As far as anyone is concerned, the user performed this action and they performed it from their home IP address. The attack leaves very few footprints and more likely than not will go unnoticed until it is too late.

We want to prevent these types of attacks against our app. It's not that we have anything of high value to protect. We do not, however, want to allow our app to become compromised in any way that affects our users, either by compromising their data or by placing blame for a compromise or attack on them.

Again, the ASP.NET MVC framework comes to the rescue with another handy attribute.

ValidateAntiForgeryToken

The `ValidateAntiForgeryToken` attribute can be placed on individual action methods or an entire controller:

```
[HttpPost]
[ValidateAntiForgeryToken]
public ActionResult Create(RecipeEditViewModel recipe)
```

The attribute works in partnership with the `HtmlHelper.AntiForgeryToken()` method:

```
@model BrewHow.ViewModels.RecipeEditViewModel

@{
  ViewBag.Title = "Create";
}

<h2>Create</h2>

@using (Html.BeginForm()) {
  @Html.AntiForgeryToken()
  @Html.ValidationSummary(true)
```

When a response is posted to an action method that is decorated with the ValidateAntiForgeryToken, the attribute looks at the data being posted for a valid request verification token—the markup added to the page by the AntiForgeryToken HTML helper. If a valid token is not found, as would be the case with a CSRF, the runtime throws an exception before the action method can be invoked.

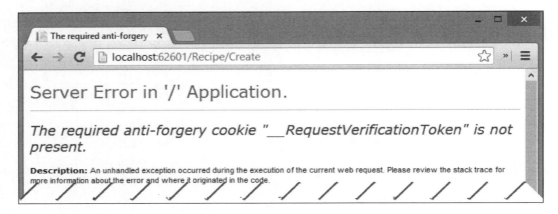

If, however, the token is found as illustrated in the following source code, the submit will succeed:

```
<form action="/Recipe/Create" method="post">
<input name="__RequestVerificationToken" type="hidden"
  value="31Kxb3eIeUEmZIfY5QwBj_
  kVGUgKsHxvLAkOjEtX7ZCPb6AJz9vUVD5M7DW6OedEUnlhqKlaP
  _k1_aGelGeoWDuzMJFvxKoUSCocittWPCo1" />
<fieldset> <!-- … --!>
```

The placement of this token is transparent to the user, but it does protect them against naïve attempts to hijack their authentication ticket to the app.

AJAX is allowed

The inclusion of the anti-forgery token does not prevent you from using AJAX functionality to submit a form against an action requiring the anti-forgery token. You can still do this. You simply need to add the RequestVerificationToken key/value pair to the POST request.

Cross-Site Scripting (XSS)

Cross-Site Scripting is an attack that can occur when a user injects client-side script into a page in an attempt to gather information or infect the computers of other users. Specific things that can occur as a result of an XSS attack are the forcible download of viruses and bots, theft of cookies containing identifying information and/or login credentials of a user, or the ability to modify the content of a site.

XSS attacks usually occur when a user is allowed to submit HTML content to a site as part of a form submission.

Assume that we wanted to let users submit formatted HTML to our app in the `GrainBill` and `Instruction` fields of our recipe creation and editing views. Without careful implementation on our part, it would be possible for users to submit HTML content with embedded script that could be used to hijack a user's session.

Even if we only let trusted users submit HTML content, we would still be exposing ourselves because there's nothing preventing our trusted users' browsers from being hijacked by another site and then being directed at our app.

Since it is exceptionally hard to prevent XSS attacks, the ASP.NET MVC framework simply blocks the submission of HTML by default.

Any submission of HTML results in a response similar to the one shown in the following screenshot:

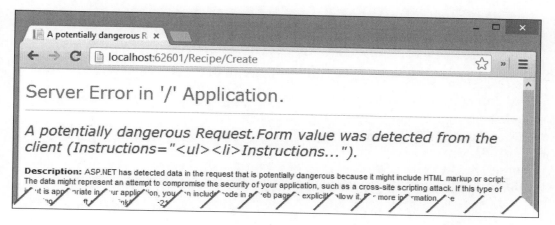

If we decide it is necessary for our users to submit HTML to our app, there are a couple of steps we can take to enable the capability. The enabling of HTML submission means we will still need to write our own HTML sanitizer to make sure that no malicious content is being uploaded to our site. The following information is simply that: information. While we will learn how to enable HTML submission, we will not enable it in our app beyond this chapter.

Don't do it

I do not recommend trying to implement your own HTML sanitizer. There are entire teams developing tools to properly sanitize posted HTML content to remove the malicious content. Not only does the sanitizer have to remove properly formatted HTML, it needs the ability to remove improperly formatted HTML as well. You can thank the loosely implemented rendering engines of legacy browsers for that one.

ValidateInput attribute

The easiest way to allow for submission of HTML is to use the `ValidateInput` attribute. This attribute can enable or disable input validation at both the action method and controller level. We can modify our RecipeController's `Create` action method to bypass input validation:

```
[HttpPost]
[ValidateInput(false)]
[ValidateAntiForgeryToken]
public ActionResult Create(RecipeEditViewModel recipe)
```

Now, when we create a new recipe with HTML as we did previously, the submission is successful.

Using the `ValidateInput` attribute should be a means of last resort. The problem is that by using `ValidateInput` we have allowed all input sent to the action to bypass input validation. We now have to sanitize not only the `GrainBill` and `Instruction` properties, but the `Title` field as well. And if we add a new field to the view and to the model at some point later we will have to remember to sanitize the input for it.

A better approach is to explicitly mark properties of our model to allow for the input of HTML.

AllowHtml

The `AllowHtml` property can be added to the property of a view model to inform the model binder to bypass input validation for that property and that property only. This explicit declaration is more secure than the `ValidateInput` method and should be used before `ValidateInput`.

To allow HTML to be used in the values of our `GrainBill` and `Instructions` properties, the `RecipeEditViewModel` class needs to be modified to include the `AllowHtml` input. Make sure you remove the `ValidateInput` attribute we added a few minutes ago:

```
[AllowHtml]
[Display(Name = "Grain Bill")]
[DataType(DataType.MultilineText)]
public string GrainBill { get; set; }

[AllowHtml]
[Display(Name = "Instructions")]
[DataType(DataType.MultilineText)]
public string Instructions { get; set; }
```

When we submit a recipe containing formatted HTML in the `GrainBill` and `Instructions` properties, we are successfully returned to our list (and we receive an exception when we try and submit HTML in the `Name` property).

If we view the details of our recipe by clicking on the name in the list view, we see we did indeed submit and save HTML, but that HTML is being displayed rather than rendered.

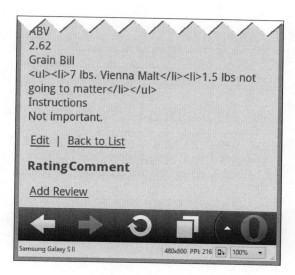

We need to modify the view to display the fields in their raw format.

Html.Raw

If you recall a few chapters back, we discussed how the Razor engine automatically encoded our properties. This encoding converts the angle brackets (<>) into &lt and &gt. These codes are then rendered in the browser as < and > respectively and do not instruct the browser to render the intended HTML. We need to modify the view to render the raw content of the property and bypass the HTML encoding using the Raw method on the HtmlHelper class.

In the Details view for the RecipeController, we need to modify the output of the Instruction and GrainBill properties to use Html.Raw in lieu of Html. DisplayFor:

```
<div class="display-label">
  @Html.DisplayNameFor(model => model.GrainBill)
</div>
<div class="display-field">
  @Html.Raw(Model.GrainBill)
</div>

<div class="display-label">
  @Html.DisplayNameFor(model => model.Instructions)
</div>
<div class="display-field">
  @Html.Raw(Model.Instructions)
</div>
```

Now when we view the output of the Details view, our HTML submission is rendered appropriately as seen in the following screenshot:

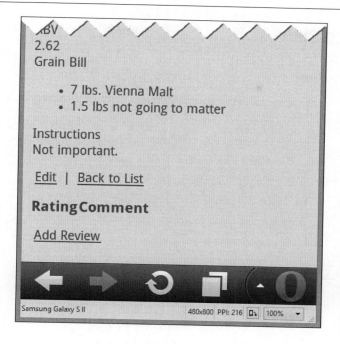

And since we know it works, we can undo it. Without proper scrubbing of the input, we don't want to allow just any HTML markup to be submitted.

Summary

In this chapter, we learned how to validate the input our app receives from our users. Validation, in this sense, means not only ensuring data is in the proper format but that it can be deemed safe or as safe as possible since rule #1 is, again, not to trust data submitted by our users.

In the next chapter, we will look at authorization and authentication for our app including support for authenticating with a Google account. We will use these features to prevent the creation and editing of recipes by anonymous users and prevent users from editing the recipes of others. We will also allow authenticated users to create a library of recipes for quick access to their favorites.

9

Identifying and Authorizing Users

Up to this point, BrewHow has been an entirely anonymous app. Anyone can post recipes to share with the community and anyone can review those recipes. This model is fine if this is the only functionality we wish to provide to users, but we have loftier aspirations. We want our users to be acknowledged for their contributions and accountable for their reviews. We may also add functionality that requires the app to know who they are. We need to provide a means for our users to authenticate themselves with our app.

In this chapter, we explore the ASP.NET Membership frameworks that provide authentication and authorization to our application. We will create new users in our application using the `SimpleMembership` membership provider and look at the new support for external authentication providers such as Google and Facebook. We will then restrict portions of our application to authenticated users. We will complete the chapter by tying together everything we've learned to allow users to create a recipe library to store their favorite recipes.

User authentication

User authentication allows us to validate that a user is who they say they are. There are several ways we could go about authenticating users in our app, but the typical scenario – and the scenario upon which we will focus – will be to allow our users to authenticate themselves to our app using a username and password.

ASP.NET supports two types of authentication out of the box: Windows authentication and Forms authentication.

Windows authentication

When using Windows authentication, an app authenticates the identity of the user against a Windows domain controller. In this scenario, the user's Windows credentials are used in an attempt to authenticate with the app. This type of authentication is typically used in intranet scenarios in which users are centrally managed.

Forms authentication

Forms authentication is the type of authentication you are most likely familiar with. Forms authentication allows a user to supply a username and password of their choice to the system. After successful authentication, the user is assigned a cookie that is submitted by the browser in any future requests to validate the identity of the user.

This type of authentication is predominately used in apps designed for the Internet. Given that our app will be accessed from the Internet, we will use forms authentication.

Authenticating BrewHow users

Out of the box, apps built using the Internet application template support forms authentication and provide facilities for users to log in and create accounts for our app. We can validate this by looking at the `authentication` node in the `web.config` file:

```
<system.web>
  <!-- -->
  <authentication mode="Forms">
    <forms loginUrl="~/Account/Login" timeout="2880" />
  </authentication>
  <!-- -->
</system.web>
```

The authentication node sets the authentication mode to `Forms` authentication and sets the login URL of our app to be `~/Account/Login`. Looking at the `Login` action of the `AccountController` class, we see the action is invoking the `WebSecurity.Login` method for the user and redirecting them to the URL they initially attempted to reach if login is successful:

```
if (ModelState.IsValid && WebSecurity.Login(model.UserName,
    model.Password, persistCookie: model.RememberMe))
{
    return RedirectToLocal(returnUrl);
}
```

The WebSecurity class used to authenticate the user is part of the SimpleMembership API, a membership provider incorporated into ASP.NET MVC 4 from the WebMatrix project.

SimpleMembership

SimpleMembership provides a smaller, improved set of tooling to manage user accounts than the tooling provided in previous versions of ASP.NET. Unlike the original ASP.NET Membership Provider API that required a version of SQL Server with stored procedure support, SimpleMembership works with SQL Server, SQL CE, LocalDB, and any other database with an Entity Framework provider.

Initializing the SimpleMembership database is as simple as calling WebSecurity. InitializeDatabaseConnection. In our app, this call is currently occurring inside the InitializeSimpleMembershipAttribute class located in the Filters folder of our solution:

```
WebSecurity
  .InitializeDatabaseConnection(
    "DefaultConnection",
    "UserProfile",
    "UserId",
    "UserName",
    autoCreateTables: true
  );
```

The InitializeDatabaseConnection method is defined as follows:

```
public static void InitializeDatabaseConnection(
  string connectionStringName,
  string userTableName,
  string userIdColumn,
  string userNameColumn,
  bool autoCreateTables
)
```

Inside our InitializeSimpleMembershipAttribute, we tell the SimpleMembership provider to initialize the database using the connection string DefaultConnection. The user profile information will be stored in the UserId and UserName fields of the UserProfile table. We also instruct SimpleMembership to create the tables housing all of the membership information by setting the parameter autoCreateTables to true.

Of course all of this setup means little if the code within the attribute never executes. To ensure that the membership tables exist when needed, the Internet application template applies `InitializeSimpleMembershipAttribute` to the `AccountController`:

```
[Authorize]
[InitializeSimpleMembership]
public class AccountController : Controller
```

By applying it to the `AccountController` class, the code ensures that the membership tables are created if and only if the account controller is invoked. This provides us with a form of lazy initialization for our membership provider. It also provides us the opportunity to change our app to use Windows authentication without creating the membership schema.

> The membership tables will be created during the first invocation of the account controller. If you desire to use Windows authentication, change the `web.config` file before you launch the app.

The tables within the membership schema are accessed through `UsersContext` — a secondary EF context defined in the `AccountModel.cs` file in the `Models` folder of our solution:

```
public class UsersContext : DbContext
{
  /* ... */
  public DbSet<UserProfile> UserProfiles { get; set; }
}
```

This context has actually been invoked several times during our testing so we should have already created our membership schema. Click on the **Show All Files** button in **Solution Explorer** to display all hidden files in our solution:

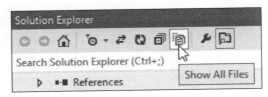

If you now expand the `App_Data` folder, you should see there are actually two databases, one for the BrewHow context and one that is holding the membership schema:

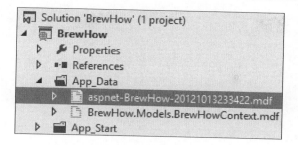

Double-click on the membership database to open it in the **Database Explorer**.

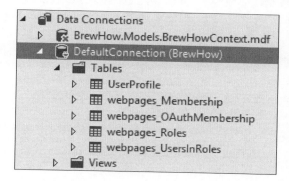

The first thing you should note is that the database contains the UserProfile table defined in the UsersContext context. We also have four other tables that are constructed by the SimpleMembership provider during our call to InitializeDatabaseConnection because we passed a value of true in the autoCreateTables parameter. These tables house information about website membership and support the management and application of roles within the app.

Customizing authentication

There are obviously a lot of steps involved in setting up the membership for our application in this as-needed scenario. Since our app is only going to use the SimpleMembership provider and implement forms authentication, we can get rid of the code supporting this as-needed scenario and apply some customization.

SimpleMembership initialization

Since the InitializeSimpleMembershipAttribute exists solely to provide lazy initialization, the easiest way to simplify the code is to remove the attribute and move the InitializeDatabaseConnection method into Global.asax.

Open up `Global.asax.cs` and add the following code at the top of the `Application_Start` method:

```
WebSecurity.InitializeDatabaseConnection(
    "DefaultConnection",
    "UserProfile",
    "UserId",
    "UserName",
    autoCreateTables: true);
```

Since we are initializing the membership database at application start, we can delete the attribute from the `AccountController` definition and delete the `InitializeSimpleMembershipAttribute.cs` file from our solution.

Unifying contexts

There's really no reason for us to have two separate databases for our app. The users of our app and the recipes they create are intertwined. We can unify the databases and, in doing so, unify `BrewHowContext` and `UsersContext`—the two contexts currently used to store and retrieve information from the database.

We will begin by changing the `DefaultConnection` connection string in the `web.config` file. We want to unify the databases into a new database file named `BrewHow.mdf` with a catalog name of `BrewHow`. The new connection string is shown in the following code:

```
<connectionStrings>
  <add
    name="DefaultConnection"
    connectionString="Data Source=(LocalDb)\v11.0;Initial
    Catalog=BrewHow;Integrated
    Security=SSPI;AttachDBFilename=|DataDirectory|\BrewHow.mdf"
    providerName="System.Data.SqlClient" />
</connectionStrings>
```

We modified the `DefaultConnection` connection string because it's actually the only connection string in a configuration file. The membership functionality is already using this connection string, but the `BrewHowContext` class is looking for a connection string named `BrewHow.Models.BrewHowContext`. We covered this in *Chapter 4, Modeling BrewHow in EF5*.

To tell the BrewHow context to use the `DefaultConnection` connection string, we need to modify the `BrewHowContext` constructor as shown in the following code:

```
public BrewHowContext()
  : base("DefaultConnection")
{
}
```

The next step is to add the `UserProfile` class—the class that represents a user of our app as defined in our call to `InitializeDatabaseConnection`—to `BrewHowContext`. This class is currently defined in the `AccountModels.cs` file. Since it's actually going to be part of our data model, we should move it into its own file in the `Models` folder. Create a new file in our `Models` folder named `UserProfile.cs` and move the `UserProfile` class defined in `AccountModels.cs` into this file:

```
[Table("UserProfile ")]
public class UserProfile
{
  [Key]
  [DatabaseGeneratedAttribute
    (DatabaseGeneratedOption.Identity)]
  public int UserId { get; set; }
  public string UserName { get; set; }
}
```

To complete the merging of our contexts, we need to move the `UserProfile` class into `BrewHowContext`. This requires us to modify both the `BrewHowContext` class and the `IBrewHowContext` interface:

```
public interface IBrewHowContext
{
  IDbSet<Models.Recipe> Recipes { get; set; }
  IDbSet<Models.Review> Reviews { get; set; }
  IDbSet<Models.Style> Styles { get; set; }

  IDbSet<Models.UserProfile> UserProfiles { get; set; }

  int SaveChanges();
}
```

```
public class BrewHowContext : DbContext, IBrewHowContext
{
  public IDbSet<Models.Recipe> Recipes { get; set; }
  public IDbSet<Models.Review> Reviews { get; set; }
  public IDbSet<Models.Style> Styles { get; set; }
  public IDbSet<Models.UserProfile> UserProfiles { get; set; }

  public BrewHowContext()
    : base("DefaultConnection")
  {
  }
  /* ... */
}
```

Of all the changes made, changing the connection string was actually the most disruptive one. We made several changes to the context, but the database identified by the connection string doesn't actually exist. That means there's really nothing to migrate. And given the migrations we've applied have all been incremental in the development of our app, there's nothing we've done that we would roll back; we're still discovering the domain of BrewHow. It's time to start over with a new database.

Begin by deleting all of the migration files from the `Migrations` folder. Do NOT delete the `Configuration.cs` file as our `Seed` method is still valid. Open the **Package Manager Console** and run the `Add-Migration` command to set the initial migration. Once the command has finished and created the initial migration, run the `Update-Database` command to create our unified BrewHow database schema and seed it with our sample data.

The UserProfile repository

To keep with our established design pattern, we need to create a repository for the `UserProfile` data model. Examining the code within `AccountController`, we see our app currently supports the creation and retrieval of a user profile by username. This functionality needs to be moved to a repository. Following the other patterns in our project, the repository for user profiles also needs to support the marshalling of our data model to and from our domain model. The interface for `IUserProfileRepository` is defined in the following code. The implementation is as straightforward as for the other repositories and is available in the code accompanying this book:

```
public interface IUserProfileRepository
{
  UserProfileEntity GetUser(string username);
  void Save(UserProfileEntity userProfileEntity);
}
```

The `UserProfileEntity` type is the domain entity for the `UserProfile` model and contains an identical set of fields:

```
public class UserProfileEntity
{
  public int UserId { get; set; }
  public string UserName { get; set; }
}
```

AccountController contexts

The final step is to modify our `AccountController` class to use an injected implementation of our `IUserProfileRepository` interface. Open up the `AccountController` class and add a constructor that accepts an `IUserProfileRepository` parameter. Make sure you're assigning the parameter to a member variable of the class:

```
private readonly IUserProfileRepository _userProfileRepository;

public AccountController(
  IUserProfileRepository userProfileRepository)
{
  this._userProfileRepository = userProfileRepository;
}
```

The only location in our entire project that was using the `UsersContext` was inside the `ExternalLoginConfirmation` method of `AccountController`. It determines if a user with a given username exists and then creates the user or returns an error indicating the user already exists in the database:

```
using (UsersContext db = new UsersContext())
{
  UserProfile user = db
    .UserProfiles
    .FirstOrDefault(
    u =>
    u.UserName.ToLower() == model.UserName.ToLower());
  if (user == null)
  {
    // Create the new user.
  }
  else
  {
    // Return an error.
  }
```

This code needs to be adjusted to use the implementation of IUserProfileRepository passed to the constructor of the controller:

```
UserProfileEntity user = this
  ._userProfileRepository
  .GetUser(model.UserName.ToLower());
if (user == null)
{
  this._userProfileRepository.Save(
    new UserProfileEntity
    {
      UserName = model.UserName
    });
  // Do other stuff.
}
else
{
  // Return an error.
}
```

Open up the app in the browser by pressing *Ctrl + F5* on the keyboard or selecting **Start Without Debugging** from the **DEBUG** menu to initialize the membership tables. After successfully starting the app, expand the App_Data directory and you will see our new unified database:

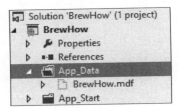

Double-click on the **BrewHow** database to open up **Database Explorer**. If you expand the **Tables** node, you will see all of the tables necessary for our application to function in a single database:

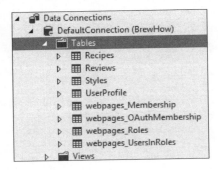

Registering and logging in

Now that the membership tables are properly configured, we should be able to register an account and log in. Start by launching the app and clicking on the **Register** link at the top of the page:

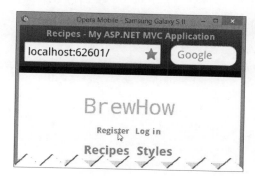

On the registration page, enter the credentials for the user you wish to create. When you are done, click on the **Register** button:

After you click on the **Register** button you are automatically logged into the app and greeted with your new username:

It works! Unfortunately, you are also taken to the old /Home/Index action—the original homepage we replaced with our /Recipe/Index action. The Internet application template has a couple of magic strings in it we need to replace. In this particular scenario, we need to modify the AccountController class in three separate action methods: LogOff, Register, and RedirectToLocal.

In all three of these action methods, we need to replace the following code:

```
return RedirectToAction("Index", "Home");
```

This preceding code will be replaced by the following code:

```
return RedirectToAction("Index", "Recipe", new { area="" });
```

Now all registration, login, and logout actions will redirect users to the RecipeController's Index action and our SimpleMembership provider is now successfully providing authentication services to our application. We can even open up the UserProfile table in the **Database Explorer** and see the user we just created:

	UserId	UserName
▶	1	brewmaster
*	NULL	NULL

In addition to providing support for usernames and passwords in our database, the SimpleMembership provider can be extended to allow us to authenticate against external sources such as Google and Facebook.

External authentication

Enabling external authentication for our app is fairly straightforward. If we open up the `AuthConfig.cs` file in our `App_Start` folder and look at the `RegisterAuth` method we will see four external providers that are available:

```
public static void RegisterAuth()
{
  // To let users of this site log in using their accounts
  // from other sites such as Microsoft, Facebook, and
  // Twitter, you must update this site. For more information
  // visit http://go.microsoft.com/fwlink/?LinkID=252166

  //OAuthWebSecurity.RegisterMicrosoftClient(
  //    clientId: "",
  //    clientSecret: "");

  //OAuthWebSecurity.RegisterTwitterClient(
  //    consumerKey: "",
  //    consumerSecret: "");

  //OAuthWebSecurity.RegisterFacebookClient(
  //    appId: "",
  //    appSecret: "");

  //OAuthWebSecurity.RegisterGoogleClient();
}
```

We will enable Google authentication for BrewHow.

Registering with an external account

To enable Google authentication we need to uncomment the `OAuthWebSecurity.RegisterGoogleClient();` line in the `RegisterAuth` method and recompile the application. When we launch the application and click on the **Log in** link, our dialog now provides us the ability to login with a Google account.

Clicking on the button labeled **Google** takes us to the Google **Sign in** page:

After entering our account information, Google, in typical OAuth fashion, asks us to grant certain permissions to the BrewHow app. In this case, it's asking to provide our email address to BrewHow:

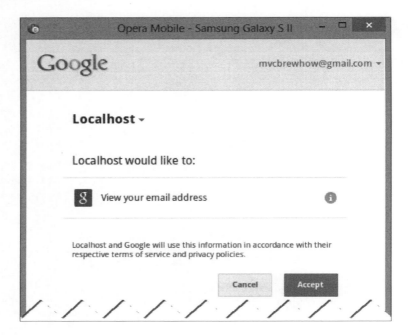

Clicking on **Accept** will take us back to our app where we are asked to provide a username. The default username for our linked account is our Google account address:

Accepting the default values and clicking on the **Register** button logs us into BrewHow with our Google account.

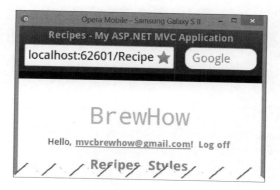

If an existing user already has a BrewHow account and wishes to use their Google account instead, we can also provide the ability to associate an external account with their existing BrewHow account.

Associating an external account

If you are currently logged into the application with your Google account, log out of the application and log in with the local account you created. If you're following along, the local account we created earlier in the chapter had a username of **brewmaster**. We will go to our profile and associate a Google account with our local BrewHow account.

To view your profile, click on your username in the greeting. Once on your account profile, scroll to the bottom and you will see a button labeled **Google**. Clicking on this button will allow you to associate your Google account with your local account:

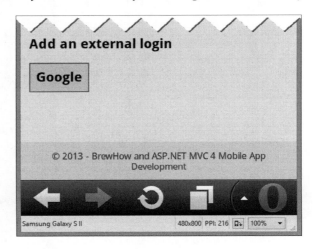

We can now successfully authenticate users in BrewHow. Time to authorize their actions.

Authorization

Authentication gives us a means to identify our users, but it is authorization that provides us a mechanism to enable or restrict the actions authenticated users may perform.

Restricting access

In ASP.NET MVC, access is restricted through the use of the `Authorize` attributes that may be placed on controllers or actions. If the `Authorize` attribute is at the controller level, anonymous users may be granted access to specific actions via the `AllowAnonymous` keyword.

The Authorize attribute

If you take a look at the `AccountController` class, you will see the class declared with the `Authorize` attribute. However, the `Login` action is decorated with the `AllowAnonymous` attribute:

```
[Authorize]
public class AccountController : Controller
{
  [AllowAnonymous]
  public ActionResult Login(string returnUrl)
  {
    ViewBag.ReturnUrl = returnUrl;
    return View();
  }
  /* ... */
}
```

The application of the `Authorize` attribute states that only authenticated users may access the account controller. The `AllowAnonymous` attribute serves as an override to the `Authorize` attribute and grants anonymous access to the `Login` action.

Authorizing user contributions

In the BrewHow app, all anonymous users should be able to browse the site and look at the recipes. However, we'd like only authenticated users to be able to contribute recipes or provide reviews.

Open the `RecipeController` class in the `Controllers` folder of our solution and apply an `Authorize` attribute to both `Edit` actions and both `Create` actions. This will restrict these actions to authenticated users. Likewise, open the `RecipeController` class in the `Review` area of our solution and apply the `AuthorizeAttribute` to both `Create` actions. Following is a partial copy of the `RecipeController` from the `Review` area to illustrate the application of the `Authorize` attribute:

```
public class RecipeController : Controller
{
  [HttpGet]
  [Authorize]
  public ActionResult Create(int id)
  {
    return View();
  }
```

```
[HttpPost]
[Authorize]
[ValidateAntiForgeryToken]
public ActionResult Create(
  int id,
  ReviewEditViewModel reviewEditViewModel)
{
  /* ... */
}
/* ... */
}
```

Open our app in the browser and make sure you are not currently logged in. From the home page, click on the link labeled **Create New** to attempt and create a recipe. You will be prompted to log in. You are prompted for login because the action now requires the user to be authenticated.

Of course it's bad form to show a user an action they cannot perform. We need to clean up the views to hide any activity that is unavailable to anonymous users.

> The `Authorize` attribute also allows you to further restrict access to a controller or action by specifying the group of roles or users who are permitted. Simply pass the users or roles to the attribute as `[Authorize(Users="andy, brewmaster")]` or `[Authorize(Roles="Administrators")]`. The BrewHow app will only be restricting access to authenticated users, so the use of `[Authorize]` is sufficient for our needs.

Cleaning the UI

Open up the view for the `RecipeController`'s `Index` action method and locate the following code:

```
@Html.ActionLink("Create New", "Create")
```

This is the portion of code that displays the **Create New** link on the `Index` view for `RecipeController`. To hide this link from unauthenticated users, change the code to the following:

```
@if (Request.IsAuthenticated) {
  @Html.ActionLink("Create New", "Create")
}
```

When we open our app in the browser, assuming we're not logged in, the link disappears:

We can validate the code works by logging in and returning to our Index view:

Make sure to apply this same logic to the **Edit** link on the recipe detail screen and the **Add Review** link on the partial view for reviews.

Content ownership

The BrewHow app has been locked down, in a manner of speaking. We only allow authenticated users to create and edit recipes or to submit reviews. Lacking, however, is any concept of ownership; any user can edit any recipe. Our users are submitting recipes to share them, not to have them altered by another user. The content on our site needs to be protected, allowing editing of content only to the user originally submitting it. We need to introduce the concept of ownership.

While ownership determinations could be used to enable or disable a large set of functionality, our implementation of ownership is concerned only with whether or not an entity can be edited.

Enabling ownership

For us to enable ownership, we need to modify our schema to associate a `UserProfile` with `Recipes` and `Reviews`. This will allow us to assign a user as the contributor or reviewer of a recipe.

Open up the `Recipe` class in the `Models` folder and add a `Contributor` property of type `UserProfile`. This will set up a relationship between a recipe and the user who created it:

```
public UserProfile Contributor { get; set; }
```

We also need to set up a relationship between `Review` and `UserProfile` to determine the user submitting a review. Adding the following property to the `Review` class can accomplish this:

```
public UserProfile Reviewer { get; set; }
```

Once created, we need to map the `UserProfile` properties of `Recipe` and `Review` to a `UserProfileEntity` property on `RecipeEntity` and `ReviewEntity`. This mapping will occur inside `ReviewRepository` and `RecipeRepository`. This model-to-entity mapping is presented in the code accompanying this book.

UserProfile schema mapping

Left to its own devices, Entity Framework would do a sufficient job of creating the relationships between `UserProfile` and the other models now referencing it. We however want to exert a little control on this process. We need to modify the `OnModelCreating` method in `BrewHowContext` to specify the name of the foreign keys. These modifications will ensure the `Recipe` and `Review` models require a `UserProfile`:

```
modelBuilder.Entity<Recipe>()
    .HasRequired(s => s.Contributor)
    .WithMany()
    .Map(m => m.MapKey("ContributorUserId"));

modelBuilder.Entity<Review>()
    .HasRequired(r => r.Reviewer)
    .WithMany()
    .Map(m => m.MapKey("ReviewerUserId"));
```

Not all is as simple as adding new properties and mapping values. UserProfile creation is handled by the SimpleMembership API and the preceding code marks the relationship between a Recipe or Review and UserProfile as required. This means the current seeding of our database inside the Seed method will not work as it is written. Adjustments need to be made to the Seed method to support the new required relationships to the UserProfile model.

Seeding users

Seeding the SimpleMembership tables is a little more complicated than invoking the API. If we simply add the following to the Seed method, invoking the Update-Database command in the **Package Manager Console** would throw an error:

```
WebSecurity.InitializeDatabaseConnection(
  "DefaultConnection",
  "UserProfile",
  "UserId",
  "UserName",
  autoCreateTables: true);

var membership = (SimpleMembershipProvider)
Membership.Provider;

if (membership.GetUser("brewmaster", false) == null)
{
  membership
    .CreateUserAndAccount(
    "brewmaster",
    "supersecret"
    );
}
```

This occurs because the default membership configuration is not picked up by the context in which the Update-Database command runs. By explicitly declaring the membership provider information in our web.config within the system.web section we can resolve this issue:

```
<roleManager enabled="true"
  defaultProvider="SimpleRoleProvider">
  <providers>
    <clear/>
    <add name="SimpleRoleProvider"
      type="WebMatrix.WebData.SimpleRoleProvider,
      WebMatrix.WebData"/>
  </providers>
</roleManager>
```

```
<membership defaultProvider="SimpleMembershipProvider">
  <providers>
    <clear/>
    <add name="SimpleMembershipProvider"
      type="WebMatrix.WebData.SimpleMembershipProvider,
      WebMatrix.WebData" />
  </providers>
</membership>
```

If we now insert the code at the beginning of this section into our `Seed` method, we can insert users using the `SimpleMembership` API. The seeding of our `Recipe` can then locate this user and assign it to the `Contributor` property of a recipe:

```
var brewMaster = context
  .UserProfiles
  .First(u => u.UserName == "brewmaster");

/* ... */
context.Recipes.AddOrUpdate(
  recipe => recipe.Name,
  new Recipe
  {
    Name = "Sweaty Brown Ale",
    Style = brownAle,
    OriginalGravity = 1.05f,
    FinalGravity = 1.01f,
    Slug = "sweaty-brown-ale",
    Instructions = "None",
    GrainBill = "None",
    Contributor = brewMaster
  },
  /* ... */
);
```

Applying the ownership migration

Having configured the relationships between our models, we are ready to create a migration to represent ownership. Go ahead and create a new migration by running `Add-Migration Ownership` in the **Package Manager Console** window.

Once the migration script has been generated, we're still not ready to apply it to our database. Remember, our new model created a required relationship to `UserProfile` from the `Recipe` and `Review` models. Our migration will currently fail because any attempt to add a foreign key constraint on the columns referencing `UserProfile` will fail for existing rows in the table. They currently have no value in these foreign key columns and a value of `null` is unacceptable:

```
AddColumn("dbo.Recipes",
  "ContributorUserId",
  c => c.Int(nullable: false));
AddColumn("dbo.Reviews",
  "ReviewerUserId",
  c => c.Int(nullable: false));
AddForeignKey(
  "dbo.Recipes",
  "ContributorUserId",
  "dbo.UserProfile",
  "UserId",
  cascadeDelete: true);
AddForeignKey(
  "dbo.Reviews",
  "ReviewerUserId",
  "dbo.UserProfile",
  "UserId",
  cascadeDelete: true);
CreateIndex("dbo.Recipes", "ContributorUserId");
CreateIndex("dbo.Reviews", "ReviewerUserId");
```

We need to seed the column before the foreign key constraint is placed on it. If we place the following code between the `AddColumn` and `AddForeignKey` statements, our problem should be resolved:

```
Sql(@"Update dbo.Recipes
  Set ContributorUserId = (
    select UserId
    from dbo.UserProfile
    where username = 'brewmaster')");
Sql(@"Update dbo.Reviews
  Set ReviewerUserId = (
    select UserId
    from dbo.UserProfile
    where username = 'brewmaster')");
```

We can now run the `Update-Database` command and everything will work. Examining the database, we see the seeded `UserProfile` is indeed associated to the `Recipe` as `ContributorUserId`:

	RecipeId	Name	ContributorUserId
1	1	Sweaty Brown Ale	1
2	2	Festive Milk Stout	1
3	3	Andy's Heffy	1

Handling ownership in the `Seed` method is great for sample data, but we also need to handle the ownership of content within the app itself.

Assigning ownership

Within the app, ownership is handled by the assignment of a `UserProfileEntity` to the `RecipeEntity`'s `Contributor` property or the `Review`'s `Reviewer` property. To construct a `UserProfileEntity`, we will create a factory class named `UserProfileEntityFactory`. This class first checks to make sure we're operating within the context of an HTTP request (if we're not then we won't be able to construct the entity). If we're not, then we won't be able to construct the entity. It then pulls the `UserId` and `UserName` of the current authenticated user from the `WebSecurity` class mentioned at the start of this chapter:

```
public class UserProfileEntityFactory : IUserProfileEntityFactory
{
  public UserProfileEntity Create()
  {
    var context = HttpContext.Current;

    if (context == null)
    {
      throw new InvalidOperationException(
        "The request is not occurring within a valid HTTP
          context.");
    }

    if (!context.Request.IsAuthenticated)
    {
      return null;
    }

    return new UserProfileEntity
    {
      UserId = WebSecurity.CurrentUserId,
      UserName = WebSecurity.CurrentUserName
    };
  }
}
```

The class definition of our factory implements a new interface, `IUserProfileEntityFactory`. This implementation can be injected anywhere the creation of a `UserProfileEntity` is needed as an `IUserProfileEntityFactory` abstraction. By using a factory, we have encapsulated the dependencies on `WebSecurity` in our `UserProfileEntity` construction. By injecting the concrete implementation as an interface, we are afforded the flexibility to change the implementation of `IUserProfileEntityFactory`, perhaps to a different security provider, without having an effect on the app.

And having the ability to create a new `UserProfileEntity` for a user allows us to assign ownership as follows:

```
recipeEntity.Contributor =
  this._userProfileEntityFactory.Create();
```

Everything is in place for us to assign ownership of content within our app. We now need to enforce those assignments.

Enforcing ownership

For us to enable ownership, we need to determine whether or not the user accessing the content is the user that originally submitted the content. This determination is pretty straightforward. We simply need to compare the `UserId` of the authenticated user to the `UserId` of the contributor. If they match, the authenticated user is the contributor of the content. If they don't match, the user isn't the contributor.

Just as we did actions unavailable to anonymous users earlier in the chapter, we need to restrict a user's actions based upon whether or not they own the content presented to them. Since these actions are presented in the view, we need to inform the view whether or not the user can perform some action. This is done through the view models.

Adjusting the view model

Recipes have a `Contributor` property and reviews have a `Reviewer` property to define ownership, but our controllers currently allow any authenticated user to edit content, theirs or otherwise. We need to communicate to the views the actions a user may take and we need to enforce those actions within the controllers themselves.

To inform the recipe detail view as to whether or not the user can edit a recipe, we need to modify the `RecipeDisplayViewModel` to contain a `CanEdit` property. While we have the view model open, let's go ahead and add a `Contributor` property to represent the username of the contributor:

```
[Display(Name = "Contributor")]
public string ContributedBy { get; set; }

public bool CanEdit { get; set; }
```

Using the `CanEdit` property, we can adjust the view to limit access to the **Edit** link on the `Display` view of `RecipeController`:

```
@if (Model.CanEdit) {
  @Html.ActionLink("Edit", "Edit", new
  {
    id=Model.RecipeId,
```

```
        slug = Model.Slug
    })
    @:|
}
```

Now the **Edit** link is only accessible to the user if `CanEdit` is true, restricting access to only the owner of the recipe.

Of course, that's not enough. Users, particularly malicious users, will find new and inventive ways to do something you don't want them to do. We need to ensure these ownership rules are enforced on the backend.

Ensuring ownership

When a new `RecipeEntity` is constructed from a view model, the `Contributor` property is assigned an instance of `UserProfileEntity` using the `IUserProfileEntityFactory`. This relationship between recipe and contributor is then persisted into the database for later retrieval via the repository. When a request is made to view the details of a recipe, the `Details` action now has the information necessary to set the `CanEdit` property of the view model. It simply needs to compare the `CurrentUserId` property of `WebSecurity` to the `UserId` of the contributor. If they match, then the current user is the creator of the recipe and can edit it:

```
if (Request.IsAuthenticated)
{
  viewModel.CanEdit =
    WebSecurity.CurrentUserId ==
    recipeEntity.Contributor.UserId;
}
```

Pretty straightforward. This small little piece of code ensures a user is the contributor of content before setting the `CanEdit` property to true. And of course we trust our users, but on the off chance they inadvertently try and submit changes to a recipe they didn't contribute, we need to validate ownership before committing the changes to the repository. You know… just in case.

Validating ownership

Validating ownership is in line with the mantra of never trusting data from users. This means validating all data, not only the data we expect them to change. Consider the scenario of a user requesting to edit a recipe. One downside to having human readable URLs, or any URL whose pattern is easily guessed, is the ability for a user to pretty easily figure out how to alter them to find information they may be interested in.

If you examine the `Edit` action of the `RecipeController` responding to HTTP GET requests, you will note the action takes a single parameter: the `id` of the recipe to retrieve for editing:

```
public ActionResult Edit(int id)
```

This is pretty easy to alter. Any half-intelligent user will realize they can get a different recipe by changing `/Recipe/Edit/1` to `/Recipe/Edit/2` and submitting the request to the server. When the action is invoked, it is its responsibility to validate that the user is the owner of the recipe being requested:

```
var recipeToEdit =
  this
  ._recipeRepository
  .GetRecipe(id);

if (!CanEdit(recipeToEdit))
{
  // Simply return the user to the detail view.
  // Not too worried about the throw.
  return RedirectToAction("Details", new { id = id });
}

return View(ToEditModel(recipeToEdit));
```

In our `Edit` action, we load the recipe requested and attempt to validate that the user is the owner. If we determine the user is the owner, we send them to the Edit view with the recipe they've elected to edit. If they're not the owner, we simply redirect them back to the `Details` page. We could throw an error, log a security violation, or perform a whole set of other actions, but sending them back to the details page is pretty benign and requires little effort on our part.

Whether presenting or persisting an edit for any user, loading of the original item from the repository should occur. It is against the loaded entity that ownership should be determined. This is necessary to prevent the user from altering the owner in the information they send back to the server.

A recipe library

Our app is nearing feature completion. To make the app ready for initial launch, we need to add one final feature: a recipe library. Users can use the recipe library to store recipes they find on our site for quick access. Adding this new feature will put together almost all of the information presented thus far in this book. We will also look at a couple of new techniques you can add to your tool belt.

To implement this feature, we need to adjust the data model to enforce a relationship between users and recipes. We then need to create a new repository to represent the library and a controller to act upon the domain at the request of the user. There will be a view to present the recipes in the user's library to the user and allow them to remove recipes from their library. Adding recipes to the library will occur through a modification to the recipe list of `RecipeController`. The addition and removal of recipes to and from the library will leverage jQuery to make these actions asynchronous. And, given a library is associated with a user, all actions associated with the library may only be performed by authenticated users.

The library data model

The library is an abstract concept. It is simply a relationship between a user and a recipe. It has no name and no data. We will make the collection of recipes within a library accessible by adding a `Library` property to the `UserProfile` data model:

```
public virtual ICollection<Recipe> Library { get; set; }
```

While it's an abstract concept, we still need a location to store this relationship. All we really need to maintain the relationship is the ID of the user and the ID of the recipe. This relationship will be configured to store the ID of the user and the ID of the recipe in a table named `UserRecipeLibrary`. Like other mappings we've implemented, this mapping will be set up within the `OnModelCreating` method of the `BrewHowContext` class:

```
modelBuilder.Entity<UserProfile>()
  .HasMany(r => r.Library)
  .WithMany()
  .Map(
  m =>
  {
    m.MapLeftKey("UserId");
    m.MapRightKey("RecipeId");
    m.ToTable("UserRecipeLibrary");
  });
```

This mapping tells Entity Framework that the user profile has many recipes associated with it through the library property. There is no complementary relationship, we can't get a list of users that have the recipe within their library. This relationship is mapped into the `UserRelationshipLibrary` table using the `UserId` and `RecipeId` as the keys of the relationship.

To modify the data model to reflect this relationship, use the `Add-Migration` and `Update-Database` commands with which you should be intimately familiar. Once complete, we can begin to write the repository representing this domain entity.

The library repository

The library repository needs to provide a means to add and remove recipes to and from a user's library and retrieve all of the recipes available from it. Its implementation should be straightforward given it's the fourth repository we've now implemented. The interface for the library repository is defined as follows:

```
public interface ILibraryRepository
{
    void AddRecipeToLibrary(int recipeId, int userId);
    IQueryable<RecipeEntity> GetRecipesInLibrary(int userId);
    void RemoveRecipeFromLibrary(int recipeId, int userId);
}
```

You can see there is no library class being returned. As I said at the start of this section, the library is an abstract concept. If we were to expand the concept to allow a user to add filters, change the name, or create multiple libraries, we would need to make the appropriate model adjustments. As it is currently defined, returning a list of recipes is sufficient for our needs.

The library controller

Creating a controller should also be fairly familiar to you by now. The LibraryController needs to support the ability to add and remove recipes from a library as well as present the list of recipes contained within a library to the user. Following is the code for the three actions supported by the LibraryController:

```
public ActionResult Index(int page = 0)
{
    var recipesInLibrary = this
        ._libraryRepository
        .GetRecipesInLibrary(WebSecurity.CurrentUserId);

    var viewModel = new PagedResult<RecipeEntity,
        RecipeDisplayViewModel>(
        recipesInLibrary,
        page,
        this._displayModelMapper.EntityToViewModel);

    return View(viewModel);
}

[HttpPost]
```

```
[ValidateAntiForgeryToken]
public ActionResult Create(int id)
{
    int userId = WebSecurity.CurrentUserId;

    this
        ._libraryRepository
        .AddRecipeToLibrary(id, userId);

    return Json(new { result = "ok" } );
}

[HttpPost]
[ValidateAntiForgeryToken]
public ActionResult Delete(int id)
{
    int userId = WebSecurity.CurrentUserId;

    this
        ._libraryRepository
        .RemoveRecipeFromLibrary(id, userId);

    return Json(new { result = "ok" });
}
```

If you read through this, you might have noticed a couple of small differences from the other controllers we've written. For starters, you might notice the _displayModelMapper member variable. Remember our controllers are responsible for converting the domain objects to objects ready for the view. It so happens that both our RecipeController and LibraryController operate on the same view models. Since we shouldn't duplicate code unless we absolutely have to, the recipe mapping functionality was moved out of the recipe controller into a mapping class. To be consistent, the same changes were applied to the styles controller and its mappings. The code for this and the other refactoring work completed in this chapter is available in the code accompanying this book.

You might also notice the Create and Delete actions are returning a JsonResult via the Json method of Controller. The entire management of a user's library will be through AJAX calls to the library controller. We should go back and provide support for users who have disabled JavaScript at some point, but we are making the assumption it's not necessary to do this to make the library available to the majority of our users.

The JSON return value simply returns an anonymous type with a single property of `result`. We will look for this property with a value of `ok` within the jQuery code in our view.

The library view

The view for our library is almost a straight copy of the `Index` view of `RecipeController`. It presents the list of recipes in a user's library. It has an additional column previously unavailable on the recipe list. This column allows users to remove a recipe from their library using the `ActionLink` HTML helper:

```
@Html.ActionLink(
  "Remove from Library",
  "Delete",
  "Library",
  new { id = item.RecipeId },
  new {
    @class = "remove-recipe",
    data_id = @item.RecipeId
  })
```

There is nothing special about this action link. If a user were to click on it as it's presented they would receive a 404 error. There is no delete action within the `LibraryController` that responds to an HTTP GET. There is, however, one that responds to a POST and our view uses jQuery to convert this link into an AJAX POST:

```
$(".remove-recipe").click(function(event) {
  event.preventDefault();
  $link = $(this);
  $.post($link.attr('href'),
  { __RequestVerificationToken:
    $("input[name=__RequestVerificationToken]").val() },
    function (response) {
      if (response.result == "ok") {
        $link.closest('tr').remove();
      }
    }
  );
});
```

A full discussion of jQuery is beyond the scope of this book, but a brief overview of the code is as follows. jQuery attaches itself to all elements on the page with a CSS class of `remove-recipe` using a jQuery selector. This is the class currently assigned to all of the remove links on our page. When the user clicks on the link, the navigation event is prevented by calling `preventDefault`. Instead, jQuery performs a POST to the URL specified in the HREF attribute of the link and adds to it the value of the `__RequestVerificationToken` input. This is the input placed on the page by the `AntiForgeryToken` HTML helper:

```
@Html.AntiForgeryToken()
```

Our controller's `Delete` action is invoked with an HTTP POST and receives the anti-forgery token as required by the `ValidateAntiForgeryToken` attribute on the action. It removes the recipe from the user's library and returns `ok`. The jQuery code receives the response and checks for the `ok`. When received, the row is removed from the page.

A similar action has been applied to the `Index` view of `RecipeController` to allow users to add recipes to their library. This link and the `Library` link in the primary navigation of our app are only presented to authenticated users. The `LibraryController`'s `Index` view is shown in the following screenshot:

The recipe library is now complete.

Summary

In this chapter we learned about authentication and authorization. We learned how to create users and how to allow users with external authentication to register for our site. We also learned how to secure portions of our app such that only authenticated users could effect change.

This chapter ended with the creation of a recipe library. This library represents the sum of the knowledge we've put together thus far. It also represents the completion of the functional requirements for our app. In the next couple of chapters, we will look at ways to increase the performance and user experience of our app, beginning with the discussion of asynchronous actions and bundles. The final chapters of this book will focus on taking our fully functional MVC 4 app and creating a truly unique mobile experience for our users.

10
Asynchronous Programming and Bundles

Having met our minimum requirements for functionality, our app has been published and is available on the Internet. Before we've had a chance to blink, BrewHow.com is inundated with users at a rate we had barely ever imagined. Within weeks, popular technology news outlets are talking about us being the biggest IPO in history. We begin to wonder what we will do with our new found wealth when, suddenly, we wake up.

Saddened it was just a dream, we begin to wonder what we would do if we were ever so fortunate to have the types of scaling problems some of the recent technology darlings have suffered. We decide we need to know more about building responsive apps.

In this chapter, we are going to explore how to make our app more responsive to the users by improving performance on the server side. These improvements will focus on how our app can get information to the users more efficiently and with less wait time. To accomplish this, we will explore, respectively, asynchronous programming and bundles.

Asynchronous programming

Asynchronous programming is a technique we can use to execute computationally heavy or I/O-heavy tasks that might normally block our application, such as making a request of a web service or performing expensive file I/O. These tasks can be sent to an independent thread until they have completed. While these expensive operations execute in the background, the application can go about servicing the needs of the user.

Most frameworks provide a mechanism to either await the completion of some task that has been queued for background execution or to provide a callback to be invoked when a background task is complete. The .NET framework is no different and, in Version 4.0, asynchronous programming was greatly simplified with the introduction of the **Task Parallel Library (TPL)**.

Task Parallel Library

The TPL provides an abstraction to the lower-level threading mechanisms within the .NET framework used to provide parallelism and concurrency. Defined in `System.Threading` and `System.Threading.Tasks`, this library allows us to focus on how we might break up our app into asynchronous tasks and leaves the worry of thread scheduling, partitioning, and cancellation to the framework.

Most of the work we will be doing for providing asynchronous functionality in our app will involve the use of the TPL `Task` class defined in `System.Threading.Tasks`.

Task

The `Task` class is used to encapsulate a unit of work to be executed asynchronously or in parallel with other tasks. We might choose to execute work within a `Task` class if it is believed that the work will take a long time to complete, will be I/O intensive, or will block the execution of a user's interaction with our app for an unacceptable amount of time.

To create and manage tasks, the `Task` class provides us with a fluent API by which we can create, schedule, execute, and cancel tasks.

Creating a Task

While there are several ways we can go about creating and executing a `Task` class within the TPL, the most commonly used method is through the static `Factory` property of the `Task` class:

```
var longTask = Task
  .Factory
  .StartNew(() => DoLongRunningTask());
```

The above code creates and starts a new `Task` that executes the code within the `DoLongRunningTask` method. Behind the scenes, the runtime creates a new thread on which the `DoLongRunningTask` method is executed. As written, this code provides no means by which the task can inform us of its completion.

This fire-and-forget approach can be used within applications that need to execute background tasks but aren't too concerned about knowing when a task has completed or what the return value of a task was.

We, however, are writing a mobile web app, and within a web app running on IIS starting threads and hoping they complete successfully is not recommended. Any unhandled exception that occurs within your web app will, in fact, bring down the process if it's not associated with an active request. Since we probably don't want to do that, we need to await the completion of any tasks we start within the context of a request.

Awaiting completion

Let's begin looking at how to await the completion of a task by examining the following code:

```
Task<bool> ingredientCheck = Task
  .Factory
  .StartNew(() =>
  {
    return IsIngredientInStock(ingredient);
  });
```

This code constructs a new task that executes the IsIngredientInStock method in the background and then returns the result. This hypothetical method goes out and checks our favorite homebrew supply store for an ingredient. If we assume the IsIngredientInStock method has a return type of bool, the ingredientCheck variable to which our new task is assigned is of type Task<bool>. The return type is actually inferred from the generic StartNew method being invoked.

To await the completion of the task assigned to our ingredientCheck variable, we simply call its Wait method:

```
ingredientCheck.Wait();
var taskResult = ingredientCheck.Result;
```

The return value of the method is available via ingredientCheck's Result property. And since the ingredientCheck variable is Task<bool>, the Result property is of type bool.

Instead of checking our favorite homebrew store for an ingredient, what if we wanted to check multiple stores? The TPL provides us with the ability to wait for the completion of multiple tasks using the static `WaitAll` method of the `Task` class.

```
var task1 = Task
  .Factory
  .StartNew(() => { return CheckStore1(ingredient); });
var task2 = Task
  .Factory
  .StartNew(() => { return CheckStore2(ingredient); });

Task.WaitAll(new Task[] { task1, task2 });
// Nothing below this will execute until both tasks complete.
```

The call to `Task`'s static `WaitAll` method is blocking. It will not let any further code execute on the current thread until both `task1` and `task2` have completed.

The Wait* methods such as `Wait`, `WaitAll`, and `WaitAny` are provided to allow us to yield execution until a given task or group of tasks have completed. These methods do exactly as their name implies; they wait until a task or group of tasks complete before proceeding.

If the needs of our app dictate we do not simply wait for the completion of a task, but prefer instead to be notified when it is complete, we can register a callback with the task.

Completion callbacks

Callbacks are supported within the TPL through the `Task` class's `ContinueWith` method. The `ContinueWith` method is defined within the `Task` class as follows:

```
public Task ContinueWith(Action<Task> continuationAction)
```

As a parameter, the `ContinueWith` method expects an `Action` to which the `Task` class whose completion is being awaited is passed as a parameter. The code within the `Action` parameter to `ContinueWith` will not execute until the preceding `Task` has completed. We can use this functionality to chain `Tasks` in addition to handling task completion.

By way of example, if we simply wanted to log a message to the console when the `DoLongRunningTask` method has completed, we could write the code as follows:

```
var longTask = Task
  .Factory
```

```
.StartNew(() => DoLongRunningTask())
.ContinueWith((previousTask) =>
{
    Console.WriteLine("Long Running Task Completed.");
}
```

The code within the `ContinueWith` method will not be invoked until `DoLongRunningTask` has completed.

As you can see, the TPL and the fluent API by which we use it allows us to write multi-threaded code in a manner more in line with how we think, linearly. Its introduction in .NET 4.0 was a huge step forward compared to the traditional methods of asynchronous programming involving the use of `AsyncCallback`, `IAsyncResult`, and others.

In .NET 4.5, the framework introduced two new C# keywords to further simplify asynchronous programming: `async` and `await`.

Async

The `async` keyword is a modifier just like `static` or `const`. It is used to mark a method declaration as asynchronous. Its use comes with a couple of restrictions. A method marked with the `async` modifier must have a return type of `Task`, `Task<TResult>`, or `void` and the method may not take any `ref` or `out` parameters.

To declare an `async` method having no return value, you declare the method to be of type `Task`:

```
async Task JustDoIt()
{
    // Do your thing
}
```

If a method defined as `async` needs to return a value, it must be declared as `Task<TResult>` where `TResult` identifies the type of the `Task`'s return value:

```
async Task<TResult> ReturnSomethingLater()
{
    TResult returnVal;
    // Do some operation.
    return returnVal;
}
```

When an asynchronous method is used for an event handler requiring a void type, we can declare the asynchronous method to be of type void:

```
async void ImRarelyUsed()
{
  // Do my job.
}
```

These void methods behave differently than those that return a Task or Task<TResult> and should not be used for the common asynchronous tasks we are presenting here.

Use of the async modifier comes with a lot of restrictions as you can see. There is one more restriction worth mentioning. Methods marked with the async modifier must contain the await operator.

Await

The await operator is generally seen as the companion to the async modifier. It is used to identify the point within an async method where the runtime is to suspend processing until the asynchronous task has completed:

```
var asyncTask = DoBackgroundWork();

// Do some additional work while
// the background task completes.

await asyncTask;
```

In the preceding sample code, the method DoBackgroundWork returns Task or Task<TResult>. After the method is invoked, the caller goes about completing other work while the background task executes. It is only when the await operator is invoked that the caller awaits the completion of the asynchronous task.

Await is actually a bit of a misnomer. The caller of await is simply paused; the current thread is not blocked. Rather, the remainder of the code beyond the await operator is signed up as a continuation of the current thread and the thread is free to go about doing other work. When the task associated with the await operator has completed — in this example, DoBackgroundWork — it invokes the continuation of the paused thread and any code beyond the await keyword.

If the await operator is not present in a method marked with the async modifier, the method will be treated as synchronous and the compiler will generate a warning.

Asynchronous programming is a topic usually associated with desktop or backend server apps. This is unfortunate because we can use the new `async` and `await` keywords to apply asynchronous programming concepts to our mobile web app.

Asynchronous controller action methods

Before we dive into discussing asynchronous controller actions, it might help to understand how incoming requests to our controllers are handled by the framework and IIS.

When IIS receives a request for a resource, it hands the request off to a handler for that request—for ASP.NET MVC, the request is handed off to ASP.NET. ASP.NET, in turn, hands the request off to a thread pool inside the .NET framework dedicated to handling web requests. This process leaves IIS free to handle inbound requests as it simply delegates requests to the appropriate handler. Since request processing for the majority of web apps takes only a couple of seconds to execute within the framework, this thread hand-off process all but guarantees IIS will be able to handle all inbound web requests.

If, however, the majority of web requests end up being long-running requests, requests that are invoking web services, performing operations on the file system, and so on, then the thread pool within the .NET framework can become exhausted. When this happens, IIS will begin queuing requests. If the request queue becomes full, IIS will begin returning HTTP status code 503 to clients, indicating the server is busy.

Asynchronous controller actions provide the ability to offload work from the request threads to worker threads. When a request comes in to the web server, the server grabs a thread from the thread pool. The thread pool, upon seeing an asynchronous operation may be executed, schedules the asynchronous operation and is then returned to the thread pool. Upon completion of the asynchronous operation, the web server is notified and it retrieves another thread from the pool to complete the request and return a response to the client.

Asynchronous actions take just as long to complete as synchronous action methods. They simply allow us to free up resources to handle additional request processing when we need to complete operations that may be CPU, network, or I/O bound, typically long-running operations in response to a web request.

Creating asynchronous actions

Prior to ASP.NET MVC 4, asynchronous action methods were only supported within a controller that extended the `AsyncController` base class. Each asynchronous action followed the event-based asynchronous pattern where the initial method had an `Async` suffix and the completion method had a `Completed` suffix:

```
public class HomeController :AsyncController
{
  public void IndexAsync()
  {
    AsyncManager.OutstandingOperations.Increment();
    Task.Factory.StartNew(() => ExecuteAsyncTask());
  }

  private void ExecuteAsyncTask()
  {
    // Do asynchronous work.
    AsyncManager.OutstandingOperations.Decrement();
  }

  public ActionResult IndexCompleted()
  {
    return View();
  }
}
```

With the introduction of the `async` modifier in .NET 4.5, the creation of asynchronous actions has been greatly simplified:

```
public class HomeController : Controller
{
  public async Task<ActionResult> IndexAsync()
  {
    var asyncTask = Task
    .Factory
    .StartNew(DoBackgroundWork());
    // Do some work.
    await asyncTask();
  }
}
```

In fact, the declaration of asynchronous actions is no different than the declaration of any other asynchronous method marked with the `async` modifier.

> The use of the `Async` suffix is not mandatory and makes no difference to the runtime. It is, however, a recommended convention to follow.

An asynchronous recipe controller

Let us assume our app is putting undue stress on the web server because the recipe controller is spending the majority of its time retrieving objects from the database and converting them to view models. This stress is causing our web server to return an HTTP status code of 503, to some users of our app. We have looked at our schema and database and have made the determination that our schema is properly indexed and maintained. We do not have the budget or the resources to set up a web farm. We do know, however, that if the web server was not waiting for us to process these requests our users would not be receiving these intermittent 503 messages. It appears it is time for us to make the `RecipeController` class's often used actions asynchronous.

Following is the asynchronous action for retrieving the `Index` action of `RecipeController`:

```
public async Task<ActionResult> Index(int page = 0)
{
  var recipeListTask = Task.Factory.StartNew(() =>
  {
    var recipes = _recipeRepository.GetRecipes();

    var viewModel = new PagedResult<RecipeEntity,
      RecipeDisplayViewModel>(
      recipes,
      page,
      this._displayViewModelMapper.EntityToViewModel);

    return viewModel;
  });

  return View(await recipeListTask);
}
```

HttpContext is null

There is one very important piece of information to remember when dealing with asynchronous tasks. The current `HttpContext` is not assigned to the thread on which the asynchronous task is executing. If you need access to it, you will need to find a way to pass it or the data you need from it into the task. An example of this can be found in `LibraryController` in the code accompanying this book.

Having optimized the actions within our `RecipeController`, the next option is to reduce the number of inbound requests to our web server—without reducing the number of visitors, mind you—and to reduce the amount of time the web server spends sending responses back to our clients. We can do this using bundles.

Bundles

In ASP.NET MVC 4, the term bundle refers to one or more files, typically JavaScript or CSS, registered as a group with the runtime.

When a request for a bundle is made, the files comprising the bundle are appended to each other in a process called **bundling**. The bundled file then undergoes a **minification** process during which the file is stripped of comments and whitespace and the local variables' names, if present, are shortened.

Through the use of bundles, a client can reduce the number and size of requests it must make to the server to retrieve content. When applied to the world of mobile app development, bundling can have a substantial impact on an app's perceived performance.

CDN support

While not discussed in this chapter, bundles also support the use of common Content Delivery Networks such as those provided by Microsoft and Google.

Creating bundles

Our BrewHow mobile app currently contains six registered bundles. These bundles are registered within the `BundleConfig` class contained in the `AppStart` folder of our project.

```
public class BundleConfig
{
    public static void RegisterBundles(
        BundleCollection bundles)
    {
        bundles.Add(new ScriptBundle("~/bundles/jquery")
        Include("~/Scripts/jquery-{version}.js"));

        // Code removed for brevity.
        bundles.Add(new ScriptBundle("~/bundles/modernizr")
          .Include("~/Scripts/modernizr-*"));

        bundles.Add(new StyleBundle("~/Content/css")
          .Include("~/Content/site.css"));

        // More code removed for brevity...
    }
}
```

When the application starts, the `RegisterBundles` method is invoked from within `Global.asax.cs` to register our bundle definitions. The bundle definitions contain the bundle type and the file (or files) to include in the bundle. The bundle type itself identifies the location at which the bundle can be requested.

 While three of the bundles were omitted from the code above for brevity, the three bundles displayed were not chosen randomly. They illustrate the use of differing bundle types and the support for wildcards when defining bundles.

Bundle types

Within the `RegisterBundles` method, two different types of bundles are registered with the runtime: `ScriptBundles` and `StyleBundles`. These bundles contain what you might expect: scripts (specifically JavaScript) and styles (specifically CSS).

While these are the only two types of bundles supported out of the box, Microsoft realized you might desire to support bundling on other types of files written in other languages. To support this, the framework has a base `Bundle` class you can use to add support for additional types.

Adding support for new bundle types is no small task, as you must write your own custom transform that implements the `IBundleTransform` interface. The `StyleBundle` and `ScriptBundle` use a tool called `WebGrease` under the hood to perform the transforms of JavaScript and CSS. Other packages available via NuGet provide support for languages such as LESS and CoffeeScript. Before you run off and write your own, I'd recommend checking to see if your language is already supported.

Wildcard support

If we look at the following bundle definitions, we will notice they are including files within the bundle using wildcard mechanisms:

```
bundles.Add(new ScriptBundle("~/bundles/jquery")
    .Include("~/Scripts/jquery-{version}.js"));

bundles.Add(new ScriptBundle("~/bundles/modernizr")
    .Include("~/Scripts/modernizr-*"));
```

Support for wildcards allows us to include related files together without having to enumerate each one in an `Include` on the bundle. The bundles themselves are smart enough to make some decisions about files to include in the event where there are collisions. If you happen to have a minified version of jQuery, the Visual Studio debug version of jQuery, and the standard version of jQuery sitting within a directory, the wildcard rules supported within the bundle will include the minified version of the file if you are targeting a release build or the standard jQuery version if you are not.

All is not rainbows and unicorns within the land of wildcard support. Wildcard includes will add files to the bundle in alphabetical order. If you are unfortunate enough to have your scripts written in such a way that alphabetical order is not the same as dependency order you will need to create multiple bundles, create a class implementing the `IBundleOrderer` interface to support your ordering, or include the files in the bundle using the `Include` method in the order in which they must execute.

Wildcard support should be used sparingly.

Consuming bundles

Now that we know what bundles are and how they're created, let's take a quick look at how we can consume them.

If you open up the layout page, `_Layout.cshtml`, you will see two lines at the top:

```
@Styles.Render("~/Content/css")
@Scripts.Render("~/bundles/modernizr")
```

These lines query the runtime for a style bundle and a script bundle with locations of `~/Content/css` and `~/bundles/modernizr` respectively. There is also a line of code at the bottom to include the jQuery bundle:

```
@Scripts.Render("~/bundles/jquery")
```

Launching the site to examine the source code of the recipe list, we can see the two bundles at the top translate to the actual files included in them:

```
1  <!DOCTYPE html>
2  <html lang="en">
3      <head>
4          <meta charset="utf-8" />
5          <title>Index - My ASP.NET MVC Application</title>
6          <link href="/favicon.ico" rel="shortcut icon" type="image/x-icon" />
7          <meta name="viewport" content="width=device-width" />
8          <link href="/Content/site.css" rel="stylesheet"/>
9
10         <script src="/Scripts/modernizr-2.5.3.js"></script>
11
12     </head>
13     <body>
14         <header>
15             <div class="content-wrapper">
16                 <div class="float-left">
17                     <p class="site-title"><a href="/Recipe/Index">your logo
   here</a></p>
18                 </div>
19                 <div class="float-right">
20                     <section id="login">
21
22         Hello, <a class="username" href="/Account/Manage"
   title="Manage">brewmaster</a>!
23  <form action="/Account/LogOff" id="logoutForm" method="post"><input
   name="__RequestVerificationToken" type="hidden"
   value="uRWo1Jw31B8aektyCUrctOlA9CmDdWyIPUubPxPRChHn9kgRv36FWI0nxTcekCoRLS2fTohjI
   ZcPrhjEM9pKrKCxHmi2FZxsj5E7HBLOX101" />             <a
   href="javascript:document.getElementById('logoutForm').submit()">Log off</a>
24  </form>
```

If we look at the content of the `styles.css` and `modernizer.js` files in the browser, we would find them identical to the versions stored on the disk. So what gives? Isn't using the bundle supposed to combine and minify each definition? Well, the answer is it depends.

The intelligence of the bundle process extends beyond wildcard file inclusion. If we were to examine the `web.config` file, we would see our app is currently compiled in debug mode.

```
<compilation debug="true" targetFramework="4.5" />
```

If the bundles are being processed when the site is currently in debug mode, the bundle process simply adds links to all of the files in their current form to the page. This is actually a desired behavior; you don't want to try and debug minified JavaScript or CSS.

Setting the `debug` property to `false` will enable the bundle process and will change the output of the page to actually reference the bundles and not the individual files.

> The bundling and minification behavior of bundles can also be turned on by setting the `EnableOptimizations` property of the `BundleTable` class to `true`. If this is done, setting the `compilation` node's `debug` property to `true` in the `web.config` will no longer have an effect on the process as the `EnableOptimizations` property supersedes any other configuration.

```
 1  <!DOCTYPE html>
 2  <html lang="en">
 3      <head>
 4          <meta charset="utf-8" />
 5          <title>Index - My ASP.NET MVC Application</title>
 6          <link href="/favicon.ico" rel="shortcut icon" type="image/x-icon" />
 7          <meta name="viewport" content="width=device-width" />
 8          <link href="/Content/css?v=WMr-pvK-1dSbNXHT-cT0d9QF2pqi7sqz_4MtK104wlw1"
    rel="stylesheet"/>
 9
10          <script src="/bundles/modernizr?
    v=jmdBhqkI3eMaPZJduAyIYBj7MpXrGd2ZqmHAOSNeYcq1"></script>
11
12      </head>
13      <body>
14          <header>
15              <div class="content-wrapper">
16                  <div class="float-left">
17                      <p class="site-title"><a href="/Recipe/Index">your logo
    here</a></p>
18                  </div>
19                  <div class="float-right">
20                      <section id="login">
21
22          Hello, <a class="username" href="/Account/Manage"
    title="Manage">brewmaster</a>!
23  <form action="/Account/LogOff" id="logoutForm" method="post"><input
    name="__RequestVerificationToken" type="hidden" value="3rutY2UTd09n-cJ-
    vOWN7NkawXZggVjavhyw8tMNemYIhikoRN_OEN2JrMOep6-wGXNdX5LfKvxa-
    au2WF1Eean4nOLXvheR4sBDrY07jjI1" />            <a
```

You should notice the query strings following each of the bundle links within the source. These query strings are a hash used to represent the content of the bundle and help to break the cache in browsers whose implementation holds script and css files longer than requested. When the content of any file in a bundle has changed, a new hash is generated resulting in a new query string and, therefore, a new link. When the browser encounters the new link it will be unable to find the file in its cache and will again retrieve it from the server.

Examination of the file contents shows that the content has indeed been minified.

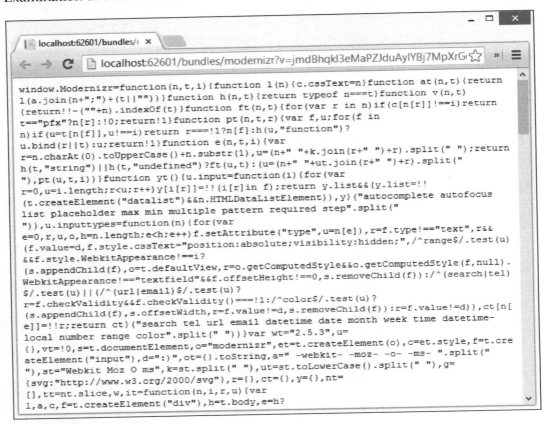

This may not seem like a big change, but the performance increases can be pretty substantial, especially for sites designed around smart clients with heavy scripting. Even on our small app running on localhost there is a measurable increase in performance.

Opening the **Network** tab within Chrome's **Developer Tools** window, we can see our site took 405 ms to load from localhost and complete a data transfer of 307 kilobytes without minification.

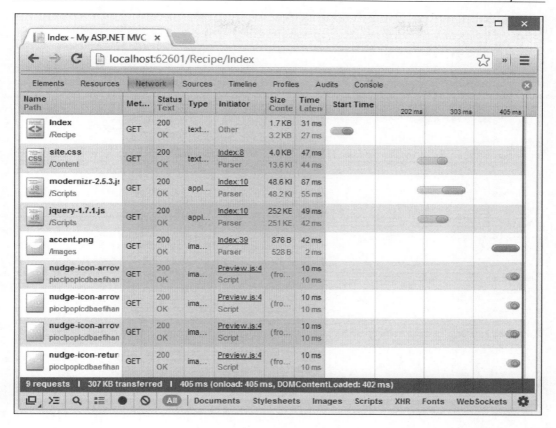

If we look at the exact same request for the release version of the site we see that load time dropped to 322 ms. This is not a huge drop, but we're loading from localhost so we shouldn't expect to see big numbers for such a small site.

The bigger difference is in the amount of data we sent from the server to the client. We dropped from 307 kilobytes to 52.5 kilobytes, essentially dropping the data volume to 1/6th its former value.

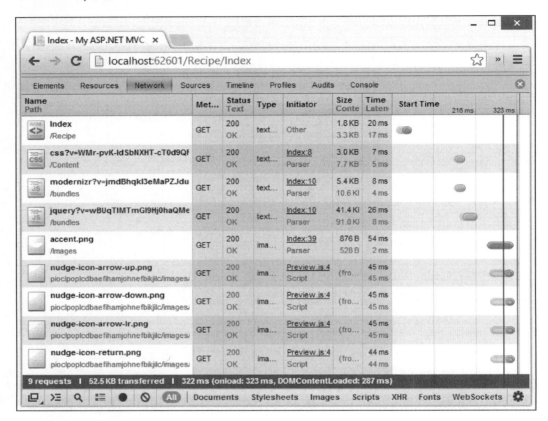

Summary

In this chapter we learned multiple ways to improve the performance of our app for the betterment of our server and our users. We learned how to perform multiple tasks simultaneously through the use of the TPL and how to free IIS to handle requests while we perform long-running processes within asynchronous controller actions.

We also learned about bundles and how we can use them to make the footprint of our site smaller in terms of both bandwidth and request chattiness.

In the next chapter we will focus on user experience as we explore SignalR and how it enables us to provide real-time interaction and feedback with our users.

11

Coding for the Real-time Web

As the lines between web apps and traditional desktop apps blur, our users have come to expect real-time behavior in our web apps—something that is traditionally the domain of the desktop. One cannot really blame them. Real-time interaction with data, services, and even other users has driven the connected revolution, and we are now connected in more ways than ever before. However valid this desire to be always connected and immediately informed of an event, there are inherent challenges in real-time interactions within web apps.

The first challenge is that the Web is stateless. The Web is built on HTTP, a protocol that is request/response; for each request a browser makes, there is one and only one response. There are frameworks and techniques we can use to mask the statelessness of the Web, but there is no true state built into the Web or HTTP.

This is further complicated as the Web is client/server. As it's stateless, a server only knows of the clients connected at any one given moment, and clients can only display data to the user based upon the last interaction with the server. The only time the client and server have any knowledge of the other is during an active request/response, and this action may change the state of the client or the server. Any change to the server's state is not reflected to the other clients until they connect to the server with a new request. It's somewhat like the uncertainty principle in that the more one tries to pin down one data point of the relationship, the more uncertain one becomes about the other points.

All hope is not lost. There are several techniques that can be used to enable real-time (or near real-time) data exchange between the web server and any active client.

Simulating a connected state

In traditional web development, there has not been a way to maintain a persistent connection between a client browser and the web server. Web developers have gone to great lengths to try and simulate a connected world in the request/response world of HTTP.

Several developers have met with success using creative thinking and loopholes within the standard itself to develop techniques such as long polling and the forever frame. Now, thanks to the realization that such a technique is needed, the organizations overseeing the next generation of web standards are also heeding the call with server-sent events and web sockets.

Long polling

Long polling is the default fallback for any client and server content exchange. It is not reliant on anything but HTTP—no special standards checklists or other chicanery are required.

Long polling is like getting the silent treatment from your partner. You ask a question and you wait indefinitely for an answer. After some known period of time and what may seem like an eternity, you finally receive an answer or the request eventually times out. The process repeats again and again until the request is fully satisfied or the relationship terminates. So, yeah, it's exactly like the silent treatment.

Forever Frame

The **Forever Frame** technique relies on the HTTP 1.1 standard and a hidden `iframe`. When the page loads, it contains (or constructs) a hidden `iframe` used to make a request back to the server. The actual exchange between the client and the server leverages a feature of HTTP 1.1 known as **Chunked Encoding**. Chunked Encoding is identified by a value of `chunked` in the HTTP `Transfer-Encoding` header.

This method of data transfer is intended to allow the server to begin sending portions of data to the client before the entire length of the content is known. When simulating a real-time connection between a browser and web server, the server can dispatch messages to the client as individual chunks on the request made by the `iframe`.

Server-Sent Events

Server-Sent Events (SSE) provide a mechanism for a server to raise DOM events within a client web browser. This means to use SSE, the browser must support it. As of this writing, support for SSE is minimal but it has been submitted to W3C for inclusion into the HTML5 specification.

The use of SSE begins by declaring an `EventSource` variable:

```
var source = new EventSource('/my-data-source');
```

If you then want to listen to any and all messages sent by the source, you simply treat it as a DOM event and handle it in JavaScript.

```
source.onmessage = function(event) {
    // Process the event.
}
```

SSE supports the raising of specific events and complex event messaging. The message format is a simple text-based format derivative of JSON. Two newline characters separate each message within the stream, and each message may have an `id`, `data`, and `event` property. SSE also supports setting the retry time using the `retry` keyword within a message.

```
:comment

:simple message
data:"this string is my message"

:complex message targeting an event
event:thatjusthappened
data:{ "who":"Professor Plum", "where":"Library", "with":"candlestick"
}
```

As of this writing, SSE is not supported in Internet Explorer and is partially implemented in a few mobile browsers.

WebSockets

The coup de grâce of real-time communication on the Web is WebSockets. WebSockets support a bidirectional stream between a web browser and web server and only leverage HTTP 1.1 to request a connection upgrade.

Once a connection upgrade has been granted, WebSockets communicate in full-duplex using the WebSocket protocol over a TCP connection, literally creating a client-server connection within the browser that can be used for real-time messaging.

All major desktop browsers and almost all mobile browsers support WebSockets. However, WebSocket usage requires support from the web server, and a WebSocket connection may have trouble working successfully behind a proxy.

With all the tools and techniques available to enable real-time connections between our mobile web app and the web server, how does one make the choice? We could write our code to support long polling, but that would obviously use up resources on the server and require us to do some pretty extensive plumbing on our end. We could try and use WebSockets, but for browsers lacking support or for users behind proxies, we might be introducing more problems than we would solve. If only there was a framework to handle all of this for us, try the best option available and degrade to the almost guaranteed functionality of long polling when required.

Wait. There is. It's called **SignalR**.

SignalR

SignalR provides a framework that abstracts all the previously mentioned real-time connection options into one cohesive communication platform supporting both web development and traditional desktop development.

When establishing a connection between the client and server, SignalR will negotiate the best connection technique/technology possible based upon client and server capability. The actual transport used is hidden beneath a higher-level communication framework that exposes endpoints on the server and allows those endpoints to be invoked by the client. Clients, in turn, may register with the server and have messages pushed to them.

Each client is uniquely identified to the server via a connection ID. This connection ID can be used to send messages explicitly to a client or away from a client. In addition, SignalR supports the concept of groups, each group being a collection of connection IDs. These groups, just like individual connections, can be specifically included or excluded from a communication exchange.

All of these capabilities in SignalR are provided to us by two client/server communication mechanisms: **persistent connections** and **hubs**.

Persistent connections

Persistent connections are the low-level connections of SignalR. That's not to say they provide access to the actual communication technique being used by SignalR, but to illustrate their primary usage as raw communication between client and server.

Persistent connections behave much as sockets do in traditional network application development. They provide an abstraction above the lower-level communication mechanisms and protocols, but offer little more than that.

When creating an endpoint to handle persistent connection requests over HTTP, the class for handling the connection requests must reside within the `Controllers` folder (or any other folder containing controllers) and extend the `PersistentConnection` class.

```
public class MyPersistentConnection: PersistentConnection
{
}
```

The `PersistentConnection` class manages connections from the client to the server by way of events. To handle these connection events, any class that is derived from `PersistentConnection` may override the methods defined within the `PersistentConnection` class.

Client interactions with the server raise the following events:

- `OnConnected`: This is invoked by the framework when a new connection to the server is made.

- `OnReconnected`: This is invoked when a client connection that has been terminated has reestablished a connection to the server.

- `OnRejoiningGroups`: This is invoked when a client connection that has timed out is being reestablished so that the connection may be rejoined to the appropriate groups.

- `OnReceived`: This method is invoked when data is received from the client.

- `OnDisconnected`: This is invoked when the connection between the client and server has been terminated.

Interaction with the client occurs through the `Connection` property of the `PersistentConnection` class. When an event is raised, the implementing class can determine if it wishes to broadcast a message using `Connection.Broadcast`, respond to a specific client using `Connection.Send`, or add the client that triggered the message to a group using `Connection.Groups`.

Hubs

Hubs provide us an abstraction over the `PersistentConnection` class by masking some of the overhead involved in managing raw connections between client and server.

Similar to a persistent connection, a hub is contained within the `Controllers` folder of your project but instead, extends the `Hub` base class.

```
public class MyHub : Hub
{
}
```

While a hub supports the ability to be notified of connection, reconnection, and disconnection events, unlike the event-driven persistent connection a hub handles the event dispatching for us. Any publicly available method on the `Hub` class is treated as an endpoint and is addressable by any client by name.

```
public class MyHub : Hub
{
    public void SendMeAMessage(string message)
    { /* ... */ }
}
```

A hub can communicate with any of its clients using the `Clients` property of the `Hub` base class. This property supports methods, just like the `Connection` property of `PersistentConnection`, to communicate with specific clients, all clients, or groups of clients.

Rather than break down all the functionality available to us in the `Hub` class, we will instead learn from an example.

Real-time recipe updates

Within our BrewHow mobile app, it would be nice to receive notifications of new recipe additions when we are looking at the recipe list. To accomplish this, we will use the `Hub` mechanism provided by the SignalR framework to accomplish real-time notification of additions to the BrewHow recipe collection.

Installing and configuring SignalR

SignalR, like most modern .NET frameworks, is available as a NuGet package: `Microsoft.AspNet.SignalR`. We can install the package by entering the following into the **Package Manager** console:

```
Install-Package Microsoft.AspNet.SignalR
```

In addition to several assembly references to our project, the SignalR package also adds a new JavaScript file: `jquery.signalR-1.1.2.min.js`—your version may vary depending upon when you're actually reading this. This JavaScript file contains all the abstractions needed by the client web browser to communicate with both types of SignalR endpoints: persistent connections and hubs.

The SignalR JavaScript file is only one part of the client puzzle. To enable SignalR support in our app, we need to add references to the SignalR JavaScript library as well as to invoke the handler, `/signalr/hubs`, used to create a JavaScript proxy for any hubs within our project. These references will be placed in `_Layout.cshtml`.

```
@Scripts.Render("~/bundles/jquery")
<script
    src="~/Scripts/jquery.signalR-1.1.2.min.js"
    type="text/javascript"></script>
<script
    src="~/signalr/hubs"
    type="text/javascript"></script>
@RenderSection("scripts", required: false)
```

We must also register the `/signalr/hubs` route with the runtime. We can do this by simply invoking the `MapHubs` extension method for the route collection where we register the other routes for our app.

```
routes.IgnoreRoute("{resource}.axd/{*pathInfo}");
routes.MapHubs();
routes.MapRoute(
    name: "BeerByStyle",
```

Note that the hub route is placed before all other `MapRoute` calls or other methods we may use to register routes. We do this because route selection is made on first match, and we don't want to inadvertently register something before SignalR within our route table.

Creating the recipe hub

We need to provide a hub to which clients can connect to receive notifications about new recipe additions.

Right-click on the `Controllers` folder of our project and select **Add | New Item...**.

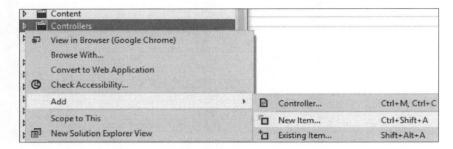

In the **Add New Item** dialog box, search for SignalR and choose the **SignalR Hub Class**. Name the class `RecipeHub.cs` and click on **Add**.

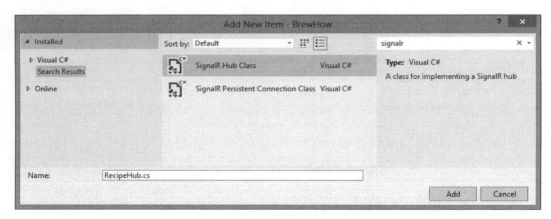

We need to modify the `RecipeHub` class generated by Visual Studio. As stated earlier, clients are going to receive notifications about new recipes, but no client is ever going to post directly to this hub to communicate with the server. As such, we simply need to create an empty hub.

```
namespace BrewHow.Controllers
{
    public class RecipeHub : Hub
    {
    }
}
```

An empty class may appear rather meaningless at first glance, but SignalR cannot create a proxy for clients to interact with the server without a class declaration.

Modifying the recipe list view

The recipe list view needs to be modified to connect to the recipe hub. The first order of business is to supply the recipe list with an ID. The ID will be used to locate and modify the list using jQuery. Assign the recipe list an ID of `recipe-list`.

```
<table id ="recipe-list">
```

We can now add some JavaScript that will connect to the recipe hub and upon the notification of a new recipe, append new recipes at the bottom of our table with a background color of yellow.

```
$(function () {
    $.connection.hub.start();
    var recipeHub = $.connection.recipeHub;
    recipeHub.client.recipeAdded = function (recipe) {
        var tr = $("#recipe-list").find('tbody')
            .append(
                $('<tr>').css('background-color', '#ff0')
                    .append($('<td>')
                        .append($('<a>')
                        .attr('href', '/Recipe/Details/'
                            + recipe.RecipeId
                            + "/" + recipe.Slug)
                        .text(recipe.Name))
                    )
                    .append($('<td>')
                        .append($('<a>')
                        .attr('href', '/Recipe/'
                            +recipe.StyleSlug)
                        .text(recipe.Style))
                    )
                    .append($('<td>'
                        + recipe
                            .OriginalGravity
                            .toFixed(3)
                        + '</td>'))
                    .append($('<td>'
                        + recipe
                            .FinalGravity
                            .toFixed(3)
                        + '</td>'))
```

```
@if (Request.IsAuthenticated) {                .append($('<td>'
    @:                                                + 'Add to Library'
    @:                                                + '</td>'))
    @:
    }
                    );
        }
});
```

The JavaScript code is contained within a closure, ensuring it is only invoked once and cannot be invoked by any outside source. The very first line of code starts the hub connections on the client:

```
$.connection.hub.start();
```

The `connection` object is an object added to jQuery by the SignalR JavaScript. The `hub` property of the connection object provides a reference to the hub infrastructure of the SignalR client library. The call to the `start` method initializes the SignalR client and prepares the proxy code generated by the `/signalr/hubs` call in our `_Layout.cshtml` page to receive notifications from the server.

Next, the JavaScript establishes a connection to our recipe hub:

```
var recipeHub = $.connection.recipeHub;
```

On examining this code carefully, you will see that the connection to our `RecipeHub` class is identified in the connection class as `recipeHub`. The `/signalr/hubs` call that generates the proxy classes for the hubs within our app adds each hub it finds to the `connection` object using a camel-cased version of the hub class name: `RecipeHub` becomes `recipeHub`, `MyHub` becomes `myHub`, and so on.

The next line of code registers a method on the client to be invoked by the server when a new recipe is added.

```
recipeHub.client.recipeAdded = function (recipe) {
```

We could call this method anything we wanted — well anything except a name that matches a server-side method within the hub. It is the act of declaring a function on the client and assigning it to the `client` property of the hub that makes the method available to the server.

The rest of the code simply takes the `RecipeDisplayViewModel` object it receives and appends it to the table with a yellow highlight.

Publishing event notifications

We have talked about responding to clients from within a `Hub` or
`PersistentConnection` based class. However, our `RecipeHub` class is empty and
we have no other hub. Not to fret. We can notify other users of our app that this
event occurred by placing code into the `Create` method of the `RecipeController`
class after a recipe is saved to the repository.

```
var context = Microsoft.AspNet.SignalR.
    GlobalHost
        .ConnectionManager
        .GetHubContext<RecipeHub>();
context
    .Clients
    .All
    .recipeAdded(
        _displayViewModelMapper
            .EntityToViewModel(recipeEntity)
    );
```

This code begins with retrieving the context of our `RecipeHub` class. We do this
using the `GetHubContext<T>()` method of the SignalR `ConnectionManager`.
We then prepare to make a broadcast to all clients of the `RecipeHub` class using
the context's `Clients.All` property.

Sir Arthur C Clarke said:

> *"Any sufficiently advanced technology is indistinguishable from magic."*

I will let you be the judge as to whether or not it's magic, but to invoke the
`recipeAdded` method we defined and assigned to the `client` in JavaScript, we
simply invoke it here passing the data we wish to return. The runtime handles the
event dispatching for us and informs all clients of the `RecipeHub` class that we are
invoking the `recipeAdded` method. If there is such a method on the client it will
be invoked by the SignalR client code.

There is one more change required to make this work. Our repository currently
doesn't set the `RecipeId` property of a `recipeEntity` class when it has been created.
As we use the recipe's ID to provide links to the details from the list, we need to
make sure it's available to all clients to which the broadcast is sent. This change is
fairly simple. Just modify the repository to set `RecipeId` after changes to the Entity
Framework context have been made.

```
recipeEntity.RecipeId = newRecipeModel.RecipeId;
```

Everything should work now. We just need two clients simultaneously connected to test it.

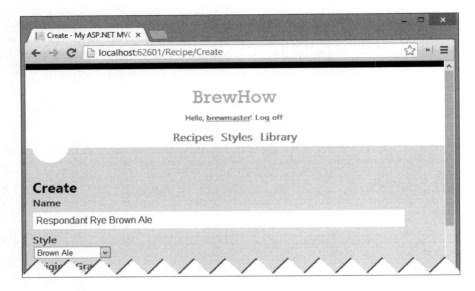

Upon adding the recipe in Google Chrome, it magically appears within Opera Mobile in the recipe list.

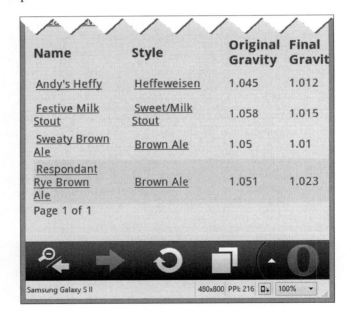

Summary

In this chapter we took a look at SignalR. The SignalR framework gives us unprecedented control of the communication between the browser and web server enabling real-time communication. This technology can be leveraged in games, real-time status updates, or to mimic push communications within a mobile web app.

We have taken a pretty wide look at ASP.NET MVC 4 up to this point and have called out considerations we need to make when building mobile web apps. In the next chapter, we will begin to drill down into the mobile web and look at the tools and techniques available to us in the latest version of the .NET Framework. We will begin with mobile templates.

12
Designing Your App for Mobile Devices

We have developed a fairly complete app in very short order. Our app has worked well on the desktop browser and is actually fairly usable on mobile devices (we will address this in detail very soon). This is in large part due to the work done by Microsoft and the new application templates they have provided. These templates are based on a set of new standards: HTML5 and CSS3.

This chapter will focus on HTML5 and CSS3, the support for these new standards in most mobile browsers, and the ability to use these standards to design next-generation mobile web applications.

HTML5

HTML5 is a marked switch from its predecessors. Instead of concerning itself with markup identifying the structure of the data, HTML5 is a semantic language focused on markup that provides meaning to the content.

In addition to these semantic tags, HTML5 introduces native support for embedded video and audio, browser-local database storage, a drawing canvas, form controls, WebSockets, and enough other features to fill an entire book—several actually. With new features, HTML5 also reduces the amount of markup we have to write to generate a standards-compliant document.

There's certainly more to HTML5 than we can cover in a single chapter, so we'll focus on the features most important to our application at this time: markup changes, semantic tags, custom data attributes, and the new form controls. We will also introduce the local storage and geolocation services provided by HTML5, as they can be used to greatly enhance the experience of mobile apps.

Markup changes

Let's begin our examination of these markup changes by looking at a traditional minimally compliant XHTML 1.1 document.

```
<!DOCTYPE HTML PUBLIC "-//W3C//DTD HTML 4.01//EN" "http://www.w3.org/
TR/html4/strict.dtd">
<html lang="en">
    <head>
        <meta http-equiv="Content-Type" content="text/html;
charset=utf-8">
        <title>BrewHow</title>
        <link rel="stylesheet" href="styles.css" type="text/css">
    </head>
    <body>
    </body>
</html>
```

Right away, you can tell this isn't something that most people are going to type out by hand. HTML4 and XHTML 1.1 place much of the burden of compliance on the author. This is unfortunate given the parser could infer a good portion of the markup involved in compliance.

In this regard, HTML5 has been designed to reduce the amount of work required to produce a standards-compliant document.

The DOCTYPE tag

The DOCTYPE tag we see at the start of every HTML document isn't actually an HTML tag. HTML was originally developed in tandem with **Standard Generalized Markup Language (SGML)**, an ISO standard intended to use markup languages to describe markup languages. HTML4 is based on SGML, which requires the declaration of a DOCTYPE.

The DOCTYPE declaration contains several pieces of information that together make up the **Document Type Definition (DTD)**. DTD is very formal, strictly defining the document beneath the header. As HTML4 is a true derivative of SGML, the DOCTYPE header is a required piece of markup—warts and all.

As HTML5 is not based on SGML and hence carries none of the overhead associated with it, we can shorten the declaration. So, in HTML5:

```
<!DOCTYPE html PUBLIC "-//W3C//DTD XHTML 1.1//EN"
"http://www.w3.org/TR/xhtml11/DTD/xhtml11.dtd">
```

becomes:

```
<!DOCTYPE html>
```

When a browser sees this minimal DOCTYPE declaration, it will attempt to parse and render the document using the latest engine it has.

 It should be noted that HTML5 is not case-sensitive. DOCTYPE, DocType, doctype, and DoCtYpE are all treated the same. Whichever format you choose to use, just make sure you're consistent throughout your documents—for your sake, not that of the parser.

The character set

The default character set for XML and HTML 4.0 is Unicode, specifically ISO 10646. This isn't something that's necessarily enforced. Rather, this standard exists to dictate to all XML parsers and web browsers that they must behave as if they are internally using Unicode. As we want to play well with others, it benefits us and consumers of our documents to identify the character set in which our document is written, so that the clients can map our character set to Unicode.

In HTML4 documents, the character set was specified using a meta tag to identify Content-Type of the document:

```
<meta http-equiv="Content-Type" content="text/html; charset=utf-8">
```

Given that the type of the document is identified in large part by the DOCTYPE tag, HTML5 introduces a new charset attribute for the meta tag making the declaration of our character set much more succinct:

```
<meta charset="utf-8" />
```

Type attributes

When declaring scripts, styles, or other external media to be loaded, we traditionally had to provide the content type of the external media via the type attribute. For JavaScript, we had to identify the type as text/javascript. For CSS, we had to provide a content type of text/css.

```
<link rel="stylesheet" href="styles.css" type="text/css">
```

Given that the browsers can infer this information, the type attribute has been made optional in HTML5 so that our link tag to load our stylesheet may now be written as follows:

```
<link rel="stylesheet" href="styles.css" />
```

Want to learn more?

There are several additional attribute modifications made in HTML5 you may not encounter everyday. For instance, the `script` tag's `async` attribute can instruct the browser to load and immediately execute external JavaScript without waiting for a page to complete. I encourage you to research the HTML5 standard, currently in candidate recommendation status at `http://www.w3.org/TR/html5/`.

Putting it all together, our boilerplate HTML5 template is much cleaner and much easier to visually parse than the HTML4 markup presented at the start of this section.

```
<!DOCTYPE html>
<html lang="en">
    <head>
        <meta charset="utf-8" />
        <title>BrewHow</title>
        <link rel="stylesheet" href="styles.css" />
    </head>
    <body>
    </body>
</html>
```

Visual Studio 2012 support

Visual Studio 2012 is aware of all these new markup changes and provides support for them in the default template used by our BrewHow app.

If we open up the `_Layout.cshtml` file in our project, you will see the first four lines of the file are the following:

```
<!DOCTYPE html>
<html lang="en">
    <head>
        <meta charset="utf-8" />
```

It would seem that Visual Studio has done the work of simplifying our markup. Let's learn a bit about the semantic tags of HTML5, and see if Visual Studio will offer us the same support for them as it does the cleaner markup.

Semantic tags

As mentioned in the introduction of this chapter, semantic tags allow us to apply context to our content. Using a simple example, one might declare a footer in HTML4 by using a `div` tag.

```
<div id="footer"></div>
```

In HTML5, `footer` is a valid tag and as such, our footer declaration now provides meaning to the markup.

```
<footer></footer>
```

The semantic tags in HTML5 were not blindly chosen. Rather, much research was done to look at content on the Web and from that content, the most commonly used class names and IDs were compiled and collapsed into the new semantic tags.

Instead of providing a list of all of the tags introduced in HTML5, it's probably easier if we look at the HTML5 markup already present in our project. Our `_Layout.cshtml` template already provides us with several HTML5 semantic tags that have been highlighted in the following code snippet:

```html
<body>
    <header>

        <!-- snip -->
            <section id="login">
                @Html.Partial("_LoginPartial")
            </section>
            <nav>
                <ul id="menu">
                    <li>@Html.ActionLink("Recipes", "Index",
"Recipe")</li>

                    <!-- snip -->
                </ul>
            </nav>
        </div>
    </div>
    </header>
    <div id="body">
        <!-- snip -->
    </div>
    <footer>
        <!-- snip -->
    </footer>
        <!-- snip -->
    </body>
```

It seems, once again, Visual Studio has simplified the process for us. Let's examine each of these tags in a little more detail and see if there are any other markup changes we need to make.

The article tag

An `article` tag identifies independent content within a page. You might use the `article` tag to identify a blog post or, in the case of our app, a recipe. The general rule of thumb to follow when using an `article` tag is to ask whether or not the content within the `article` tag makes sense on its own. If it does, an `article` tag is appropriate. There is no `article` tag present in our template, but it is nonetheless an important tag in the HTML5 landscape and we will be leveraging it in the remainder of this book.

The header tag

The `header` tag is precisely what its name implies. It is used to identify the header of a sectioned piece of content. In this context, sectioned content is not specific to the `section` tag discussed in the following section. It instead means that any logical grouping of a page such as section, article, or the document itself may contain a header to identify the content contained within.

Given the scope of the header within our template, we can ascertain that this header refers to the content of the entire page.

The section tag

A section is a group of content that may or may not contain a header and footer. It is used to break up larger content groupings into smaller chunks.

In the code in `_Layout.cshtml`, `section` tags are used to identify the portion of the header specific to login functionality and the section of the page as a whole that is specific to the general content of the page.

One could also apply the `section` tag within an article to break it up into chapters.

The nav tag

The `nav` tag is used to indicate navigation typically at the site level. Screen readers and other browsers may actually omit the initial loading of this tag to provide the user with access to the primary content of the page being loaded first.

Our `_Layout.cshtml` file contains a `nav` section that contains links to the recipe list, the style list, and the user's library.

The footer tag

As noted in the tag descriptions, these tags are independent of each other and no tag is required to be nested within another one. We could apply `header` and `footer` tags to an `article` tag, a `section` tag, or as done in our `_Layout.cshtml` file, an entire document. Likewise, articles may contain child articles and each article may be broken into sections. The whole idea behind semantic markup is to provide meaning to our content that may then be interpreted by others.

> Other HTML5 tags include `address`, `aside`, `date`, `figure`, `figcaption`, `hgroup`, `mark`, and `time`. For a complete list of HTML5 tags, I recommend the HTML5 candidate recommendation at `http://www.w3.org/TR/html5/`.

The new templates in Visual Studio do a pretty good job of using the new HTML5 tags, so there are only a few modifications we should make. We will examine these modifications using the recipe details view.

Modifying recipe details

Before we start making modifications, let's take a snapshot of how recipe details appear to the user in the web browser.

The following is the portion of the markup used to display the details of a recipe:

```html
<h2>Details</h2>
<fieldset>
    <legend>Recipe Details</legend>

<!--Fields describing the recipe -->
</fieldset>
```

If the existing markup is run through an HTML5 outliner such as the one located at `http://gsnedders.html5.org/outliner/`, it will generate the following outline:

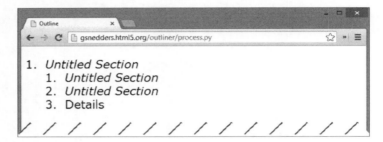

There are a couple of things that we could change to make the current markup meaningful. First, there's an h2 tag that is used to identify the information below as **Details**. This seems woefully insufficient; it certainly isn't descriptive of the content. Second, our recipe detail content would make sense outside of the context of our site, a description deserving of an article tag.

Knowing how we can better apply markup to our content, we can adjust the detail view to look like the following:

```html
<article id="recipe-detail">
    <header>
        <h2>Recipe for @Model.Name</h2>
    </header>
    <fieldset>
        <legend>Recipe Details</legend>
        <!--Fields describing the recipe -->
    </fieldset>
</article>
```

These changes to the markup had no effect on how our app appears in the user's browser other than the change to display the recipe name in the header. These changes did have a significant effect on how the markup is parsed and interpreted. If we run the new markup through the same parser, we get the following outline:

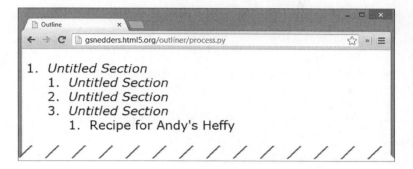

The first section is the page itself. Contained within the page are the login section, the menu contained within the nav tag, and the content section. Within the content section is our recipe article—the third (and new) untitled section. Were each section named, and ideally you should only use the section tag if you can apply a header to it, we'd have a well-outlined page. We will go ahead and apply appropriate titles to the other form pages within our app. To see these changes, you may consult the code accompanying the book.

In addition to these new semantic tags, HTML5 provides the ability to associate private data to any HTML tag via a new set of attributes collectively known as custom data attributes.

Custom data attributes

Custom data attributes are sometimes referred to as data-* attributes, and with good reason. Provided that the attribute starts with data- and anything following the - is longer than a single character, the attribute is classified as a custom data attribute and will be treated as such. We actually used one of these data-* attributes when we implemented our recipe library.

Custom data attributes are completely ignored by the browser or by any other user agent retrieving the markup. They will have no effect on page parsing or page rendering. It will be treated as if it is simply not there. Likewise, the user or any second-hand consumer of the page should ignore these attributes as well.

The specification actually refers to these attributes as private. That does not mean they do not show up in the source of the browser or they are somehow mysteriously removed from the source in transit to the browser. If a user views the source for the page or if an external agent elects to parse the `data-*` attributes from a page in our app, they are certainly free to do so. Private, in this case, implies intent and not actual implementation. We should not store sensitive information in these attributes.

Things we can store in these attributes are things for which the tag has no existing attribute. We certainly wouldn't store an element title here because the HTML standard specifies that all tags support the `title` attribute. We might, however, store some initial value for a field or specify the role for a tag or container.

```
<a href="#" data-initiallink="{oldlink}">Changing Link</a>
```

Our use for these attributes is practically unlimited and they are one of the most powerful features of the HTML5 specification.

Form controls

HTML5 introduces new form control types that allow for a better data input for the user. These controls are accessible through the `type` attribute of the `input` tag and provide a better data input experience for the user of the app. The new input types supported are enumerated as follows:

- `color`: This presents the user with a color-picker.
- `date`: This provides the user a mechanism to select a date.
- `datetime`: This allows the user to enter a date and time, including a time zone.
- `datetime-local`: This allows the user to enter a date and time local to them.
- `email`: This allows the user to enter an e-mail address.
- `month`: This provides the user a mechanism to select a month.
- `number`: This permits the user to enter a number.
- `range`: This presents the user a control, typically a slider, to select a value within a range.
- `search`: This converts the input to a search box.
- `tel`: This is used to collect phone numbers.
- `time`: This provides a control for the user to enter a time without a time zone.
- `url`: This presents the user a control for entering a URL.
- `week`: This allows the user to enter a specific week.

You may ask yourself how some of these differ. In truth, these types are cues to the browser as to how to gather the information being requested. When these inputs types are encountered, most browsers will provide a custom control in place of the traditional textbox associated with an input.

If the `input` type isn't supported or if the browser doesn't support HTML5 (or specifically HTML5 form controls), the browser will render an input of type `text`. This is as the standard dictates. Unknown input types are to be treated as text.

Our app is already leveraging some of these new form controls. If we go to look at the form we created for adding a review, we will see that Opera Mobile presents the form as follows:

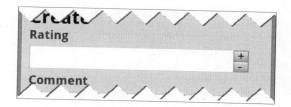

The ASP.NET MVC runtime is actually generating the following output for the rating control based on the validation rules we added from `System.ComponentModel.DataAnnotations`.

```
<input class="text-box single-line"
    data-val="true"
    data-val-number="The field Rating must be a number."
    data-val-required="The Rating field is required."
    id="Rating" name="Rating"
    type="number"
    value="" />
```

You will note that among the `data-*` attributes, the type of the input is set to `number`. Chrome and Opera see this and provide a custom input control to the user to indicate that a number is to be entered. Not only is the input customized to help the user input a number, it will actively refuse any input that cannot be converted to a number and, by proxy, enforce some of our validation rules.

Local storage

Local storage is a dictionary-like storage mechanism supported by most browser vendors. It differs from the traditional way of storing data with the client — cookies — in that information stored in a browser's local storage is not sent to the server with each request. Access to the data in local storage is through key/value pairs and each dictionary is accessible only to the site that created it.

Assume we have a variable named localStorage that is a reference to the browser's local storage mechanism. We could place information in local storage in one of the following ways:

```
localStorage["key"] = value;
localStorage.setItem("key", value);
```

Likewise, retrieving data from the dictionary would look like the following:

```
var value = localStorage["key"]
var value = localStorage.getItem("key");
```

Data is actually stored in the dictionary as a string, so you will need to do the type conversion yourself upon retrieval.

Geolocation

The geolocation API provides location-based services to the browser. If you ever need to know where your users are, this is the API for you. Invocation of this API will notify your users of its access and requires their permission.

Access to geolocation services is through the navigator.geolocation property. This property supplies a single method, getCurrentPosition, which takes a callback method as a parameter.

```
navigator.geolocation.getCurrentPosition(tell_me);
```

In the preceding example, the tell_me callback will be invoked by the geolocation API and will provide not only latitude and longitude, but also information such as speed and heading.

There are a lot of exciting possibilities when leveraging HTML5 and fortunately for us it is supported by most mobile browsers. If you have doubts about the features your target browser supports, you should look at the feature compatibility table provided at mobilehtml5.org.

CSS3

As HTML5 is to HTML 4, CSS3 is to CSS2. It is the next incarnation of cascading style sheets bringing with it several improvements, such as namespaces, regions, filters, and conditional styles.

And yet again, as with HTML5, the depth and breadth of CSS3 is enough to fill up a series of books. In fact, it is so large that the working group for CSS3 has broken the standard up into a series of modules you can view at `http://www.w3.org/Style/CSS/current-work`.

We will focus on media types, selectors, and media queries as they are applicable to mobile development, but before we start I would like to remind you all to remember when dealing with CSS the C means cascading. Styles will be applied to elements in the order they appear. Be precise with your styles and make sure your elements and styles have meaningful names.

Media types

Media types have existed for some time and are not new to CSS3, but they deserve a brief mention as most people are not familiar with them. In a nutshell, media types can be used to specify different styles for different rendering types. If I want to apply one set of styles or a stylesheet to a page when it is being viewed on a screen and one set of styles or a stylesheet to a page when it is being printed, I can use media types to control this.

```
<link href="styles.css" media="screen" rel="stylesheet">
<link href="print-styles.css" media="print" rel="stylesheet">
```

The media types supported at the time of this writing are `all`, `aural`, `braille`, `embossed`, `handheld`, `print`, `projection`, `screen`, `tty`, and `tv`.

We will largely make use of the `all` media type throughout the remainder of this book.

CSS selectors

CSS selectors provide us a mechanism to select a tag or set of tags based on a piece of selection criteria. The selection criteria may be something as simple as the type of the tag, or something much more complex such as every seventh child starting with the fourth child of a node.

There are several types of selectors and their usage varies by type, so we will briefly discuss each of the types and review a couple of samples to arm us with just enough information to be dangerous. This information will, however, allow us to do some further reading on the topic and deepen our CSS-fu.

Type selectors

CSS type selectors allow us to apply a style to all elements of a specific type. Several examples of type selectors can be found in our BrewHow app's `Site.css` file.

```
html {
    background-color: #e2e2e2;
    margin: 0;
    padding: 0;
}
```

This selector says that for each `html` tag (OK, yes, there's only one), set the `background-color`, `margin`, and `padding` attributes. Type selectors are rather straightforward.

ID selectors

ID selectors allow us to apply styling to an element with a specific ID. Note that it applies to an element as in any conforming document, and element IDs are unique. ID selectors are denoted with the # character.

```
#body {
    background-color: #efeeef;
    clear: both;
    padding-bottom: 35px;
}
```

When rendered, any element with an ID of `body` will have the preceding style applied to it.

Attribute selectors

If you want to select an element or a set of elements based on the values of an attribute or the existence of an attribute, you will want to use attribute selectors. Attribute selectors are denoted by brackets (`[]`) and their selection criteria allow you to apply conditions on the values.

```
#loginForm input[type="checkbox"],
#loginForm input[type="submit"],
```

```
#loginForm input[type="button"],
#loginForm button {
    width: auto;
}
```

This excerpt of code form our `Site.css` stylesheet sets the width of all checkbox, submit, and button inputs contained within any element with an ID of `loginForm`. Attribute selectors are not limited to the `type` attribute and they're not limited to an equivalency check. Any attribute of any element may be queried. The following table enumerates the conditions you can apply to an attribute selector:

Condition	Matches
[attr]	Matches any element with the attribute {attr}, regardless of attribute value.
[attr=value]	Matches any element with the attribute {attr} having a value of {value}.
[attr~=value]	If the attribute {attr} is a list of whitespace-separated words, the condition will match assuming one of the words is equal to {value}.
[attr|=value]	If the value of the attribute {attr} equals {value} or begins with {value-}, the condition will evaluate to `true` and result in a match.
[attr^=value]	Matches if the attribute value {attr} begins with {value}.
[attr$=value]	Matches if the attribute value {attr} ends with {value}.
[attr*=value]	If the value of the attribute {attr} contains the value {value}, the condition results in a match.

Class selectors

Classes may also be used as CSS selector criteria. A class selector is typically denoted with a dot (.).

```
.float-left {
    float: left;
}
```

Any class to which the `float-left` class is applied will have the `float: left` style applied to it.

As `class` is also an attribute of an element, you may use attribute selectors to locate and select elements of certain classes.

Universal selectors

Universal selectors are denoted by an asterisk (*). They are global and are rarely seen in practical application because their existence is implied. The example class selector presented in the previous section could also be re-written as:

```
*.float-left {
    float: left;
}
```

The asterisk makes the universal scope of the selector explicit.

Pseudo-class selectors

One of the more powerful classes of selectors in CSS3 is the pseudo-class selectors. These selectors allow us to apply simple functions to our selectors. Denoted by the use of a colon (:), pseudo-class selectors provide a mechanism to get information about the markup that is contained outside the **Document Object Model (DOM)**.

One of the most commonly seen set of pseudo-class selectors are the `:link`, `:visited`, `:active`, and `:hover` selectors that are applied to anchor tags.

```
a:link, a:visited,
a:active, a:hover {
    color: #333;
}
```

Other pseudo-class selectors provide a mechanism to retrieve the children at specific positions, checked, enabled, or disabled elements. One particularly interesting pseudo-class selector is the `:nth-child` selector that allows us to specify an occurrence and an offset for the selection. `:nth-child(4n-1)` would select every fourth child of an element starting with the third child.

CSS selectors allow us to query the elements on a page, but CSS media queries allow us to query the capabilities of the media on which the page is being displayed.

CSS media queries

CSS media queries provide a mechanism for us to selectively apply styles based on information ascertained about the features of a specific (or the current) media type. A media query involves the use of a media type and one or more feature queries that must evaluate to true before the styles associated with the query will be applied.

Media queries can be applied using the traditional media attribute of the `link` tag or using the `@media` keyword within a CSS file.

```
<link
    rel="stylesheet"
    media="all and (orientation:landscape)"
    href="landscape.css">
@media all and (orientation:landscape) { /* styles */ }
```

Media features

When combined with a media type, media features complete the media query's functionality. One important note about media features is that most features support a `min-` or `max-` prefix. For instance, the `width` media feature supports both the `min-` and `max-` prefixes meaning that not only can the width be queried, but so can the `max-width` and `min-width`.

Feature	min- or max- prefix	Description
width	Yes	Used to query the current, minimum, or maximum width of the media device.
height	Yes	Used to query the current, minimum, or maximum height of the media device.
device-width	Yes	Used to determine the actual width of the device screen. This is different than the width of the current window.
device-height	Yes	Used to determine the actual height of the device screen. This is different than the width of the current window.
orientation	No	Used to query the orientation of the media. Valid values are portrait or landscape.

If we inspect our `Site.css` stylesheet, we currently have a media query present.

```
@media only screen and (max-width: 850px)
```

We will talk about the functionality this line presents when we talk about responsive design later in this chapter.

The viewport meta tag

The last piece of information that is rather important when talking about designing for the mobile web is the `viewport meta` tag.

Most mobile browsers assume, and rightfully so, that any page they attempt to render is authored for and intended to be viewed in a desktop browser. In this scenario, mobile browsers will render the page at 980 pixels wide (typically, but some browsers may use an alternative resolution) and then scale the rendered page to fit on the screen of the device. For devices of lower resolution, even our emulated Samsung Galaxy S II in our Opera Mobile emulator with a width of 480 pixels, this means the page is rendered and then scaled down to less than 50 percent of its original size. This makes for some hard reading and leaves users frustrated.

The `viewport meta` tag, currently in our `_Layout.cshtml` file as `<meta name="viewport" content="width=device-width" />` is a `meta` tag used to instruct mobile devices as to the resolution and scaling factor with which they should render a page when displaying it to the user. Our `meta` tag, by setting the content width to the width of our device, tells the browser to render the page in native resolution, 480 pixels wide for our Opera Mobile emulator.

> There are numerous attributes and attribute values available for the `viewport meta` tag. While the settings provided here are the default ones, I recommend you read a little more about this tag and determine if there's a better value or set of values for your intended use.

And it is this value that allows us to do a little responsive design in our application.

A responsive design

And now we've come full circle. In *Chapter 3, Introducing ASP.NET MVC 4*, we talked about responsive design and what it means to develop apps that attempt to present themselves properly within any browser window, and to continually respond to changes in the size of the browser window or in the content that the page itself is displaying.

In the previous section, we learned there was a `@media` tag located in our `Site.css` file.

```
@media only screen and (max-width: 850px)
```

This media tag contains beneath it a set of styles that applies to all screen media types that have a maximum width of 850 pixels—that is to say most mobile devices.

We also learned that our `_Layout.cshtml` file contains the `viewport meta` tag telling the mobile browser to render the page in its native resolution. Let's take a moment to put it all together.

When we load any page in a web browser that has a resolution of 850 pixels or less, we will get one set of styles applied to make the page usable at that resolution. Setting the viewport to use the native resolution of the mobile device and loading this page in Opera applies the set of styles contained within the media definition.

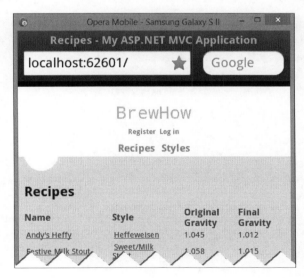

The same rules apply if the browser window on our desktop falls below 850 pixels; it receives the same treatment as our mobile emulator.

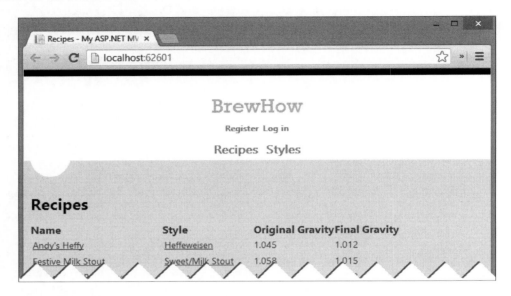

However, if we increase the resolution of a browser to a width outside the 850 pixels, say 1,024 pixels, the page looks markedly different.

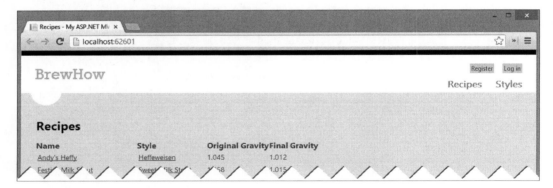

Our navigation and logo are now no longer centered, but are right and left justified respectively to make better use of the newly available horizontal resolution. Even small things such as the background for the **Log in** link have changed. Our site has adjusted to the width of the medium in which it is being displayed. This is the essence of responsive design.

A responsive list

To make our site more responsive, we will make a couple of adjustments to the recipe list. First, showing original gravity and final gravity is great for those that know how to compute the alcohol content of a recipe based on those numbers, but it shouldn't be a required skill for our users. We need to add the `PercentAlcoholByVolume` property of our `RecipeDisplayViewModel` class to the list.

Unfortunately, our list is already cramped on a mobile device. Adding another field to the display will make it practically unusable. To accommodate this, we will make the design responsive. For displays less than or equal to 600 pixels across, we will show only the alcohol by volume. If the display is greater than 600 pixels in width, we will show the alcohol by volume, original gravity, and final gravity.

We will begin by adding a style named `hide600` to `Site.css` located in the `Content` folder of our project. The style is defined as follows:

```
@media only screen and (max-width: 600px) {
    .hide600 {
        display: none;
    }
}
```

This style states that whenever the screen is below 600 pixels wide set `display` for the element to which the style is applied to `none`. This essentially hides the element. When the width of the screen goes back out beyond 600 pixels, this style is not defined. This resets the value of `display` to whatever it was by default.

We need to apply this style to the original gravity and final gravity columns. Remember to do this in the table headers, table cells, and in the JavaScript that responds to the SignalR hub. We are also going to add the `PercentAlcoholByVolume` property before the gravity fields, so remember to adjust the list in the same places. The following is the code for the adjusted table headers. The complete code can be found in the bundle accompanying this book:

```
<tr>
    <th>
        @Html.DisplayNameFor(model => model[0].Name)
    </th>
    <th>
        @Html.DisplayNameFor(model => model[0].Style)
    </th>
    <th>
```

```
            @Html.DisplayNameFor(model => model[0].PercentAlcoholByVolume)
        </th>
        <th class="hide600">
            @Html.DisplayNameFor(model => model[0].OriginalGravity)
        </th>
        <th class="hide600">
            @Html.DisplayNameFor(model => model[0].FinalGravity)
        </th>
    @if(Request.IsAuthenticated) {
        <th>
        </th>
    }
    </tr>
```

If we load the page in Google Chrome, we see that all columns are present. The width of the window is outside the 600 pixels at which we hide the gravity columns.

Our Opera Mobile browser, however, has a width of 480 pixels. Viewing the page there has a different column set.

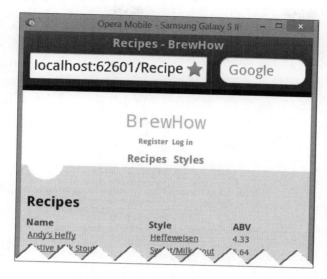

Dealing with responsive design issues isn't that difficult, but there are always situations where you have neither the time nor the desire to create an entirely responsive layout. In these scenarios, you may opt to use one of the publicly available responsive design frameworks such as ZURB's **Foundation** or Twitter **Bootstrap**. These toolkits provide you with a complete set of templates and classes to assist you in your responsive design needs.

Summary

In this chapter, we learned about HTML5 and the fact that its origins are from study and analysis of how HTML is actually used. The output of this research is a new semantic markup focused on what the content is, not how it's to be displayed. We also looked at CSS3 and its ability to best display content based on the abilities of the client through the use of selectors and media queries. Using these technologies in conjunction with browser support for viewport control, we can control the user experience through a technique known as responsive design.

In the next chapter, we will learn about the functionality built into ASP.NET MVC 4 that allows us to target specific mobile devices, and we will customize our application to provide a better mobile experience to our users.

13
Extending Support for the Mobile Web

In the previous chapter, we learned how to design and style our app in such a way that it looked and functioned more or less the same on both a mobile platform and a desktop browser. The responsive design approach may be fine for some apps, but there are some things to be considered before making the final decision of allowing the client to handle all mobile presentations.

Developing a mobile web app requires us to present information to our users quickly and easily with as little overhead as possible. While these are good design goals in general, the usage patterns of mobile users dictate these goals to be the focus of our design efforts. Mobile users want to launch our app, get the information they need, and get out. To accommodate this usage scenario, we may decide we need a substantially different experience than what can be accomplished through client-side presentation determinations through responsive design, media queries, and viewport tags.

The alternative to client-side determination is, of course, to make presentation determinations on the server before the data is sent to the client. This approach has its own set of drawbacks. For starters, determining the capabilities of a client on the server is nontrivial. Even if you account for every device at the time of your app's release, new devices with new capabilities are being constantly released.

You also run the risk of duplicating a substantial amount of code on the server in views that are specific to a mobile device or mobile device family. The ideal solution, then, is to make presentation decisions through a combination of client-side and server-side determination.

It just so happens that ASP.NET MVC 4 ships with support for making server-side presentation determinations that we can couple with our existing client-side responsive design logic.

Mobile views

If we examine our layout page, `_Layout.cshtml`, we see that a bulk of our app's presentation layout is contained within this file. It then seems logical that if we create a layout page specific to mobile devices, we would certainly be on the fast path to offloading some of the presentation logic from the client to the server.

As we have already seen, convention over configuration is pervasive in the ASP.NET MVC 4 framework. One of the slickest extension points in my opinion is the ability to use a `.Mobile` extension within the name of a view, partial view, or layout to target mobile devices. We will begin extending our support to the mobile web with a mobile layout.

A .Mobile layout

Begin by creating a copy of the `_Layout.cshtml` file in `~/Views/Shared`, and rename the copy to `_Layout.Mobile.cshtml`. The contents of the `Shared` folder is shown in the following screenshot:

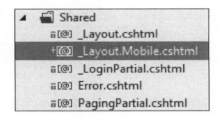

Open up the new `_Layout.Mobile.cshtml` file and locate the line used to display the app title.

```
<p class="site-title">@Html.ActionLink("BrewHow", "Index", "Recipe",
new { area = "" }, null)</p>
```

Replace the text `BrewHow` with `BrewHow Mobile`. We will use this text to validate that our new layout is being used when requests are made by a mobile device.

```
<p class="site-title">@Html.ActionLink("BrewHow Mobile", "Index",
"Recipe", new { area = "" }, null)</p>
```

We have now created a layout page that will be used by all requests from a mobile browser. Seriously, that's all we had to do. If we launch our application in our Opera Mobile emulator, we will see that the new mobile layout page is indeed being used by the runtime as is evident by the presence of our title change.

To prove this is not a trick, here is how the page appears in Google Chrome:

As mentioned at the start of this section, this technique works for all views, not just layouts. Anytime we want to create views and partial views that target mobile devices, we can simply append .Mobile to the name of the view.

Mobile users need quick and easy access to the information. Keeping this in mind, we should modify the remainder of our views to provide the minimum amount of necessary information in the order of importance. It's time to mobilize BrewHow.

Mobilizing BrewHow

Let's examine the home page of our app—a page with the primary purpose of returning a list of recipes to the user—shown in the following screenshot:

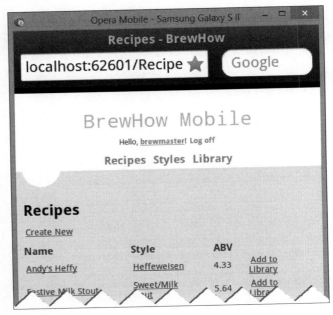

Our recipe list page begins with a title that serves as a link to return to the home page, a greeting, and a list of navigation links across the top of our page allowing the user to get to the **Recipes** list (the home page), a **Styles** list, and their **Library** page. This is followed by a page title and a link to create a recipe. It is only after all of this page filler that we arrive at the content of the page, a list of recipes presenting the name, style, and alcohol content of each recipe. There is an additional link to add a recipe to the user's library if they are logged in. We also need to keep in mind that we are hiding some of the content based on our responsive design effort in *Chapter 12, Designing Your App for Mobile Devices*.

If we make an honest assessment of our app as it appears in our Opera Mobile emulator, it's rather hard for us to actually see the content. We certainly couldn't be able to read it if we were walking, exercising, or doing any other activity we're often doing while using our mobile devices. We need to address these shortcomings.

Removing content

The first thing we need to do is remove the extraneous content from our recipe list. This is, by far, the biggest improvement we can make to our app. It not only brings to the forefront the relevant content, but it will also allow us to better utilize the smaller screen inherent with most mobile devices.

Let's start from the top. The title and greeting are useful to the user. While we could style them to make them smaller, they serve a need: to notify the user where they are and to notify them they are logged into the app.

With regards to the navigation links, if we think about how a user will use our app, they're typically going to login, search for a recipe or find one in their library, view the information about the recipe, and leave. They're almost never going to click the Styles link. The **Styles** link can be removed.

Our recipe list also requires some attention as you can see in the following screenshot:

Create New

Name	Style	ABV	
Andy's Heffy	Heffeweisen	4.33	Add to Library
Festive Milk Stout	Sweet/Milk Stout	5.64	Add to Library
Respondant Rye Brown Ale	Brown Ale	5.25	Add to Library
Sweaty Brown Ale	Brown Ale	5.25	Add to Library

Page 1 of 1

Alcohol content isn't going to be the primary search criteria for must users. We can remove this column, as well as the two hidden columns for original and final gravities. This will create a little bit of space for the recipe name and style so that our display isn't so cramped.

It would seem that the only change to be made to the _Layout.Mobile.cs file is to remove the **Styles** link. The bulk of our changes are going to occur on the pages containing the actual content. Go ahead and remove the **Styles** link from the _Layout.Mobile.cs file.

As for the content pages, start by copying the `Index.cshtml` file in our `Views\ Recipe` folder and rename the copied file to `Index.Mobile.cshtml`. The new content of the `Recipe` folder is shown in the following screenshot:

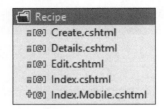

Open the mobile view you just created in Visual Studio and apply the identified edits. The list in the file should match the following code:

```
<table id ="recipe-list">
    <tr>
        <th>
            @Html.DisplayNameFor(model => model[0].Name)
        </th>
        <th>
            @Html.DisplayNameFor(model => model[0].Style)
        </th>
        <th>
@if(Request.IsAuthenticated) {
        <th>
        </th>
}
    </tr>
@foreach (var item in Model) {
    <tr>
        <td>
            @Html.ActionLink(
            item.Name,
            "Details",
            new { id=item.RecipeId, slug=item.Slug })
        </td>
        <td>
            @Html.ActionLink(
            Html.DisplayFor(modelItem => item.Style).ToHtmlString(),
            "Style",
            "Recipe",
            new { style = item.StyleSlug },
```

```
                    null)
                </td>
    @if (Request.IsAuthenticated) {
            <td>
                @Html.ActionLink(
                "Add to Library",
                "Create",
                "Library",
                new { id = item.RecipeId },
                new { @class = "add-recipe", data_id = @item.RecipeId })
            </td>
    }
        </tr>
    }
    </table>
```

We should make the same changes to the library's `Index` view.

As for the view showing the details for a recipe, there is a lot of information that can be removed. Create a `Details.Mobile.cshtml` file and remove category, original gravity, final gravity, alcohol by volume, and contributor from the new mobile view. We can also remove the `Name` field from the `Details` view, as it is presented in the title of the page and in the page header.

We are now showing minimal functional content for our users. All we need to do now is prioritize the order in which it is presented.

Prioritizing content

While it is possible that users of our app will be adding new beer recipes from their mobile devices—tablets are mobile devices after all, it is certainly of lower importance than being able to find a recipe. By placing the link to create a new recipe at the top of our list, we are forcing the user to scroll down to get to the content they're looking for. We don't want to take away this ability; we simply want to relocate it at the bottom of our page.

In our `Index.Mobile.cshtml` view, move the following code to the bottom of the view below the paging control. Feel free to change the text on the link to `Create Recipe`.

```
<p>
    @if (Request.IsAuthenticated) {
        @Html.ActionLink("Create New", "Create")
    }
</p>
```

If we build and launch the app in our Opera Mobile emulator, we should see a substantially different, and much more mobile friendly, user experience awaiting us.

The support for mobile templates is a pretty powerful gift from Microsoft. But with great power comes great responsibility. We really need to understand how this is working.

How it works

You're never too old to believe in magic. Unfortunately, magic is not what's at the root of this process. The .NET Framework maintains a list of "known" browsers and their capabilities. When an incoming request is processed, the list of known browsers is consulted to determine if the user agent of the client is a match for a known browser. If a match is found and the capability of that browser identifies it as a mobile browser, the request will be processed using any `.Mobile` views that exist.

On standard 64-bit installations of the .NET Framework, the list of browsers is located on the filesystem at `C:\Windows\Microsoft.NET\Framework64\v4.0.30319\Config\Browsers`. The content of this folder is pictured in the following screenshot:

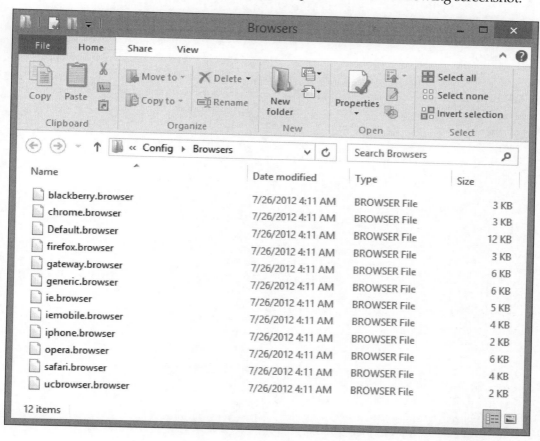

If we look inside one of these files, we see a fairly simple XML file. The following is the content of the browser definition file, `iphone.browser`. This file contains the identifying information and capabilities for iPhone, iPad, and iPod.

```
<browsers>
    <!-- Mozilla/5.0 (iPhone; U; CPU like Mac OS X; en)
AppleWebKit/420+ (KHTML, like Gecko) Version/3.0 Mobile/1A543a
Safari/419.3  -->
    <gateway id="IPhone" parentID="Safari">
        <identification>
            <userAgent match="iPhone" />
        </identification>
```

```xml
        <capabilities>
          <capability name="isMobileDevice" value="true" />
          <capability name="mobileDeviceManufacturer" value="Apple" />
          <capability name="mobileDeviceModel" value="IPhone" />
          <capability name="canInitiateVoiceCall" value="true" />
        </capabilities>
    </gateway>


    <!-- Mozilla/5.0 (iPod; U; CPU like Mac OS X; en)
AppleWebKit/420.1 (KHTML, like Gecko) Version/3.0 Mobile/4A93
Safari/419.3  -->
    <gateway id="IPod" parentID="Safari">
        <identification>
            <userAgent match="iPod" />
        </identification>


        <capabilities>
            <capability name="isMobileDevice"            value="true"
/>
            <capability name="mobileDeviceManufacturer" value="Apple"
/>
            <capability name="mobileDeviceModel"         value="IPod"
/>
        </capabilities>
    </gateway>


  <!-- Mozilla/5.0 (iPad; U; CPU OS 4_3 like Mac OS X; en-us)
AppleWebKit/533.17.9 (KHTML, like Gecko) Version/5.0.2 Mobile/8F191
Safari/6533.18.5  -->
  <gateway id="IPad" parentID="Safari">
    <identification>
      <userAgent match="iPad" />
    </identification>


    <capabilities>
      <capability name="isMobileDevice" value="true" />
      <capability name="mobileDeviceManufacturer" value="Apple" />
      <capability name="mobileDeviceModel" value="IPad" />
    </capabilities>
  </gateway>
</browsers>
```

The `gateway` node in the definition file is used to identify a specific browser or browser family. In the `iphone.browser` file, each gateway node contains an attribute named `parentID` and each attribute has a value of `Safari`. What you are seeing is browser definition inheritance.

For the iOS platform that powers each of Apple's mobile device brands, the browser is a derivative of Safari. Therefore, each browser definition in the `iphone.browser` definition file inherits the user agent matches and capabilities of the `gateway` node with an `id` of Safari. The capabilities of the Safari browser are defined in the `safari.browser` file.

If we want to add support for new mobile browsers, we can certainly add new files into this collection but that seems a little tedious. The argument could be made that if we're trying to identify a device that falls outside of those captured with the `.Mobile` extension, we're likely trying to do something device-specific. The ASP.NET MVC 4 Framework provides us with a simpler way of targeting those specific devices than editing browser definition files—display modes.

Serious detection

If you're serious about browser detection and capability testing on the server side, there are several public (`http://wurfl.sourceforge.net/`) and commercial products (`http://51degrees.mobi/`) available to use in lieu of these methods.

Display modes

Display modes are new to ASP.NET MVC 4. They allow us to target specific devices based on some matching criteria contained in an `HttpContext`, typically a user-agent string. Upon a match, the display mode identifies the suffix appended to any view specific to the device. It is actually this technology underlying the `.Mobile` suffix we just learned about.

Display modes are represented by an implementation of the `IDisplayMode` interface defined in `System.Web.WebPages`. At application startup, implementations of `IDisplayMode` can be registered with the current `DisplayModeProvider`.

We will be creating and registering an instance of `IDisplayMode` for the Asus Nexus 7. Our new display mode will use a suffix of `nexus7` for any Asus Nexus 7 specific views. This means that the layout file `_Layout.nexus7.cshtml` will be used for any request to our site made by an Asus Nexus 7.

Supporting Asus Nexus 7

We must first identify a request from an Asus Nexus 7 with the device's browser's user-agent string if we are to effectively target it. The Nexus 7 ships with Google Chrome for Android as the default browser, and this browser identifies itself with the following user-agent string (your definition may be slightly different):

```
Mozilla/5.0 (Linux; Android 4.1.1; Nexus 7 Build/JRO03D)
AppleWebKit/535.19 (KHTML, like Gecko) Chrome/18.0.1025.166
Safari/535.19
```

Right away, we can identify the string Nexus 7 within the user agent. We will use that to target the device.

Creating the display mode

To target the Nexus 7, we need to create an instance of a class that implements IDisplayMode. The IDisplayMode implementation must satisfy two criteria; it must identify a request as coming from a Nexus 7 and it must specify the suffix for views specific to the device.

The .NET Framework ships with a default implementation of IDisplayMode named DefaultDisplayMode that is sufficient for our needs. The DefaultDisplayMode class has a constructor that takes a single parameter used to specify the suffix associated with the display mode.

```
var nexus7DisplayMode = new DefaultDisplayMode("nexus7");
```

The DefaultDisplayMode class also has a ContextCondition property that is defined as follows:

```
public Func<HttpContextBase, bool> ContextCondition { get; set; }
```

We can use this lambda property to interrogate the HttpContext of an incoming request, and see if the user-agent string contains the string Nexus 7, thus identifying the request as coming from our targeted device.

Our full DefaultDisplayMode definition is as follows:

```
var nexus7DisplayMode = new DefaultDisplayMode("nexus7")
{
    ContextCondition = (context =>
        context
            .GetOverriddenUserAgent()
            .IndexOf(
```

```
                "Nexus 7",
                StringComparison.OrdinalIgnoreCase
            ) >= 0)
    };
```

Registering the display mode

Display modes need to be registered with the display mode provider when our application starts and before any inbound request is processed. Registering our display mode with the display mode provider is as simple as the following:

```
DisplayModeProvider
    .Instance
    .Modes
    .Insert(0, nexus7DisplayMode );
```

We are inserting the display mode for the Nexus 7 at position 0 because we want it to supersede any other display modes that may match the device. Much like routes, the first match found is the one to be used.

To be consistent with our other code, we need to put this code in the App_Start folder of our project and invoke it from the Application_Start method of the MvcApplication class in our Global.asax.cs file.

Right-click on the App_Start folder and create a new class named DisplayModeConfig.cs with the following content:

```
public class DisplayModeConfig
{
    public static void RegisterDisplayModes()
    {
        DisplayModeProvider
            .Instance
            .Modes
            .Insert(0,
                new DefaultDisplayMode("nexus7")
                {
                    ContextCondition = (context =>
                        context
                            .GetOverriddenUserAgent()
                            .IndexOf(
                                "Nexus 7",
```

```
                            StringComparison
                                .OrdinalIgnoreCase
                ) >= 0)
            }
        );
    }
}
```

In the `Application_Start` method of the `MvcApplication` class in `Global.asax.cs`, add the following line of code:

```
DisplayModeConfig.RegisterDisplayModes();
```

We're now ready to test our work.

Testing with Nexus 7

The last step is to see if we've successfully defined and registered our display mode for Nexus 7. Make a copy of the `_Layout.Mobile.cshtml` file in the `Views/Shared` folder and name it `_Layout.Nexus7.cshtml`. After renaming the file, open it up and change the title from `BrewHow Mobile` to `BrewHow Mobile Nexus 7`. When you are done, build and launch the site.

If you have a Nexus 7 handy, navigate to the site on your local network. You should be greeted with our Nexus 7 specific page:

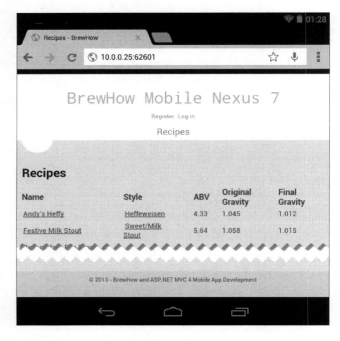

Accessing IIS Express from your local network requires you to edit the address bindings in the `IISExpress\config\applicationhost.config` file located in your `Documents` folder. You may also need to launch Visual Studio 2012 as an administrator.

Notice that our display mode for the Nexus 7 supersedes any other matches. If a display mode matches, the suffix and only the suffix associated with the display mode will be used. As you can see in the preceding screenshot, we were presented with the standard list within the Nexus 7 layout master because we matched a suffix of `nexus7`.

Summary

In this chapter, we learned about creating mobile views and about targeting specific devices with tailored content. The goal was the quick and accurate delivery of content to our users. These server-side tools are best used in combination with some client-side presentation determinations. Coupled with the responsive design techniques we learned in *Chapter 12, Designing Your App for Mobile Devices*, it's possible to build truly solid web apps that function well on both standard desktop and mobile platforms.

If, however, we want to create a truly mobile experience for our users, we have to take our mobile app to the next level. In the next chapter, we examine one of the most popular client-side presentation toolkits available: jQuery mobile. With jQuery mobile, we will modify BrewHow to look and feel like a native mobile app.

14
Improving the User Experience with jQuery Mobile

In the previous chapter, we learned about creating views that are specific to mobile devices. These views used responsive design and adaptive rendering techniques in addition to content alteration to make our app look and perform better within the user's browser. With that said, it still looked and felt like a web app. What we really want to do is provide our users with an experience that will make them forget they are looking at a web app. We can provide this experience using jQuery Mobile.

jQuery Mobile is a user interface framework targeting mobile browsers. It is intended to help provide a device-native look-and-feel to mobile web apps with a write-once approach.

jQuery Mobile is able to target multiple browsers simultaneously because it employs a progressive enhancement approach. Simply stated, progressive enhancement is a design methodology allowing for the baseline content and layout to target a wide array of browsers. As the content is displayed to the user, enhancements within the capability of the viewing browser are made to the content via CSS and JavaScript.

Arguably the most appealing feature of jQuery Mobile is the use of semantic markup. Through the use of custom data attributes, the data-*, attributes we learned about in our discussion of HTML5 in *Chapter 12, Designing Your App for Mobile Devices*, we can mark HTML tags as jQuery Mobile widgets. It is then, through progressive enhancement, that only the widgets capable of being displayed to the user are enhanced with a mobile look-and-feel.

You can also instantiate jQuery Mobile widgets directly if you decide you do not want to use custom data attributes to provide presentation hints in your markup, but you will be missing out on a very powerful feature of the framework.

The best way to see how simple jQuery Mobile is to use is to actually use it, so let's get started.

Installing jQuery Mobile

Had we started our app using the Mobile Application template, we would have the jQuery Mobile library available to us immediately. Since we started our app using the Internet Application template, we need to add the library to our project. We will install it from a NuGet package using the **Package Manager Console**.

The jQuery Mobile NuGet package contains a file named _Layout.Mobile.cshtml, the same name as the mobile layout we created in the prior chapter. For us to install the package properly, we need first to delete the _Layout.Mobile.cshtml file from our existing project. It will be replaced with the one in the package. Right-click on the _Layout.Mobile.cshtml file in our project and delete it. While removing layouts, go ahead and remove the Nexus 7 layout as well. We want all mobile devices to target the jQuery Mobile layouts.

Now we can open the **Package Manager Console** by selecting **Library Package Manager** from the **Tools** menu and install the jQuery Mobile MVC package by executing the following within the console:

```
Install-Package jQuery.Mobile.MVC
```

The installation of this package modifies our project by adding a few new files in addition to _Layout.Mobile.cshtml. In short, we should find the following files included in our project:

- jQuery Mobile
- jQuery Mobile CSS files and supporting images
- jQuery
- _ViewSwitcher.cshtml, a partial view providing the ability to toggle between desktop and mobile views
- The ViewSwitcherController.cs file containing the controller used to back the view switcher partial
- A new jQuery Mobile bundle definition in BundleMobileConfig.cs

These files represent the content of the jQuery Mobile MVC NuGet package as of package version 1.0.0.

Enabling the jQuery Mobile bundle

The jQuery Mobile package includes bundles for the CSS and jQuery Mobile libraries. These bundles are defined within the `BundleMobileConfig.cs` file that has been added in the `App_Start` folder of our project.

After installing the package, we are presented with a `readme.txt` file containing the following text:

To enable default mobile view, you must add the following line as the last line in the `Application_Start` method in `Global.asax.cs`:

```
BundleMobileConfig.RegisterBundles(BundleTable.Bundles);
```

Let's open up the `Global.asax.cs` file and do as the `readme.txt` file instructs to register our mobile bundle:

```
ServiceLocatorConfig.RegisterTypes();
AreaRegistration.RegisterAllAreas();
WebApiConfig.Register(GlobalConfiguration.Configuration);
FilterConfig.RegisterGlobalFilters(GlobalFilters.Filters);
RouteConfig.RegisterRoutes(RouteTable.Routes);
BundleConfig.RegisterBundles(BundleTable.Bundles);
BundleMobileConfig.RegisterBundles(BundleTable.Bundles);
AuthConfig.RegisterAuth();
DisplayModeConfig.RegisterDisplayModes();
```

At this point, our application is now enabled for mobile devices with the jQuery Mobile environment, so let's look at what's new.

Viewing the results

Before we can launch the app, we need to make a small change to the new `_Layout.Mobile.cshtml` file. Our views are looking for a section in the layout named `Scripts`. This section does not exist in the mobile layout provided by the jQuery Mobile package. This is simple enough to fix; simply add the following code to the `_Layout.Mobile.cshtml` file before the closing body tag:

```
@RenderSection("Scripts", false)
```

Now, if we build and launch our BrewHow app, there will be no difference when viewing the app within Chrome, but the differences are rather dramatic when viewing the app within our Opera Mobile emulator:

This mobile version of the site bears little resemblance to our prior mobile version outside of content. Let's examine the new layout file for our mobile app to learn how jQuery Mobile is being used to create this new look and feel.

jQuery Mobile's layout

The new jQuery Mobile layout is rather simple. In fact, it's much smaller than the initial mobile layout we built in the previous chapter:

```
<!DOCTYPE html>
<html>
  <head>
    <meta charset="utf-8" />
    <title>@ViewBag.Title</title>
    <meta name="viewport" content="width=device-width" />
    @Styles.Render("~/Content/Mobile/css",
      "~/Content/jquerymobile/css")
    @Scripts.Render("~/bundles/jquery", "~/bundles/jquerymobile")
    <script>
      $(document).ready(function () {
```

```
        $.mobile.ajaxEnabled = false;
      });
    </script>
  </head>
  <body>

    <div data-role="page" data-theme="a">
      @Html.Partial("_ViewSwitcher")

      <div data-role="header">
        <h1>@ViewBag.Title</h1>
      </div>

      <div data-role="content">
        @RenderSection("featured", false)
        @RenderBody()
      </div>

    </div>
    @RenderSection("Scripts", false)
  </body>
</html>
```

Our new layout includes familiar elements such as the viewport `meta` tag. Also note that some elements though similar have change. For example, the styles and scripts bundles now include the jQuery Mobile styles and scripts identified in the `BundleMobileConfig.cs` file.

The rest of the changes to our mobile app are all accomplished via the magic of jQuery Mobile. Some of the changes are triggered off of markup hints such as the `data-*` attributes. Other changes, such as touch-friendly controls, are provided automatically by the framework. So let's dig a little deeper, shall we?

Data-roles and data attributes

When we learned about data attributes (`data-*`) when covering HTML5 in *Chapter 12, Designing Your App for Mobile Devices,* we learned they are really syntactic sugar. They may be used to store additional information about an HTML element but have no effect on the rendering or display of that element. This functionality is the key to jQuery's progressive enhancement. It uses this semantic markup to convert standard HTML elements into jQuery Mobile widgets. Specifically, jQuery Mobile looks for HTML elements having a `data-role` attribute and attempts to convert them to the jQuery Mobile widget identified in the attribute's value. This conversion includes the application of a control theme and widget-specific behaviors.

In our new layout, we use the `data-role` attribute to identify three standard HTML elements as jQuery Mobile widgets: `page`, `header`, and `content`. Other widget types available include buttons, list views, sliders, checkboxes, radio buttons, site navigation, and so on. The list is pretty exhaustive but is detailed completely on the jQuery Mobile site.

Each particular widget, as we will soon see, also supports a set of `data-*` data attributes that define the behavior of the widget identified in the `data-role`. For example, we could apply the data attribute `data-fixed` to the `div` with the `data-role` of `header`. The application of this attribute would prevent the header from scrolling with the rest of the page content.

And yes, while it is possible for you to declare widgets dynamically within the JavaScript, the true power of jQuery Mobile is in the semantic markup.

Form elements

In addition to using semantic markup to identify widgets, jQuery Mobile gives us several things for free. Out of the box, it will convert our standard HTML form elements to touch-friendly widgets. To do this, the jQuery Mobile library parses the DOM of our app and applies new styles, styles defined in the jQuery Mobile CSS bundle, to the form elements it finds. We do not need to provide any hints in the form of `data-roles`, we simply need to encapsulate the elements within a `form` tag and make sure each input field has an associated label.

When done properly, the change in appearance can be pretty dramatic as illustrated on our login screen:

Our login page has nice rounded corners on our inputs. The checkbox for remembering the login of our users is now touch-friendly and spans the width of the screen. The buttons for logging in with BrewHow credentials or logging in with Google have also been modified to be easier to press on a mobile device. All of this is free provided we maintain valid HTML5 markup.

Themes

If you've ever used jQuery UI, you may be familiar with the extensive theming capability it provides. jQuery Mobile follows in the footsteps of its older sibling in this regard. It has extensive support for theming throughout, supporting a total of 26 themes. Each theme is identified as a letter of the alphabet.

To apply a particular theme, simply add or change the `data-theme` data attribute to the letter of the alphabet used to identify the theme. Each widget, with the exception of headers and footers, inherits the theme of its parent unless explicitly assigned a different theme. Headers and footers default to theme a unless explicitly configured to use a different theme.

The default layout for the mobile template sets the theme on the element with the data role of page:

```
<div data-role="page" data-theme="a">
```

Following is the login page with theme "e" applied:

This was done simply by changing the value of the `data-theme` attribute from a to e.

$.mobile

In addition to changing the look of an app, jQuery Mobile will use other progressive enhancement techniques to try and make a mobile app feel as native to the device as possible. To accomplish this, jQuery Mobile will attempt to handle all requests for content asynchronously using AJAX techniques. Once the content has been retrieved, the framework then employs transitions such as sliding content in and out to better mimic a native app.

While this behavior certainly provides a better experience for the user, it alters the order and existence of the events one might be accustomed to seeing fired by jQuery or other libraries. If you are familiar with this behavior and are developing new applications, this change might not be problematic. If, however, you're converting existing apps to be more mobile friendly, are leveraging third-party libraries that hook certain page-level events such as `document.ready`, or a combination of the two, this change is significant. If you're not aware of the behavior, it can be down-right impossible to debug.

Knowing that alterations to a typical app event lifecycle would be pretty jarring, the authors of the jQuery Mobile library provided us with the `$.mobile` object we can use to override some global behaviors. Examining our new layout page shows the packages of the NuGet jQuery Mobile package have turned off these transitions knowing they're likely to cause us problems until we're familiar with the intricacies of the library:

```
<script>
  $(document).ready(function () {
    $.mobile.ajaxEnabled = false;
  });
</script>
```

jQuery Mobile also supports new events such as `mobileinit`. While our app will function fine by applying this particular overriding behavior within the `document.ready` handler, it should be noted that jQuery Mobile will begin applying markup enhancements as soon as it loads, which may be long before the `document.ready` event fires. The `mobileinit` event fires when jQuery Mobile itself is started and any overrides to the global behaviors should really be applied in response to this event notification.

View switcher

While not part of jQuery Mobile, the jQuery Mobile layout comes with a very useful partial control that can be used to toggle between the desktop and mobile versions of our app. The view switcher is separated into a partial view (_ViewSwitcher.chstml) for embedding within a view and a controller (ViewSwitcherController) used to handle requests to toggle between app versions:

```
@Html.Partial("_ViewSwitcher")
```

The partial control, itself, is fairly simple; it passes two values to ViewSwitcherController. The first value represents whether or not to use the mobile version of the site. The second value is the URL to which the user should return after the request has been processed. To accomplish the override, the controller leverages a new extension method in ASP.NET MVC 4, named SetOverriddenBrowser:

```
public RedirectResult SwitchView(bool mobile, string returnUrl) {
  if (Request.Browser.IsMobileDevice == mobile)
    HttpContext.ClearOverriddenBrowser();
  else
    HttpContext.SetOverriddenBrowser(mobile ?
      BrowserOverride.Mobile : BrowserOverride.Desktop);

  return Redirect(returnUrl);
}
```

Internally, the SetOverriddenBrowser method sets a cookie within the browser. This cookie is used by the runtime to evaluate which version of the site should be returned. If present, the value within the cookie is used. If the cookie is not present, then the default display mode for the user-agent making the request is used, be that .Mobile or a custom version like the one we created in the previous chapter.

Now knowing how all of these pieces work together, let's apply some jQuery Mobile functionality to the rest of BrewHow to make it a truly unique mobile experience.

Mobilizing BrewHow

By installing the jQuery Mobile NuGet package and using the new layout template, we could declare success on mobilizing our site. It does provide a lot of functionality out of the box and it may be sufficient for a good portion of sites out there. We, however, are looking for a much more native experience for our users. To provide this, we need to take some UI queues from the mobile apps we use on a day-to-day basis and incorporate that knowledge with what we've learned about developing for the mobile web into our app.

Adjusting the header

Most mobile apps that we use on a day-to-day basis provide us with a header providing some basic functionality or, at the very least, the title of the app. Our app should be no different.

In our header, we should include navigation to return back to the starting page of our app: the recipe list. We also want the user to know they're running the BrewHow mobile app so we should probably include a simple title. Given the user is, in fact, a user, there should be some mechanism provided to them to log in and log out of our site. Finally, we want our header to include the basic site of navigation.

Open up the _Layout.Mobile.cshtml file and replace the content of the header tag with the following code:

```
<header data-role="header">
  <a href="~/"
    data-icon="home"
    data-iconpos="notext">Home
  </a>
  <h1>BrewHow</h1>
  @Html.Partial("_LoginPartial")
  @if (Request.IsAuthenticated)
  {
    <nav data-role="navbar">
      <ul>
        <li>@Html.ActionLink(
          "Recipes",
          "Index",
          "Recipe",
          new { area = "" },
          null)
        </li>
        <li>@Html.ActionLink(
          "My Library",
          "Index",
          "Library",
          new { area = "" },
          null)
        </li>
      </ul>
    </nav>
  }
</header>
```

The other piece of code we need to modify for this functionality is the partial view for logging in: _LoginPartial.cshtml. We need to operate within the constraints placed upon us by our users' mobile devices. Showing registration and login links for unauthenticated users or an entire greeting to users currently authenticated will not fit within the space on most mobile devices.

To that end, we need to create a new partial login view for our app. Copy the _LoginPartial.cshtml file in the Shared views folder and rename the copied version _LoginPartial.Mobile.cshtml. Replace the contents of the file with the following contents:

```
@if (Request.IsAuthenticated) {
  <a href="javascript:document.getElementById('logoutForm')
    .submit()"
    data-role="button"
    class="ui-btn-right">
    Log off
  </a>
  using (Html.BeginForm(
    "LogOff",
    "Account",
    FormMethod.Post,
    new { id = "logoutForm" }))
  {
    @Html.AntiForgeryToken()
  }
}
else
{
  @Html.ActionLink(
    "Log in",
    "Login",
    "Account",
    new { area = "" },
    new { data_role="button", @class="ui-btn-right"})
}
```

The new login control will only be used for mobile devices and shows a single button to login and logout dependent upon the authenticated state of the user.

For anonymous users, our app now presents a header similar to the following:

For authenticated users, the navigation appears and should look similar to the following:

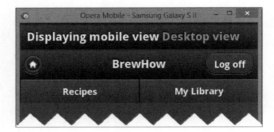

Let's examine each of the elements now present in our mobile layout.

The home button

The home button placed at the top-left of our app's header is the rendered output of the following markup:

```
<a href="~/"
   data-icon="home"
   data-iconpos="notext">Home
</a>
```

This code is simply an anchor that has two `data-*` attributes associated with it. jQuery Mobile supports several icons within the CSS files accompanying the package. To instruct jQuery to render an icon as part of a widget, we simply use the `data-icon` data attribute and set the value to one of the names supported.

Only select elements support the `data-icon` attribute. While the list of elements is limited, the entire list of icons is supported by any element supporting the data-icon attribute.

Similarly, the `data-iconpos` data attribute instructs the jQuery Mobile framework where to position the icon in relation to any text within the control.

An exhaustive list of values for `data-icon` and `data-iconpos` can be found at `http://jquerymobile.com/demos/1.1.2/docs/buttons/buttons-icons.html` at the time of this writing.

Logging in users

The appearance of our app for authenticated state has been greatly simplified in the mobile version. Instead of displaying login and register links to unauthenticated users and a greeting and logoff link to authenticated users, our mobile app simply provides a button to login or logout.

We simplified this process for a couple of reasons. First, the primary function of the app is to allow users to find recipes. While its true authenticated users may wish to pull recipes from their library, they may also simply open the app to pull a recipe from the recipe list and have no need to authenticate with the site.

The second reason for simplifying the prompting is due to space constraints on a mobile device. There simply isn't room to display register and login links to unauthenticated users. We, likewise, cannot display a greeting in the header. For the mobile version we have sacrificed the greeting entirely and are providing access to the registration process from the login page of our app where it has been all along. In today's connected world, most users can assume they will be allowed to create an account from the login page and we have designed our app with that assumption in mind.

Site navigation

The first thing to point out about navigation is that it is only available to users who have logged into the app. Adhering to the tenets of mobile app development we learned early on, we need only present information relevant to the user for the task they want to accomplish. Since only authenticated users can have a library of recipes available to them, unauthenticated users would have a single element within the navigation bar. Given the navigation bar takes up a rather large portion of the user's screen, it seems rather wasteful to take up this space with a single function, so we remove the navigation bar when users are using our app anonymously.

To apply the jQuery Mobile styling to the navigation elements contained within the `nav` element of our layout, we have simply added a `data-role` attribute with a value of `navbar`. This instructs jQuery to render the element as a `navbar` widget:

```
<nav data-role="navbar">
```

Creating a footer

Within the BrewHow app, there's not a lot of information we need to place within the footer. The desktop version of our app simply displays a copyright notice and while that may be useful, it is certainly not required for our mobile site as the space can best be used in other ways.

For BrewHow, we should move the view switcher out of the header and into the footer. By placing this at the bottom of the screen, we allow more relevant content to be placed higher up in the visible window of the app. To create a jQuery Mobile footer, we simply add the `data-role` of `footer` to the `footer` element in our mobile layout template:

```
<footer data-role="footer" data-position="fixed">
  @Html.Partial("_ViewSwitcher")
</footer>
```

You will note we also have a `data-position` data attribute in our `footer` element. The `data-position` attribute has a value of `fixed`. This attribute and value pair locks the footer at the bottom of the screen preceding any scrollable content:

Desktop footer

The desktop footer for our app needs to be adjusted as well. If a user on a mobile device elects to switch to the desktop version of our app they may need the ability to return to the mobile view. Making this change is pretty straightforward. We simply add the view switcher control to the desktop footer:

```
<footer>
  <div class="content-wrapper">
    <div class="float-left">
      <p>&copy; @DateTime.Now.Year - My ASP.NET MVC
        Application</p>
    </div>
  </div>
  @Html.Partial("_ViewSwitcher")
</footer>
```

The view switcher can be seen as it appears in the desktop footer as shown in the following screenshot:

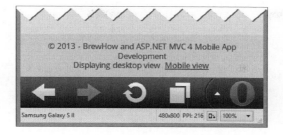

Having done a rework of our app's appearance, let's shift our focus to adjusting the content.

Configuring content

The primary purpose of our app is to collect and share homebrew recipes. These recipes are the content driver for our app. As such, we need to make them fully accessible in our mobile web app. To do this, we need to make some adjustments to how the content is laid out.

Recipe list

The recipe list is still being displayed as tabular data. The problem with this is that a table display is something not typically associated with a native mobile app. Further, when we display multiple columns across a screen with a vertical orientation, a good portion of the data will be wrapped or, in the case of a jQuery Mobile enabled app, occluded by adjacent columns. We need to convert the table to something more suitable for a mobile device display.

The jQuery Mobile listview

jQuery Mobile provides a listview widget we can use to display the recipes contained in our app. It is, as you might have guessed by now, defined through the use of the `data-role` data attribute. When applying a `data-role` value of `listview`, we can convert a standard HTML list into a jQuery Mobile listview widget. Following is the markup for the modified mobile `Index` view for `RecipeController`:

```
@model BrewHow
   .ViewModels
   .ITypedPagedResult
   <BrewHow.ViewModels.RecipeDisplayViewModel>
@{
```

```
    ViewBag.Title = ViewBag.Title ?? "Recipes";
}
<ul data-role="listview">
@foreach (var item in Model)
{
  <li>
    @Html.ActionLink(item.Name, "Details", new
    {
      id=item.RecipeId,
      slug=item.Slug
    })
  </li>
}
</ul>
<p>
  @{ Html.RenderPartial("PagingPartial", Model); }
</p>
<p>
  @if (Request.IsAuthenticated) {
    @Html.ActionLink("Create Recipe", "Create")
  }
</p>
```

This is certainly an improvement, but the information displayed on the page is still grouped closely together even after making accommodations for removing the style and the ability to add recipes to the library:

Since we're developing a mobile app we need to take into consideration the input method of our users: their fingers. To better accommodate touch input, we need to separate the content a little more to provide a better experience to our users.

We can begin to improve the experience by insetting the list, separating it from the navigation and the creation link. To inset the list, we need to apply another data attribute, called the `data-inset` data attribute, to the `ul` element and supply the attribute with a value of `true`:

```
<ul data-role="listview" data-inset="true">
```

Insetting the list results in the following change to our look and feel:

Unfortunately our content now appears a bit sparse so let's address that.

Expanded listview content

We removed the recipe style from the recipe list when we converted the display from a table to a jQuery Mobile listview widget. We actually have the ability to add the information back to the list without greatly impacting the display.

Within a jQuery Mobile listview widget, all content contained within the first anchor of a listview is styled as a listview item. If we adjust the content of the list item to contain a single anchor with multiple content items, we can successfully reinsert the recipe style to the content:

```
@foreach (var item in Model)
{
    <li>
        <a href="@Url.Action("Details", new
```

```
    {
      id = item.RecipeId,
      slug=item.Slug
    })">
      <h3>@Html.DisplayFor(modelItem => item.Name)</h3>
      <p>
        @Html.DisplayFor(modelItem => item.Style)
      </p>
    </a>
  </li>
}
```

Supplemental Listview Content

There are other ways to get additional content into a listview. jQuery Mobile ships with several additional styles, some of which can be used to control how information is displayed within a listview. If we wish to display right-aligned content, we can apply the `ui-li-aside` style to content contained within the anchor of the list item. We can also apply the `ui-li-count` style if we wish to have count bubbles appear to the right of the list item name.

We've gone from sparse to rather verbose. The addition of more content is OK provided it's relevant and meaningful. We do need to provide our users the ability to filter it down though.

Listview filters

When displaying large amounts of data, it may be desirable to provide the user with a mechanism to filter content. The listview widget provides this functionality through the use of the `data-filter` data attribute. To enable it, all we need to do is add the attribute to our listview widget and set its value to true. We can even adjust the placeholder text, the hint to the user using a data attribute:

```
<ul
  data-role="listview"
  data-inset="true"
  data-filter="true"
  data-filter-placeholder="Search for a recipe...">
```

This functionality only searches the content currently displayed in the list. We will address searching all recipes in the final chapter of this book. As for the ability to create recipes, we need to make a small tweak there.

Buttons

The final adjustment we need to make to the recipe list page is convert the link to create a new recipe into something more touch-friendly. jQuery Mobile can convert links to touch-friendly button widgets through the, you guessed it, `data-role` data attribute:

```
@Html.ActionLink(
  "Create Recipe",
  "Create",
  null,
  new { data_role = "button" }
)
```

 When providing HTML attributes to an action link that contain a dash, we must supply them to the action link HTML helper using underscores. The runtime is smart enough to convert the underscores to dashes when it renders the link to the output stream.

Our recipe list view is complete, but it's rather meaningless if the user cannot determine which screen they're actually looking at.

Navigation hints

When viewing the recipe list, it is unclear whether or not we're looking at the global list of recipes or if we're looking at the recipes within our library. We need to provide a navigation hint to clarify this to the user. To highlight a button in our `navbar` widget in the mobile layout, we need to apply the `ui-btn-active` style to the active navigation element:

```
<li>@Html.ActionLink(
  "Recipes",
  "Index",
  "Recipe",
  new { area = "" },
  new { @class="ui-btn-active" })
</li>
```

The output of all of our work is shown in the following screenshot:

The recipe list now looks, feels, and functions like a native mobile app. Time to focus on the details page.

Recipe details

When displaying the details for a recipe within the BrewHow mobile app, we need to maintain a few pieces of functionality: the ability to return to the prior page, the ability to add and view reviews for the recipe, and the ability to edit the recipe. We want to do all of this in a way supported by jQuery Mobile. Our current Detail view for the RecipeController is littered with styles and layout elements that are specific to the CSS accompanying our old mobile template. We need to do some substantial clean-up work on the Detail view for the RecipeController.

The relevant code for the new view we will use for our mobile app to display recipe details is presented as follows:

```
<article id="recipe-detail">
  <header>
    <h2>
      <a href="#"
         data-role="button"
```

```
                data-icon="back"
                data-iconpos="notext"
                data-inline="true"
                onclick="javascript:history.go(-1)">
          Back
          </a>
          @Model.Name
        </h2>
    </header>
    <section>
      <header>
        <strong>
          @Html.DisplayNameFor(model =>
            model.PercentAlcoholByVolume)
        </strong>
      </header>
      @Html.DisplayFor(model =>
        model.PercentAlcoholByVolume)
    </section>
    <br>
    <!-- Other section fields omitted -->
</article>
<div>
  @if (Request.IsAuthenticated)
  {
    @* Buttons to add to library and edit recipe *@
  }
  @Html.ActionLink("View Reviews",
    "Index",
    new
    {
    area = "Review",
    id = Model.RecipeId
    },
    new { data_role = "button" })
  @if (Request.IsAuthenticated)
  {
    @Html.ActionLink(
    "Add Review",
    "Create",
    new
    {
```

```
      area = "Review",
      id = Model.RecipeId
      },
      new { data_role = "button" });
   }
</div>
```

Let's examine how this new view meets the user requirements we identified at the start of this section.

Back button

Creating a back button uses the same technique we learned to create a home button in our header. The only significant changes of note are the value for the `data-icon` data attribute and the inline JavaScript we have attached to the anchor:

```
<a href="#"
   data-role="button"
   data-icon="back"
   data-iconpos="notext"
   data-inline="true"
   onclick="javascript:history.go(-1)">Back</a>
```

 We could use jQuery to provide the back button functionality instead of the inline JavaScript, and we should probably do this if we're writing production-ready code. If you choose to use portions of this within your own production mobile apps, please adjust accordingly.

Action buttons

The actions a user may take when viewing a recipe have been converted to buttons. These actions include the ability to add a recipe to the library, edit the recipe, review the recipe, or to view all reviews for a recipe. We also have restricted access to the library, recipe edit, and review functionality within the UI to only authenticated users. These restrictions are enforced within our controllers as well:

```
@if (Request.IsAuthenticated)
{
   @Html.ActionLink("Edit Recipe", "Edit", new
   {
      id = Model.RecipeId,
      slug = Model.Slug
   },
   new { data_role = "button" });
}
```

```
@Html.ActionLink("View Reviews", "Index", new
{
  area = "Review",
  id = Model.RecipeId
},
new { data_role = "button" })
@if (Request.IsAuthenticated)
{
  @Html.ActionLink("Add Review", "Create", new
  {
    area = "Review",
    id = Model.RecipeId
  },
  new { data_role = "button" });
}
```

All of these changes result in the new and improved recipe detail screen you see in the following screenshot:

Next stop: the ability to edit recipes from a mobile device.

Recipe edits

Our mobile app currently has no mobile-specific view for editing recipes. While it is true most of our users will use the mobile app to retrieve information quickly, there will be users who wish to make contributions to BrewHow from their mobile devices. We should, therefore, make the editing experience as pleasant as possible.

Let's begin by making a copy of the `Edit.cshtml` file in the `Views` folder for our recipe controller and rename the new copy to `Edit.Mobile.cshtml`. Once the rename is complete, open the new mobile edit view. For the most part, our mobile edit view is functional on most mobile devices. We can do a better job though.

As with the detail view, we need to support the desire for a user to return to the prior page. Adding a back button is nearly an identical exercise as defined in the detail view:

```
<a href="#"
   data-role="button"
   data-icon="back"
   data-iconpos="notext"
   data-inline="true"
   onclick="javascript:history.go(-1)">Back</a>
```

The larger change we need to make is to remove the `fieldset` and `legend` elements from our view. They will be replaced with the `fieldcontain` style.

Fieldcontain

The `fieldcontain` style is a style defined in the jQuery Mobile CSS. It is used to support responsive design when laying out forms for input. This CSS class is applied to a container that encapsulates a label and input element. It attempts to display the label and input in a manner best suited for the device.

When dealing with an exceptionally low resolution, the `fieldcontain` style will force the browser to layout the label above the input. If, however, the device rendering the page has enough horizontal resolution to display the label beside the input, then it will do so.

To apply the `fieldcontain` style to our mobile edit view, we need to move the associated labels and inputs into a single container. In the case of our view, the container is a div. We then need to apply the `fieldcontain` style to each div wrapping a label and field pair.

By way of example:

```
<div class="editor-label">
  @Html.LabelFor(model => model.Instructions)
</div>
<div class="editor-field">
  @Html.EditorFor(model => model.Instructions)
  @Html.ValidationMessageFor(model => model.Instructions)
</div>
```

The preceding code becomes as follows:

```
<div class="fieldcontain">
  @Html.LabelFor(model => model.Instructions)
  @Html.EditorFor(model => model.Instructions)
  @Html.ValidationMessageFor(model => model.Instructions)
</div>
```

The new edit view is shown in the following screenshot:

Reviews

The biggest impact to the flow of our new mobile app is the entry and viewing of reviews. In the desktop version and responsive design versions of our app, reviews appear with the details of a recipe. In the mobile realm, this probably isn't a good idea.

As discussed, when we are writing apps for mobile devices we need to make sure we're returning only the requested information to the user. The return of additional information means the user will have to wait longer for it to display on their device and will have to filter through everything presented to them in order to find the piece of information they were actually seeking.

We should still provide our users with access to reviews, but we should return them only when the user explicitly requests them. This dictates we move the reviews off to a new page. We made this assumption when we added the **View Reviews** and **Add Reviews** buttons to the recipe detail view in this chapter. If we go click on the button to view the reviews, you will see something is a bit off:

First, and most obviously, our review view has no styling associated with it. It's missing both the jQuery Mobile stylings and the stylings that would be associated with our desktop view.

Perhaps less obvious is the absence of the `viewport meta` tag. Without this tag, the browser is trying to scale a "desktop" site into the resolution of the mobile device.

Both the lack of any styling and the `viewport meta` tag hint to the absence of any layout being applied to the view. This is indeed what is happening. To understand how, we have to examine the return value of our `Index` action method in the `Review` area's recipe controller, the action responsible for returning reviews for a particular recipe. This action method has the following return value:

```
return PartialView(ToListModel(reviews));
```

It seems we made an assumption when we first wrote this method that we would only ever embed this view in another view or layout. Since the view would be embedded in another view, we only ever needed to return it as a partial view. This, of course, returns only the content of the view and makes no attempt to embed the view within a layout file such as _Layout.cshtml or _Layout.Mobile.cshtml.

Because this view is used by the desktop version of the app, we don't want to prevent the action from returning a partial view. We also don't want to create a new action method solely for returning a complete view for mobile browsers. Our views would then need to know which action to invoke and when to invoke it. What we need to do is have the controller be responsible for determining which view to use based upon the requestor. Fortunately, the ASP.NET MVC 4 framework provides us such a mechanism.

IsMobileDevice

To return a full view for a mobile site, we simply need to determine if a mobile device is making the request. We can do this using the Browser.IsMobileDevice property of the current Request:

```
if (Request.Browser.IsMobileDevice)
{
   return View(reviewList);
}
```

The action will now return a full view for mobile devices and a partial view for desktop devices or mobile browsers emulating a desktop browser. But even returning a full view is only going to solve part of our problem. Even with our work to return a full view, the response looks no different than it did before. The runtime has no layout to associate with our view.

Copy the _ViewStart.cshtml file from the root of our project's Views folder to the project's Areas/Review/Views folder. This will inform the runtime to use the same layout for this area as is being used for the other areas of our app. Now if we only had some actual mobile views in the reviews area.

Mobile views

We still need to create mobile-specific views for review listing and editing, but we can now leverage the view naming convention (.Mobile) instead of relying on complex logic in our views. In the Recipe view folder of the Review area, copy Index.cshtml and rename the copied file to Index.Mobile.cshtml. Following is the code for our new mobile review list view:

```
<h2>
  <a href="#"
    data-role="button"
    data-icon="back"
    data-iconpos="notext"
    data-inline="true"
    onclick="javascript:history.go(-1)">
    Back</a>
@ViewBag.RecipeName
</h2>

<ul data-role="listview" data-inset="true">
  @foreach (var item in Model)
  {
    <li>
      <p style="white-space: normal;">
        @Html.DisplayFor(modelItem => item.Comment)
      </p>
      <p class="ui-li-count">@item.Rating</p>
    </li>
  }
</ul>
<p>
  @if (Request.IsAuthenticated) {
    @Html.ActionLink("Add Review", "Create", new {area = "Review",
      id = ViewBag.RecipeId, name=ViewBag.RecipeName }, new {
      data_role = "button" })
  }
</p>
```

 Our rating has a class of ui-li-count. This will display itself as a count bubble as we will see shortly.

We are currently returning everything our view needs except for the name of the recipe. Our view is looking for this value in `ViewBag.RecipeName`. We need to provide this key to our users because, without it, our users would have no context by which to read the reviews. That is to say they would not be able to discern to which recipe the review belongs. This is not an issue with the desktop version of the review list because the reviews are displayed on the same page with the recipe details. Given this isn't the case with our mobile app, we need to address it.

The first step in doing this is adding a `RecipeName` property to the `ViewBag`. We can do this easily enough in our `Index` action method invoked for the recipe review list. The problem comes with populating it.

We don't want the review controllers to load the recipe if they have no real need to do so and, given this scenario, it's not warranted. We also don't want to start caching information if it's not going to be used downstream. It would seem our best option at this point is to provide the name of the recipe to the review controllers' action methods when necessary. We need to modify the `Index` action method to take the name of the recipe as an optional parameter (it's a string so it is by default nullable and therefore optional):

```
public ActionResult Index(int id, string name)
{
  var reviews = this
    ._reviewRepository
    .GetReviewsForRecipe(id);

  this.ViewBag.RecipeId = id;
  this.ViewBag.RecipeName = name;
```

Our new action now supports retrieving and passing the name to downstream views via the `ViewBag.RecipeName` property. We now need to pass the name to the action method. This, too, is fairly straightforward. We simply add it to the route data when we build action links like so:

```
@Html.ActionLink(
  "View Reviews",
  "Index",
  new
  {
    area = "Review",
    id = Model.RecipeId,
    name=Model.Name
  },
```

```
new
{
    data_role = "button"
})
```

Any data added to the route collection of an action link that is not matched when
the route is chosen is appended to the constructed link as a query string parameter.
We can validate this works by building our application and clicking on the **View
Reviews** link on a recipe detail page. We should see the following if all goes well:

And what do you know? It worked.

Summary

This chapter introduced you to jQuery Mobile and its use to generate web apps that function as if they were native to the device. Through progressive enhancement, jQuery Mobile can take any page and transform it into a truly mobile user experience.

This chapter only scratched the surface of what can be done with jQuery Mobile and, admittedly, put forth a lot of information in very few pages. For some really interesting ideas, tools, techniques, and demos, including support for browser orientation and swipe events, I recommend you visit the jQuery Mobile site at `jquerymobile.com`.

Speaking of only scratching the surface, determining what information to put in this book, chapter by chapter, was one of the most difficult things I've undertaken. There were several other items I wanted to cover that simply wouldn't fit within a book of this size. In the next chapter, we will look at some of the more interesting items that didn't make the cut and I will provide you with the starting points to implement them yourself.

15
Reader Challenges

In this book we examined a history of the mobile web, learned how to develop a web application with consideration for the mobile web, and then converted that web application to a full-fledged member of the mobile web community. We have come a long way since those first chapters but, frankly, have only begun the journey of developing mobile web apps using ASP.NET MVC 4. Had we attempted to cover the entire breadth of the subject matter, we would have a book that weighs roughly 300 pounds and would require a small forest of trees to print.

Also, had we covered everything imaginable then where would the fun be for you, the reader? I'm a firm believer that you learn best while doing and I want to challenge you to some doing.

This chapter will present a few challenges for you to complete based in part upon your readings in this book.

Full-text search

Our site currently lacks the ability for users to directly search for recipes. Our users might want to find a recipe by style, by ingredient, or simply by name. They can go to their favorite search engine if our site has been properly crawled and indexed by it, but why not embed the capabilities of a search engine on our site?

Your challenge is to use one of the following technologies and add full-text search functionality to BrewHow.

Embedded search

If you want users to be able to search the content of your site but you don't want to go through the trouble of actually writing this functionality yourself and don't mind a little co-branding, both Google and Bing offer free solutions for you.

Search boxes

Using Google Custom Search, you can place a search box on your site users can use to query your site for information. Google provides an interface to allow you to customize the look and feel of those results as they are displayed to the user. The results from the free version, of course, display the Google ads we are so accustomed to seeing, but you can pay a small fee to have these removed.

APIs

Both Google and Microsoft offer APIs to embed their search engine functionality into your site. Unlike the Google Custom Search search box, you will need to get your hands a little dirty writing code as this functionality is provided over RESTful HTTP services.

As with the Google Custom Search, these services are provided for free for nominal usage, but once you clear a certain search threshold you will need to pay for continued use of the service.

Lucene.NET

If you want to embed full-text search into your application but don't want to promote it through the use of ads (or you just don't want to pay someone else to do it for you), you may want to look at Lucene.NET. Lucene.NET is a port of the popular Java-based search engine Lucene. Like Lucene, Lucene.NET is part of the Apache Software Foundation's offerings and is licensed under the Apache License.

Lucene.NET operates on the concept of documents and indices. Indices hold a collection of documents available for search. Each document is a collection of key-value pairs. Indices can be constructed and maintained in memory or on the filesystem.

The true benefit of Lucene.NET is that it can be bin deployed. This means there's no software to install, simply bundle the assembly with your application when you deploy it and you have full-text search support at your fingertips. This makes Lucene.NET an ideal choice if your hosting provider doesn't support the full-text capabilities built into Microsoft SQL Server.

SQL Server Full-text Search

Operating on a Microsoft stack, you might be inclined to use **SQL Server's Full-text Search (SQL FTS)** capability. SQL FTS is exceptionally powerful and provides you the ability to search content based on inflection, linguistic variants (plurals, tenses, and so on), or proximity.

Instead of creating an index based off of documents, SQL FTS uses the table as the index source and populates the index based on a column or columns specified at the time the FTS index is created. Those columns can be traditional text-based columns such as char, varchar, and nvarchar or the columns may be of type image, xml, or varbinary(MAX).

SQL FTS can even be made content-aware. That means if you place a Word document within a varbinary (MAX) column, SQL FTS is smart enough to parse out the content of the document and include it in search results made against the index.

The only downside to using SQL FTS is finding a hosting provider supporting it. If you self-host SQL Server, you will need to obtain a license supporting your usage scenario.

There are other options available for performing full-text search within our app and if you find one more suitable for your needs then you should use it. Regardless of the technology, accept this challenge and implement full-text search in your app.

Socialization

If we created a high-level feature list of our site, we would see users can login, create recipes, provide comments, add items to their library, and well, that's about it. We can do so much more for our users and with our users than we are currently doing. If we want a truly social site, we need to interact with our users and let them interact with each other.

To that end, your challenge is to engage your users to participate in the BrewHow community using one or more of the following ideas.

Social media support

Obviously, if we're going to socialize BrewHow, we need to add support for existing social media. This includes support for social sites such as Facebook, Twitter, and Google+. Leveraging these social platforms, we can inform users of activity on our site and let them inform others of their activity.

Recipe additions

To inform your users and potential users of your site about new recipe additions, you can publish recipe additions to Twitter and provide a link back to your site to view the recipe. Remember the site supports anonymous access so anybody can read the recipes present.

You may also elect to publish recipe additions to Facebook or Google+, but note these media outlets are a little less acceptable of noise and in the beginning you might not want to post a message to these services every time someone adds a recipe.

Recipe sharing

Your users will likely want to share recipes they have made, intend to make, have created, or just plain find interesting. Allowing them to share this information to existing social services will bring traffic to your site and help build up the recipe base and build community.

You should enable the sharing of recipes by allowing users to tweet recipes from the site directly to their Twitter account, to Like recipes using their Facebook account, or to +1 recipes using their Google+ account.

Offline support

There are times when your users may not have access to a good Internet connection. Perhaps they have no coverage in their local homebrew supply store. Perhaps they want to keep recipes on their tablet and the tablet is only equipped with WiFi. Whatever the reason, you should support the ability for your users to store recipes offline.

Several services exist to support the offline access of web content. Two of the most popular, Pocket and Instapaper, can be placed directly on your site allowing your users to directly publish the recipe to the offline reader of their choice. These services also allow users to share the offline versions they have saved with their friends. If you provide the appropriate layouts you can use offline versions of content to drive users to your site.

Push notifications

SignalR is currently being used to publish new recipes to all users viewing the recipe list regardless of a user's interest in the recipe being published. While this is functionality you should keep, it might be more useful to the user if they were notified only of recipes they might be interested in.

Users should be allowed to keep a profile allowing them to subscribe to notifications. These notifications may be about comments to recipes they created or about the addition of recipes of certain styles. Whatever the notification, you can use SignalR to emulate the push notifications available when developing native mobile apps.

Of course the user must be viewing the site to receive these notifications. If you truly want to enable push notifications you will have to develop a native app.

Going native

Some things a mobile web app just can't do (currently). It is on the occasion when we need the power of the hardware we're running upon, unencumbered by the limitations of the browser, that we must take our apps native.

If you decide to expose BrewHow as a native app you will need to provide access to your platform to remote callers. The most convenient method we have of doing this in ASP.NET MVC 4 is through the Web API.

ASP.NET Web API

The ASP.NET Web API framework makes it simple to build RESTful services and expose those services over HTTP. These services automatically use the same model-binding techniques we learned about earlier in this book and can accept and return requests using XML or JSON.

Given HTTP is ubiquitous and XML and JSON can be parsed on all major mobile platforms, the ASP.NET Web API is ideal for you to expose your platform to outside consumers. You can, of course, choose another path to expose your application for consumption.

Note that you will want to secure the API to prevent malicious users from identifying your endpoints and trying to find exploits in your site. And, if I were the one implementing this functionality, I would make sure controllers and services are simply wrappers around the code doing the actual work. You don't want to end up maintaining your logic in two places.

Developing native apps

When developing your native apps, you could write an Android app in Java and an iOS app in Objective-C, hoping you have the time and patience to deliver nearly identical experiences to your users, or you could leverage existing tools allowing you to maintain one set of source code. There are several cross-platform development tools available in the market today.

PhoneGap and Appcelerator

PhoneGap (`phonegap.com`) and Appcelerator (`appcelerator.com`) provide development tools and frameworks allowing you to target multiple platforms from a single codebase. While you have to learn the framework itself, both of these tools allow you to develop code in languages with which you're already familiar, such as HTML, CSS, and JavaScript.

These frameworks do have their trade-offs, providing limited support for certain hardware-level features. But for 90% of the work you will want to accomplish, they are more than sufficient. Also keep in mind these frameworks are improving every day and should soon reach parity with the native development tools.

If you want to go native and don't wish to learn a new framework, language, or both, there is still hope.

Xamarin

Xamarin is unique in my experience dealing with cross-platform development tools. It provides you access to native hardware but requires you to have or obtain knowledge of how the underlying mobile operating system functions. It may sound intimidating, but you must have this knowledge as all Xamarin is doing is allowing you to target the mobile platform of your choice using C#.

Now writing code with knowledge of what iOS and Android are doing under the covers does imply the shell of your application must be specific to a platform, but we learned that with a good separation of concerns our logic can exist externally and independently of any presentation mechanism. Xamarin will allow you to write all of your mobile-side business logic in a language with which you're familiar, allowing you to focus on the problem you're trying to solve.

Summary

Every time I sit down to investigate a new feature of a framework or a nuance of an old established feature, I find I learn something new. It is that learning process we, as developers, must embrace if we are to stay current. It is why I end this book with this set of challenges. I want you, the reader, to continue your pursuit to know more about your craft. It is why I chose to write this book and why, I hope, you are reading it.

It's been a long journey, a journey I pretty well summed up in the introduction to this chapter. In the end, I hope I was able to convey just how much potential there is for developing mobile apps using the ASP.NET MVC 4 framework.

Index

Thank you for buying
ASP.NET MVC 4 Mobile App Development

About Packt Publishing

Packt, pronounced 'packed', published its first book "Mastering phpMyAdmin for Effective MySQL Management" in April 2004 and subsequently continued to specialize in publishing highly focused books on specific technologies and solutions.

Our books and publications share the experiences of your fellow IT professionals in adapting and customizing today's systems, applications, and frameworks. Our solution based books give you the knowledge and power to customize the software and technologies you're using to get the job done. Packt books are more specific and less general than the IT books you have seen in the past. Our unique business model allows us to bring you more focused information, giving you more of what you need to know, and less of what you don't.

Packt is a modern, yet unique publishing company, which focuses on producing quality, cutting-edge books for communities of developers, administrators, and newbies alike. For more information, please visit our website: www.packtpub.com.

About Packt Enterprise

In 2010, Packt launched two new brands, Packt Enterprise and Packt Open Source, in order to continue its focus on specialization. This book is part of the Packt Enterprise brand, home to books published on enterprise software – software created by major vendors, including (but not limited to) IBM, Microsoft and Oracle, often for use in other corporations. Its titles will offer information relevant to a range of users of this software, including administrators, developers, architects, and end users.

Writing for Packt

We welcome all inquiries from people who are interested in authoring. Book proposals should be sent to author@packtpub.com. If your book idea is still at an early stage and you would like to discuss it first before writing a formal book proposal, contact us; one of our commissioning editors will get in touch with you.

We're not just looking for published authors; if you have strong technical skills but no writing experience, our experienced editors can help you develop a writing career, or simply get some additional reward for your expertise.

PhoneGap 2.x Mobile Application Development Hotshot

ISBN: 978-1-84951-940-3   Paperback: 388 pages

Create exciting apps for mobile devices using PhoneGap

1. Ten apps included to help you get started on your very own exciting mobile app

2. These apps include working with localization, social networks, geolocation, as well as the camera, audio, video, plugins, and more

3. Apps cover the spectrum from productivity apps, educational apps, all the way to entertainment and games

Appcelerator Titanium: Patterns and Best Practices

ISBN: 978-1-84969-348-6   Paperback: 110 pages

Take your Titanium development experience to the next level, and build your Titanium knowledge on CommonJS structuring, MVC model implementation, memory management, and much more

1. Full step-by-step approach to help structure your apps in an MVC style that will make them more maintainable, easier to code and more stable

2. Learn best practices and optimizations both related directly to JavaScript and Titanium itself

3. Learn solutions to create cross-compatible layouts that work across both Android and the iPhone

Please check **www.PacktPub.com** for information on our titles

PhoneGap Mobile Application Development Cookbook

ISBN: 978-1-84951-858-1   Paperback: 320 pages

Over 40 recipes to create mobile applications using the PhoneGap API with examples and clear instructions

1. Use the PhoneGap API to create native mobile applications that work on a wide range of mobile devices

2. Discover the native device features and functions you can access and include within your applications

3. Packed with clear and concise examples to show you how to easily build native mobile applications

Socket.IO Real-time Web Application Development

ISBN: 978-1-78216-078-6   Paperback: 140 pages

Build modern real-time web applications powered by Socket.IO

1. Understand the usage of various socket.io features like rooms, namespaces, and sessions

2. Secure the socket.io communication

3. Deploy and scale your socket.io and Node.js applications in production

4. A practical guide that quickly gets you up and running with socket.io

Please check **www.PacktPub.com** for information on our titles

Printed in Great Britain
by Amazon.co.uk, Ltd.,
Marston Gate.